Palgrave Studies in Educational Media

There is no education without some form of media. The Palgrave Studies in Educational Media series welcomes research-based critical studies that explore these media in their socio-political contexts. These books explore textbooks and other educational technologies as sites of cultural contestation, epistemic struggles and socio-political forces. Drawing on local and global perspectives, and attending to the digital, nondigital and postdigital, the series explores how these media technologies are entangled with broader continuities, upheavals and transformations in today's society. It seeks to provide valuable and accessible resources for researchers, students, teachers, teacher trainers, policymakers, textbook authors and educational media designers interested in critical approaches to education and media technology. It is trans- and interdisciplinary, and welcomes both single authored and edited volumes that analyse how media and media practices play a role in shaping ways of knowing, identifications, subjectivations, inclusions and exclusions, economies and global political projects.

Monika Popow

Learning in the Postdigital Knowledge Society

Between Textbooks, Social Media and AI

palgrave
macmillan

Monika Popow
Polish Naval Academy
Gdynia, Poland

ISSN 2662-7361 ISSN 2662-737X (electronic)
Palgrave Studies in Educational Media
ISBN 978-3-032-21955-8 ISBN 978-3-032-21956-5 (eBook)
https://doi.org/10.1007/978-3-032-21956-5

This work was supported by Georg Eckert Institute and Monika Popow.

Cover credit: MF3d/GettyImages

This Palgrave Macmillan imprint is published by the registered company Springer Nature Switzerland AG
The registered company address is: Gewerbestrasse 11, 6330 Cham, Switzerland

Series Editors' Foreword

In 1913, Thomas Edison said that 'books will soon be obsolete in public schools'. In light of the advent of the motion picture, he claimed that 'our school system will be completely changed inside of ten years'. With every newly emerging technology, a revolution of the school system was supposed to follow: film, radio, teaching machines, the internet, mobile devices, apps, artificial intelligence. Media technologies are crucial to education: there is no education without some form of media. Conflicts over the contents of textbooks or desires to ban media (from novels and textbooks to smartphones) from schools are discussed widely in the daily news. An astonishing number of stakeholders are invested in defining what ideas about ways of knowing, living, being, thinking, feeling, imagining, hoping or fearing should be permitted to circulate among students in schools. Policymakers, educators, parents, activists, and of course young people themselves care deeply about the media used in their everyday education. These media shape and are shaped by the knowledges, affects and skills which are considered desirable or even legible in the socio-political contexts in which they are produced and used.

Given the dynamics of contemporary developments in textbooks and other media designed or adapted for use in schools, the *Palgrave Studies in Educational Media* series takes stock of current research by focusing on three developments:

First, it emphasises critical approaches to educational media. The majority of studies on educational technology tend to revolve around individual learning processes or best practices. At the same time, however, a rich body of critical work has been growing over recent decades which is informed by cultural, political, social and media theory, and science and technology studies. This work attends—empirically and conceptually—to the embeddedness of educational media technologies in cultural, social and political processes, and to the historicity of the media used in education. If we see educational media as a highly contested and thus crucially important cultural and epistemic site, then perceptive and critical studies based on thoroughly research are important to further develop these carefully critical approaches to educational media as a matter of social concern.

Second, it welcomes scholarship across disciplinary boundaries. Today's vibrant and dynamic research and critical scholarship on education and technology stems from a broad range of disciplines, including sociology, history, cultural studies, memory studies, media studies and educational sciences, and also information, computer and cognitive science. Traditionally, much of this research has engaged with specific disciplinary questions, and been published in separate disciplines, with limited reading across disciplines. Over recent years, critical studies of education and technology—or critical edtech studies—have been consolidated into the kind of interdisciplinary field which builds on previous conversations across disciplinary boundaries and communities. This series has endeavoured to contribute to this consolidation.

Third, the series attends to multiple configurations of digital, postdigital, nondigital, or hyperdigital practices. Research, policy and practice today are closely attentive to digital technologies. Yet looking at today's educational practices, it has become clear that while no social or pedagogical practices are entirely digital, very little in much of the world is entirely without digitally networked connections. Postdigital approaches—as both a diagnosis of the contemporary condition in which 'digital' is undifferentiated from 'nondigital', and a critical approach to scholarship—have overthrown the notion of digital technology as new, innovative or a solution to wicked problems. Instead, technologies are seen as intimately interwoven with other materials in daily teaching and learning. The potentials and risks of digital education emit a fascination for politicians, journalists and others concerned with the future of education, and are undoubtedly important to consider. But the co-constitution of our world through multiple, ambivalent, situated media practices is the focus for fascinating research that opens new perspectives on the contemporary world and on possible, plausible and implausible futures.

Palgrave Studies in Educational Media offers a dedicated space to bring together research on these three developments. It encourages dialogue across disciplines within the emerging space of critical studies on educational media, educational technology, education and media technology. The series showcases both empirical and theoretical work which understands these media technologies as sites of cultural contestation and socio-political forces. The focus lies primarily on schools, across all school subjects. The series is interested in both local and global perspectives, in order to explore how educational media are entangled with broader debates about continuity and change in today's society, about classroom practices, inclusions and exclusions, identifications, subjectivations, economies, infrastructuring, and global political projects. We particularly welcome contributions based on decelerated inquiry.

This book by Monika Popow explores in depth the challenges and dynamics of learning in the postdigital knowledge society with a focus on Central and Eastern Europe (CEE), where conceptions of education as both an economic and identity-forming entity meet in a unique sociopolitical space. Here, the transformation of the 'knowledge society' into a 'knowledge economy' in which education is viewed as individual capital has a fascinating impact for international educational media research as particularly illuminating tensions between knowledge, authority, and identity arise from a reshaping of education by digital infrastructures and neoliberal governance. In Poland, the state is being redefined as a facilitator of competition, leading to growing inequalities. While it can be argued that education has never been 'merely' about imparting knowledge, but always also about regulating subjectivities and identites, Popow shows in this groundbreaking study how education in CEE becomes an 'epistemic imposition' in which local knowledge production is suppressed by external epistemic hierarchies, with teachers and students orienting themselves toward Western models defined by organisations such as the OECD, World Bank or PISA.

Located firmly at the decolonial-postdigital education nexus, this book takes the example of AI use in CEE to show how (Western-shaped) dismissive attitudes towards the use of AI tools by learners highlights the gap between institutional requirements and local practices. As an alternative, Popow shows how decolonial and postdigital pedagogy can promote epistemic justice and integrate different types of knowledge into the education paradigm.

Series Editors, Palgrave Studies in Educational Media, Brunswick and Oldenburg, Germany
October 2025

Eckhardt Fuchs
Felicitas Macgilchrist

Acknowledgments I am indebted to many people and institutions who supported this work. The students and teachers who welcomed me into their classrooms shared their perspectives with generosity, even when they were at times skeptical of the research itself. Colleagues enriched my thinking through discussions, critiques, and encouragement: Prof. dr hab. Jerzy Kojkoł, Head of the Faculty of Humanities and Social Sciences at the Polish Naval Academy; Dr hab. Tomasz Maliszewski, Head of the Department of Educational Studies; Prof. dr hab. Piotr Zamojski; Dr hab. Maja Grabkowska; Dr hab. Paweł Rudnicki; and Dr. Isidora Sáez-Rosenkranz.

I am especially grateful to the Leibniz Institute for Educational Media | GEI, and to the series editors, Prof. Dr Felicitas Macgilchrist and Prof. Dr Eckhardt Fuchs, as well as to the managing editor, Dr Wendy Anne Kopisch.

I would also like to thank my partner Peter Pawlowski for his support and for providing the space that enabled my work.

While working on this book, I occasionally turned to large language model (LLM) tools. They were helpful for practical matters such as translation, improving the clarity and syntax of my English, checking consistency of terminology, light text correction, and for generating draft materials like indexes or tables of contents. Everything produced in this way was carefully checked and revised by me, and all interpretations, arguments, and final wording are entirely my own responsibility.

This book was written at a moment when artificial intelligence has begun to permeate not only classrooms but also the practice of research and writing itself. I remain cautious about these developments. The arguments presented here are grounded in ethnographic evidence, theoretical reflection, and critical analysis. If they resonate, it is because they reflect the realities of students and teachers whose experiences complicate the celebratory narratives of digital transformation. My hope is that this book contributes to a broader conversation about how education might reclaim its emancipatory purpose under conditions that too often reduce learning to compliance, data extraction, and survival. And I am aware that, in the rapid pace of technological change, this account may soon serve as a historical record. What I offer here is not a final word but an invitation: to rethink what it means to learn, teach, and know in the postdigital knowledge society, and to consider how, even in contexts marked by dependency and constraint, alternative futures can still be imagined.

Competing Interests The author declares no competing financial interests. The author is engaged in academic projects and professional collaborations related to the themes of education, digital culture, and pedagogy, but these affiliations did not influence the analysis, interpretation, or conclusions presented in this book. The analysis was carried out with the support of the GEI Fellowship in 2024.

Ethics Approval The research presented in this book was conducted between 2022 and 2024 in secondary schools in Gdańsk, Poland, employing an ethnographic design that combined participant observation, semi-structured interviews with teachers, and informal conversations with students. Access to the field was secured through formal procedures, including institutional consent, data protection agreements, and notification at the school level. Written informed consent was obtained from all teacher interviewees. Participation was strictly voluntary, and respondents were informed that they retained the right to withdraw at any time without consequence.

No formal interviews were conducted with students. Informal conversations were carried out in hallways, staffrooms, and other everyday school settings, and only after approval had been granted by school authorities and, when necessary, parental consent, in order to comply with applicable child protection standards.

All participants have been fully anonymized, with schools and individuals identified exclusively through coded references designed to safeguard confidentiality. The study was undertaken in compliance with the ethical principles of the Declaration of Helsinki and comparable institutional guidelines.

Contents

About the Author

Monika Popow holds a Ph.D. in educational studies. She has been affiliated with the Department of Educational Studies at the Faculty of Humanities and Social Studies, Polish Naval Academy in Gdynia, Poland. She is a scholar specializing in educational studies, with expertise in the areas of postdigital learning, educational media, and the integration of digital technologies into pedagogical practices. Dr. Popow's work is situated within the broader framework of postdigital theory, engaging with the challenges posed by the commodification of education, platformisation, and algorithmic governance. She has been a research fellow in the Leibniz Institute for Educational Media | GEI. Monika Popow's publications focus on the intersections of education, citizenship, and digital transformation. She is an author of "The Category of Nation in Educational Discourse: An Analysis of Identity Construction Processes in School Textbooks," Adam Mickiewicz University Press, 2015.

CHAPTER 1

Introduction

Education has long been the terrain where wider transformations are inscribed and contested. Schools and universities do not simply transmit knowledge. They produce and regulate subjectivities, demarcate what counts as legitimate expertise, and embody the ideological currents of their time. The current conjuncture is distinctive in the ways digital infrastructures and neoliberal governance converge to reshape both the meaning of knowledge and the conditions of learning. This is especially evident in Central and Eastern Europe (CEE), where the post-socialist transformation has fused the neoliberal logics of marketization with resurgent nationalisms and ideological control, embedding education in a contradictory field of modernization and retraditionalization.

This book was written out of a sense of urgency. Over the past decade, I have observed how education in Poland and across Central and Eastern Europe has been caught between the rhetoric of modernization and the persistence of inherited hierarchies—between political demands and the desire to become modern in a deeply colonial sense (Gandhi, 1998). Digital technologies entered schools with promises of democratization, inclusion, fast development and innovation. However, what I witnessed in classrooms, and what my fieldwork confirms, is that these technologies rarely transform the epistemic foundations of schooling. Instead, they are absorbed into a culture of standardization, surveillance, and test preparation, constantly disrupted by political interventions and reforms. Teachers

M. Popow, *Learning in the Postdigital Knowledge Society*, Palgrave Studies in Educational Media,
https://doi.org/10.1007/978-3-032-21956-5_1

remain anchored in transmissive pedagogies, while students navigate the demands of assessment with pragmatism, irony, and, increasingly, the help of generative tools. This contradiction—the simultaneous presence of technological novelty and pedagogical inertia—was the starting point for this book.

The project developed at the intersection of several fields of inquiry: critical pedagogy, sociology of education, discourse studies, and post-digital theory. I was drawn to the notion of the *postdigital* because it captures the saturation of digital infrastructures into everyday life without assuming rupture or neutrality (Jandrić et al., 2018). For nearly four years—interrupted by the pandemic and later by the war in Ukraine—I entered schools, trying to conduct research in a field that itself resisted easy research design. Education is a socially and politically sensitive sphere. Those who inhabit it are not always able or willing to sustain the presence of a researcher. Ultimately, I drew together material from several schools, concentrating on two comparable sites. This narrowing of scope unexpectedly allowed me to capture a wide-ranging picture of contrasting contexts. What emerged was not a story of technological progress, but of ambivalence and contradiction.

As the research confirmed, the boundary between online and offline has collapsed. Students do not "use" technology as an external resource but inhabit environments already structured by AI, platforms, algorithms, and data flows (Knox, 2019; Williamson, 2017). At the same time, these infrastructures are never experienced in the abstract. They are negotiated within classrooms where authority and meaning remain in dispute. This book is therefore as much about the lived experience of learning as it is about broader transformations of governance.

My focus on Poland and the wider Central and Eastern European region reflects both intellectual and personal commitments. Education in post-socialist societies has been shaped by overlapping trajectories of neoliberal reform, state centralization, and cultural nationalism (Silova, 2010). These trajectories have produced what Dudzikowa (2001) described as the illusion of schooling as a formative project. Schools is imagined as cultivating autonomous citizens but in practice oriented toward compliance and reproduction. By situating the postdigital within this context, the book shows that digital transformation cannot be understood in universal terms. It intersects with specific historical legacies and political formations, producing hybrid configurations of control, dependence, autonomy and resistance.

The ideal of the "knowledge society," widely popularized in the late twentieth century (Bell, 1973; Castells, 1996, 2010; Drucker, 1993), carried the promise that innovation and technological fluency would democratize access and extend participation in intellectual life. In practice this vision has largely unfolded as the knowledge economy, a regime in which education is recast in terms of employability and human capital formation (Ball, 2012; Jessop, 2002). What had once been framed as a public good—central to democracy and collective life—has increasingly been redefined as an individual responsibility and as an instrument of national and global productivity (Simons & Masschelein, 2008; Szkudlarek, 2016). In CEE, this translation has been particularly pronounced. Post-1989 reforms, carried out under the imperative of "catching up" with Western modernity, positioned education as both a vehicle for economic convergence and a tool of identity politics. On the one hand, neoliberal restructuring imposed regimes of efficiency, decentralization, and alignment with global standards (Novotný et al., 2023; Silova, 2010). On the other hand, resurgent cultural nationalism re-inscribed schools with ideological and moral functions, producing a hybrid governance where market logics coexist with patriotic curricula and centralized control (Cervinkova & Rudnicki, 2019; Dudzikowa, 2001; Filipiak, 2009).

The postdigital condition sharpens these dynamics. Following Jandrić et al. (2018), *postdigital* does not suggest the disappearance of digital technologies but rather their saturation into the very fabric of social and educational life. The distinction between online and offline has become untenable. Schools no longer use digital tools as supplements but are themselves constituted through algorithmic infrastructures and learning management systems (Knox, 2019; Williamson, 2017). These dispositifs, in Foucault's (1972) sense, are not neutral instruments but organizational logics that delimit what knowledge appears, how it circulates, and whose voices are heard. To speak of postdigital education, therefore, is to acknowledge that predictive analytics and algorithmic personalization are not peripheral features but central to the very reconfiguration of pedagogy and authority.

One of the key dynamics shaping the postdigital knowledge society in Central and Eastern Europe is what can be described, following Mignolo (2011), as epistemic imposition. This concept denotes the subordination of local forms of knowledge to externally defined epistemic hierarchies that present themselves as universal. In the CEE region, educational reforms after 1989 were framed as processes of modernization and alignment with transnational models of development. This narrative of convergence was simultaneously a narrative of epistemic dependency. Schools were asked not simply to innovate but to align with standards and pedagogical frameworks designed elsewhere. Policy vocabularies imported from the OECD, World Bank, and European Commission—terms such as "competence," "human capital," or "digital transformation"—entered national debates as neutral descriptors of progress, but in practice functioned as carriers of particular epistemological and political assumptions.

The effects of epistemic imposition are visible in everyday school practices. Teachers and students in my fieldwork frequently described the digital practices that mattered for institutional evaluation as those corresponding to Western, Anglophone models of competence: academic writing in English, familiarity with Microsoft Office, or standardized formats of presentation. By contrast, students' own digital practices—local languages on social media, hybrid memes mixing cultural references, or forms of collaborative creativity cultivated in private channels—were routinely dismissed as irrelevant or even illegitimate. In Pyżalski's (2025) recent research on the use of generative AI in Polish schools, a similar pattern emerges. Students use these tools in occasional and largely informal ways, primarily for tasks such as content creation or problem-solving, while schools neither systematically integrate these practices into teaching nor provide frameworks for their critical use. Knowledge is still understood as something transmitted in school and produced exclusively by humans. These patterns resonate with a growing body of ethnographic and platform studies on technology and education. Classic ethnographies include Garcia's (2017) study of mobile media in a Los Angeles high school, Livingstone and Sefton-Green's (2016) account of learning in the digital age, Rafalow's (2020) analysis of inequality in the tech era, and Sims's (2017) critique of techno-idealism in school reform. More recent work has extended these perspectives to platform and AI contexts: Bhatia et al. (2024) on marginalized communities' digital learning, Cone (2023) on Danish primary schools, González López and Büchner (2024) on repair practices in Argentina and Germany, Hangartner et al. (2024) on personalized learning in secondary schools, and Wagener-Böck et al. (2023) on ethnographic encounters with automation. Macgilchrist (2024) has also reflected on methodological innovation in educational ethnography. This book contributes to these debates by bringing new empirical insights from Central and Eastern Europe, a region often marginalized in global research on postdigital education.

This marginalization reflects the long-standing positioning of CEE as a semi-periphery, historically subjected to shifting regimes of epistemic authority—from socialist ideological control to neoliberal and neoliberal benchmarking. In both cases, educational legitimacy was conferred not internally but through external reference points. The arrival of digital infrastructures and AI intensifies this dependency. Platforms designed in Silicon Valley or Shenzhen define the parameters of participation, embedding Anglo-Western linguistic and cultural codes into the everyday practices of students. As a result, learners find themselves inhabiting a paradoxical condition. On the one hand, they are praised for embodying the "competences of the future" when they align with imported standards. On the other hand, when they draw on their own practices—whether regional languages, community-based knowledges, or creative uses of digital tools—these are rendered invisible or suspect within school hierarchies.

Epistemic imposition in this context produces more than an asymmetry of recognition. It shapes the very subjectivities of learners and teachers. Students internalize the idea that valuable knowledge always comes from outside, while teachers often see their task as translating local practices into externally recognizable formats. This reproduces what Mignolo (2011) terms epistemic disobedience only in fragmentary and precarious ways. Students' reversive uses of digital tools parody institutional demands, but they rarely achieve recognition as legitimate epistemologies. Instead, they oscillate between compliance with imported standards and covert practices of subversion. The result is the simultaneous valorization of external models and the delegitimization of local creativity.

Addressing the issues requires rethinking educational sovereignty. Rather than measuring schools solely against OECD frameworks or the affordances of global platforms, it is necessary to foreground the epistemic resources embedded in local contexts. This includes multilingual repertoires, community-based practices of knowledge sharing, and culturally situated ways of engaging with technology. Only then we can move beyond the repetition of external templates and begin to articulate pedagogies that are both critical and locally resonant.

This book takes these paradoxes as its point of departure. Its central claim is that learning in the postdigital knowledge society cannot be understood simply in terms of technological adoption or resistance. It must instead be analyzed as a contested field in which authority and knowledge are continuously renegotiated under the combined pressures of neoliberal governance, digital infrastructures, and cultural politics. The postdigital collapse of the online/offline divide does not automatically produce pluralism or emancipation. Rather, it reconstitutes new pedagogical relations within the logics of algorithmic governance. At the same time, the everyday engagements of students and teachers reveal spaces of creativity and resistance—however contradictory or ambivalent.

This book is written for an international readership, but it carries the imprint of its specific location. The Polish case is not unique, as it illustrates how postdigital education unfolds in societies marked by both the legacies of state socialism and the pressures of neoliberal globalization. In this respect, the study speaks to broader questions about how education is governed. Specifically, how knowledge is legitimized, and how learners are positioned in an age of algorithmic saturation. It is also, however, a book about schools as lived spaces: about teachers who see themselves as guardians of didactic traditions, and about students who oscillate between reluctance toward schooling and pragmatic resistance.

The chapters that follow are not intended as a comprehensive account of all dimensions of postdigital education. Rather, they focus on specific constructions: the discourse of learning in schools, the figure of the mechanized subject, the practices of reversive knowledge, and the broader condition of the postdigital knowledge society. The book proceeds through a dialogue between theory and ethnography, situating empirical findings within frameworks drawn from Foucault, Fraser, Jessop, Biesta, and others. Its ambition is not to offer definitive answers but to illuminate tensions, contradictions, but also possibilities.

The four chapters of this book trace these tensions across multiple scales and theoretical perspectives. Chapter 1 situates the shift from "knowledge society" to "knowledge economy" within the broader transformations of neoliberal governance, showing how discourses of learning function less as neutral descriptions than as technologies of control that frame learners as self-managing subjects. It also places these changes within the specific trajectory of Central and Eastern Europe, asking how the region's post-socialist reforms shape the conditions of knowledge production and exploring whether artificial intelligence can be understood as a paradigmatic form of educational media. Chapter 2 turns to the discursive construction of learning in schools, drawing on ethnographic material to show how students and teachers interpret, negotiate, and resist institutional frameworks. Here, the persistence of transmissive pedagogy and exam-oriented practices contrasts sharply with policy rhetoric about innovation, revealing the resilience of established hierarchies. Chapter 3 examines the identity of the learner as it is constructed within discourse, focusing on two figures: the *mechanized subject*, produced through standardized assessment, surveillance, and algorithmic infrastructures, and the practices of *reversive knowledge* that subvert institutional demands while remaining caught within their logics. Chapter 4 extends the analysis to postdigital education in the CEE context, focusing on algorithmic infrastructures, AI platforms, and digital governance. It interrogates not only how these media redistribute epistemic authority but also asks what potential—if any—the postdigital condition holds for reimagining educational media beyond the logics of neoliberal governance and epistemic coloniality.

Across these chapters, several arguments unfold. First, digital transformation in education is less a radical innovation than a selective adaptation. Technologies are incorporated to stabilize assessment, surveillance, and control rather than democratize learning. Second, the postdigital condition intensifies neoliberal logics, shifting the burden of survival and adaptability onto individuals and families (Biesta, 2019; Fraser, 2013). Third, learners are not passive recipients. Through reversive practices, students reinterpret institutional expectations and navigate pressures with pragmatism and irony, even if these tactics remain ambivalent. Finally, the CEE context emphasizes how digital transformation intersects with histories of dependence, neoliberalization, and nationalism, producing hybrid formations in which education serves both the knowledge economy and ideological retraditionalization.

Taken together, the book argues that postdigital education is not a technological breakthrough but a contested terrain where knowledge, subjectivity, and governance are inseparably entangled. What is at stake is not simply how technologies are used, but how they reconfigure the very conditions of learning. What counts as knowledge? Who is authorized to speak? Under what terms? To grapple with these dynamics is to see education less as a promise of emancipation than as an unstable negotiation of authority and recognition in the fractured landscape of the postdigital knowledge society.

References

Ball, S. J. (2012). *Global Education Inc.: New policy networks and the neo-liberal imaginary*. Routledge.

Bell, D. (1973). *The coming of post-industrial society: A venture in social forecasting*. Basic Books.

Bhatia, K. V., Arora, P., & Gupta, S. (2024). Edtech platforms from below: a family ethnography of marginalized communities and their digital learning post-pandemic. *Learning, Media and Technology*, 1–15. https://doi.org/10.1080/17439884.2024.2328693

Biesta, G. (2019). Should teaching be re (dis) covered? Introduction to a symposium. *Studies in Philosophy and Education, 38*(5), 549–553.

Castells, M. (2010). *The rise of the network society*. Blackwell. https://doi.org/10.1002/9781444319514

Cervinkova, H., & Rudnicki, P. (2019). Neoliberalism, neoconservatism, authoritarianism. The politics of public education in Poland. *Journal for Critical Education Policy Studies, 17*(2).

Cone, L. (2023). The platform classroom: Troubling student configurations in a Danish primary school. *Learning, Media & Technology, 48*(1), 52–64. https://doi.org/10.1080/17439884.2021.2010093

Drucker, P. (1993). *Post-capitalist Society*. HarperBusiness.

Dudzikowa, M. (2001). *Mit o szkole jako miejscu wszechstronnego rozwoju. Eseje etnopedagogiczne*. Oficyna Wydawnicza "Impuls".

Filipiak, E. (2009). Uczenie się w klasie szkolnej w perspektywie socjokulturowej. *Forum Dydaktyczne*, 5–6.

Foucault, M. (1972). *The archaeology of knowledge and the discourse on language*. Pantheon Books.

Fraser, N. (2013). *Fortunes of feminism: From state-managed capitalism to neoliberal crisis*. Verso.

Gandhi, L. (1998). *Postcolonial theory: A critical introduction*. Edinburgh University Press.

Garcia, A. (2017). *Good reception: Teens, teachers, and mobile media in a Los Angeles High School*. MIT Press.

González López, A. E., & Büchner, F. (2024). EdTech in a broken world: Breaking and repairing in Argentinian and German Schools. *Postdigital Science and Education*. https://doi.org/10.1007/s42438-024-00490-4

Hangartner, J., Hürzeler, D., & Aebli, N. (2024). Everyday approaches to platform-mediated personalized learning in secondary schools. *Learning, Media & Technology*. https://doi.org/10.1080/17439884.2024.2367051

Jandrić, P., Knox, J., Besley, T., Ryberg, T., Suoranta, J., & Hayes, S. (2018). Postdigital science and education. *Educational Philosophy and Theory, 50*(10), 893–899. https://doi.org/10.1080/00131857.2018.1454000

Jessop, B. (2002). *The future of the capitalist state*. Polity Press.

Knox, J. (2019). What Does the 'Postdigital' Mean for Education? Three Critical Perspectives on the Digital, with Implications for Educational Research and Practice. Postdigital Science and Education 1, 357–370. https://doi.org/10.1007/s42438-019-00045-y

Livingstone, S., & Sefton-Green, J. (2016). *The class: Living and learning in the digital age*. NYU Press.

Macgilchrist, F. (2024). Educational ethnography in an age of technoculture: exploring Noise and Glitch instead of Fetishising the new. In J. Budde, A. Wischmann, M. Meier, & G. Rißler (Eds.), *Novelty, innovation & transformation in educational ethnographic research* (pp. 16–28). Routledge. https://doi.org/10.4324/9781032629384-4

Mignolo, W. D. (2011). *The darker side of western modernity: Global futures*. Duke University Press.

Novotný, P., Dvořák, D., Dvořáková, M. (2023). Czech School Reforms: Between East and West. In: Krejsler, J.B., Moos, L. (eds) School Policy Reform in Europe. Educational Governance Research, vol 22. Springer, Cham. https://doi.org/10.1007/978-3-031-35434-2_10

Pyżalski, J. (Ed.). (2025). *Generatywna sztuczna inteligencja w polskiej szkole: Przecieranie szlaków. Badania ilościowe i jakościowe nauczycieli klas 4–8 szkół podstawowych*. NASK – Państwowy Instytut Badawczy.

Rafalow, M. H. (2020). *Digital divisions. How schools create inequality in the tech era*. University of Chicago Press

Silova, I. (2010). Rediscovering post-socialism in comparative education. In I. Silova (Ed.), *Post-socialism is not dead: (Re)reading the global in comparative education* (pp. 1–24). Emerald Group Publishing.

Sims, C. (2017). *Disruptive fixation: School reform and the pitfalls of techno-idealism*. Princeton University Press.

Simons, M., & Masschelein, J. (2008). The governmentalization of learning and the assemblage of a learning apparatus. *Educational Theory, 58*(4), 391–415.

Szkudlarek, T. (2016). *On the politics of educational theory: Rhetoric, theoretical ambiguity, and the construction of society*. Routledge. https://doi.org/10.4324/9781315712505

Wagener-Böck, N., Macgilchrist, F., Rabenstein, K., & Bock, A. (2023). From automation to symmation: Ethnographic perspectives on what happens in front of the screen. *Postdigital Science and Education, 5*, 136–151. https://doi.org/10.1007/s42438-022-00350-z

Williamson, B. (2017). *Big data in education: The digital future of learning, policy, and practice*. Sage.

CHAPTER 2

Learning as Governance: Discursive Constructions of Learning in the Postdigital Knowledge Economy

In recent decades, the functions and meanings of education have undergone a profound redefinition. Historically, education was never reducible to a single, universal purpose through diverse, often competing visions, each connected to wider cultural and political projects. In some perspectives, education appears as a national cultural project, inseparably linked to the shaping of national identity and the consolidation of community (Herder, 2002); in others, as a personalist-developmental current, focused on the learner's autonomy, self-discipline, and moral growth (Montessori, 1964); and in still others, as a democratic-civic current, treating education as the foundation of civic participation and social renewal (Dewey, 1916). There is also a critical-emancipatory vision that understands education as a practice of freedom, oriented toward unveiling oppression and fostering collective transformation (Freire, 2000). Taken together these perspectives show that education has always been a contested terrain, shaped by competing ideals ranging from individual formation to cultural reproduction and democratic engagement.

Set against this historical plurality, the contemporary discourse of the "knowledge society" (Bell, 1973; Castells, 1996) brings a significant narrowing of how education is understood. Knowledge is no longer primarily seen as a shared cultural or civic good, but increasingly framed as economic capital—an asset to be mobilized for competitiveness and productivity. Within this framing, the learner is reimagined less as a

M. Popow, *Learning in the Postdigital Knowledge Society*, Palgrave Studies in Educational Media,
https://doi.org/10.1007/978-3-032-21956-5_2

citizen or moral subject than as an entrepreneurial individual expected to continually invest in personal competences in order to remain relevant within global labor markets (Szkudlarek, 2007). This reorientation signals more than a semantic shift: it represents a reconfiguration of the political rationalities that structure education, subordinating its ethical, cultural, and democratic functions to the imperatives of capital accumulation and market efficiency. What was once envisioned as the foundation of nationhood, moral autonomy, or democratic community has been reframed as a mechanism for producing calculable, optimizable subjectivities—subjects whose value lies in their capacity to sustain the dynamics of neoliberal economies.

This chapter takes as its point of departure the reconfiguration of learning within the rationalities of neoliberal governance. Education is approached not as a neutral or technical domain of transmission but as a discursive construct that organizes and legitimates broader economic and cultural projects. Globally, policies promoting lifelong learning, knowledge economies, and digital modernization has changed learning as a mechanism of competitiveness and self-management (Simons & Masschelein, 2008). It is embedded in performative logics that privilege optimization, entrepreneurial self-fashioning, and the constant enhancement of measurable competences. Such discursive shifts exemplify what Simons and Masschelein (2008) have described as the governmentalization of learning. In this context pedagogy is becomes a technology of regulation rather than a space of emancipation. What emerges is a transformation of the learner into a responsibilized subject whose value lies in the capacity to align with the temporalities of markets and the metrics of productivity.

At stake is not only how learning is framed but also how knowledge itself is defined and mediated. Despite promises that digital infrastructures would democratize access and challenge epistemic hierarchies (Drucker, 1993; Jandrić et al., 2018), the proliferation of such infrastructures has often had the opposite effect. These technologies organize knowledge around logics of prediction, privileging what can be tracked and rendered measurable (Knox, 2019; Williamson, 2017). In doing so, they embed normative assumptions about learning within seemingly neutral systems. These assumptions frequently reinforce existing exclusions (Eubanks, 2018; Noble, 2018).

This analysis is situated within the post-1989 transformations of education in Central and Eastern Europe, where reform has been neither a straightforward transition to liberal democracy nor a simple convergence with Western models, but a contested and uneven process shaped by overlapping rationalities. In Poland, as elsewhere in the region, the restructuring of schools has combined market-oriented policies of decentralization with the reassertion of cultural traditionalism, often presented through the idea of technological progress and digital modernization (Silova, 2010; Chelcea & Druţă, 2016; Novotný et al., 2023). These developments are inflected by specific historical legacies, where neoliberal efficiency and productivity are superimposed upon traditions that positioned education as central to national formation and cultural transmission. This hybrid formation makes the region a particularly interesting site for observing how global market imperatives are translated into, and mediated by, local ideological trajectories. From Jessop's (2002, 2020) strategic-relational perspective, such formations can be understood as provisional accommodations within shifting constellations of political economy and ideology. Neoliberal logics of marketization and responsibilization are not merely overlaid upon nationalist tendencies but articulated together in ways that stabilize reform agendas and legitimate authority. This hybridization demonstrates that education in CEE cannot be read as the unfolding of a single rationality—whether neoliberal, nationalist, or technocratic—but as a dynamic field where these projects interact and reshape one another. What emerges is a system in which the technologies of governance associated with globalization and digital capitalism do not displace older imaginaries of cultural reproduction. They provide new modalities through which they are exercised.

The purpose of this chapter is not to present a linear history of educational change, but to trace how learning is discursively constructed across multiple levels: policy, institutional routine, digital media, and classroom practice. Through a combination of theoretical reflection and empirical grounding, it explores the tensions between global discourses of innovation and local experiences of constraint. Rather than accepting the vocabulary of modernization for granted, the chapter interrogates the material and epistemic conditions under which learning takes place—and asks what kinds of knowledge, agency, and relationality might still be possible within increasingly automated and unequal educational landscapes.

2.1 From Knowledge Societies to Knowledge Economies. Human and Social Capital in Neoliberal Governance

The narrative of the knowledge society, popularized in late twentieth-century accounts (Bell, 1973; Castells, 1996; Drucker, 1993), announced what appeared to be an epochal rupture. It was argued that knowledge had displaced labor and capital as the decisive resource of social and economic organization. This story carried an emancipatory promise. Education and access to knowledge were expected to erode entrenched hierarchies, democratize participation, and create new spaces for cultural and civic development. Knowledge was to become the universal currency of modern life, promising inclusion and mobility in ways that material resources could not.

In practice the knowledge society proved less a break with earlier regimes of accumulation than their rearticulation in a new form. At its center was a reconceptualization of learning—not as an intellectual, dialogical, or cultural practice, but as a form of investment, subject to the logics of accumulation, calculation, and continuous evaluation. The rhetoric of knowledge as a common good was thus progressively displaced by frameworks that treated knowledge as capital: measurable, comparable, and turned into economic advantage.

To understand the dynamics of postdigital education in Central and Eastern Europe—and in Poland specifically—it is essential to locate them within the wider trajectories of post-socialist transformation. A recurring feature across CEE has been the deployment of crisis discourse as a catalyst for reform. In contexts marked by rapid systemic change and ongoing economic uncertainty, "crisis" has served not only as a descriptive category but as a governing logic (Jessop, 2018). References to falling academic standards, perceived inefficiencies in state provision, or international competitiveness, crisis narratives have been used to legitimize reforms that intensified market orientation, tightened managerial control, and the deepened reliance on performance metrics. In Poland, these narratives were particularly pronounced. International assessments such as PISA were mobilized to dramatize national shortcomings, while discourses of "modernization" and "European integration" framed the expansion of standardized testing, the growth of private tutoring industries, and the development of quasi-market relations in schooling.

What emerges from these trajectories is a distinctively post-socialist configuration of education in which the state, once the guarantor of mass access and collective welfare, is redefined as a facilitator of competition and entrepreneurial self-governance (Jessop, 2020). This shift is accompanied by widening inequalities. Middle-class, urban, and internationally oriented families are best placed to benefit from privatized opportunities and more competitive school environments, while rural and working-class communities face chronic underinvestment and diminished prospects. Such disparities, however, are reframed through meritocratic rhetoric that emphasizes individual responsibility and effort, effectively obscuring structural asymmetries and legitimizing exclusion (Buchowski, 2006). The CEE context thereby reveals a double bind. Education is expected to align with transnational policy frameworks in order to secure integration into global knowledge economies, while it is still shaped by the historical legacies of uneven access, resources, and cultural capital. In this setting—where post-socialist restructuring intersects with neoliberal governance and the pervasive reach of digital infrastructures—education is transformed into a privileged arena for negotiating these tensions, producing subjects expected to embody the democratic aspirations of the post-1989 transition while internalizing the imperatives of neoliberal adaptability, self-management, responsibility and competitiveness.

These reforms are not merely technical adjustments to shifting social and economic conditions. They are ideological projects that actively reshape the imaginaries of education. They reorganize the moral economy of schooling, redefine institutional obligations, and embed austerity as a permanent principle of governance. In Poland, especially since 2015, these dynamics have assumed a distinctly political form. As Červinkova and Rudnicki (2019) observe, contemporary education policy reflects a combination of neoliberal managerialism with authoritarian cultural politics. This hybrid formation has produced a system in which patriotic education, centralized control, and technocracy reinforce one another. Curricula have been revised to emphasize historical continuity and moral virtue, while schools are subjected to new layers of surveillance technologies, performance audits, and evaluative dashboards. The rhetoric of "excellence" legitimizes these reforms, simultaneously narrowing the space for critical, pluralist, or emancipatory pedagogies.

These tendencies are most visible in underfunded and overburdened school environments, where symbolic appeals to tradition, sacrifice, and personal virtue mask the state's withdrawal of material support. Teachers encounter mounting workloads, declining autonomy, and deteriorating working conditions, while students learn in settings that valorize conformity, procedural compliance, and patriotic performance over reflexive engagement or intellectual risk-taking. The convergence of neoliberal and nationalist discourses thus reconfigures the subject of education: not the critical citizen or democratic participant, but the disciplined, responsibilized, and culturally "loyal" learner.

Fraser's (2009) concept of "dual injustice" helps to capture the consequences of this trajectory. On one level, there is misrecognition. Marginalized knowledges and identities are delegitimized by curricula that privilege hegemonic narratives of nation, tradition, and moral order (Popow, 2015). On another level, there is maldistribution. Structural inequalities in access to resources—between urban and rural schools, between affluent and working-class families—are deepened by austerity and privatization. Educational policy, often presented in terms of innovation, digital modernization, and moral renewal, reproduces existing hierarchies. The postdigital infrastructures of governance—such as data dashboards, algorithmic management systems and performance indicators—do not remove these exclusions but adapt them to new conditions, rendering inequality calculable, monitorable, and normalized.

In this perspective, the appearance of reform in Poland and across Central and Eastern Europe is less about genuine transformation than about continuity in a new form. What is presented as modernization or national revival often masks the persistence of exclusionary structures, now mediated by technocratic tools and nationalist rhetoric. Education became a key arena in which these dynamics converged, simultaneously carrying the legacies of socialism, the pressures of neoliberal globalization, and the authoritarian turn of national politics. It produces a postdigital formation that is both regionally specific and globally resonant. This was particularly evident in the post-1989 transition, when education was reconfigured as a central site for negotiating the shift from state socialism to market democracy. Although national authorities formally kept authority over curricula and governance, reform agendas were increasingly shaped by the policy expertise and financial leverage of international organizations, most notably the World Bank and the OECD. In the 1990s, the World Bank's conditional loans and reports such as *Higher Education: The Lessons of Experience* (1994) and *Priorities and Strategies for Education* (1996) linked educational investment to human capital formation. OECD analyses such as *Education and the Economy in a Changing Society* (1989) and *Lifelong Learning for All* (1996) promoted competitiveness, adaptability, and employability as central goals. Together, these frameworks advanced a policy vocabulary in which education was no longer conceived as a cultural or civic institution but as an engine of modernization and convergence with global markets. In this configuration, equity and democracy were subordinated to efficiency and productivity, aligning education with the broader neoliberal project of economic restructuring, but not with emancipatory or civic visions of social development.

The World Bank played a key role in the early 1990s by framing education in CEE as underfunded, inefficient, and poorly adapted to market needs. Loans and technical assistance were conditioned on structural adjustments that prioritized cost-effectiveness, privatization, and decentralization (World Bank, 1994, 1995). In Poland, the 1991 Education Act transferred responsibility for school financing from the central state to municipalities, presented as democratization but functioning largely as fiscal decentralization. Wealthier municipalities could support innovation and infrastructure, while poorer ones struggled to maintain basic standards, thereby introducing new inequalities and reframing systemic problems as matters of local capacity and managerial competence. The OECD entered somewhat later but with equal force, especially after Poland and other CEE states joined in the mid-1990s and early 2000s. Through initiatives such as PISA, it established a benchmarking regime that reshaped educational priorities by positioning countries in competitive league tables (OECD, 1992, 1996). For countries in the region, PISA results became both a source of anxiety and a benchmark of progress. Poland's strong results in 2000 and 2003 were celebrated as proof that reforms were effective. At the same time, this obscured how curricula and pedagogy were being reoriented toward test performance and international comparability rather than local needs. These changes reached schools through new forms of accountability mechanisms, and standardized assessments, privileging skills linked to the global economy—such as literacy, numeracy, problem-solving—over broader civic or ethical aims. Teachers were pressured to teach to the test. Students experienced the devaluation of local history, regional languages, and artistic or vocational subjects.

These external pressures intersected with domestic reform initiatives, producing hybrid forms of governance that combined local traditions with transnational agendas. In Poland, the *Szkoła z klasą* (School with

Class) program, launched in 2002 by Gazeta Wyborcza in cooperation with the Center for Civic Education, exemplified this dynamic. The programme promoted democratic school culture, student participation, and innovative teaching. It also aligned closely with the competence-oriented frameworks advanced by the OECD, evaluating schools on measurable indicators. Teachers often described the program as simultaneously inspiring and bureaucratic—opening space for experimentation, however tethering innovation to audit culture. The cumulative effect of such interventions was the emergence of what Jessop (2002) calls a "strategic-relational" governance of education, in which local traditions of nation-building and moral regulation were not replaced but recalibrated through neoliberal and transnational frames. In Poland, curricula continued to emphasize national history and Catholic values, but reforms were simultaneously celebrated for raising PISA results and producing a labor force suited to the knowledge economy, thereby stabilizing reform by aligning seemingly contradictory agendas: national retraditionalization and global benchmarking.

Crucially, the authority of OECD and World Bank discourses lay not only in policy advice but in their capacity to reframe what counted as legitimate knowledge about education. National debates increasingly revolved around the question of "where we stand" in PISA rankings, rather than the on the broader aims of schooling. The very language of reform—competence, accountability, efficiency—was borrowed from transnational organizations. It embedded CEE education within a discursive universe that naturalized neoliberal rationalities. This epistemic alignment represents another form of dependency. While reforms were locally enacted, their legitimacy was measured externally.

At the school level, these reform pressures produced ambivalence among educators and students. Polish teachers often expressed pride in PISA performance as a form of professional validation, even as they confronted the proceduralization of teaching that eroded autonomy through targets (Grek, 2009; Ball, 2003). Students, meanwhile, experienced an exam-centered culture in which knowledge counted primarily when convertible into test results. In that context, "digital shortcuts" (from online repositories to, more recently, generative AI) functioned as pragmatic responses to a regime that defines success via standardized benchmarks (Knox, 2019; Piattoeva, 2015; Williamson, 2017). Across the region, global reforms were refracted through local politics. In Hungary, governance first shifted to municipalities and was then recentralized after 2010, a sequence associated with widening funding inequalities despite equity-oriented rhetoric (Semjén et al., 2018). The result is a characteristic hybrid governance in CEE: neoliberal vocabularies of efficiency, human capital, and benchmarking are combined with traditions of state control, moral regulation, and nation-building (Dale, 2007; Jessop, 2002).

Lifelong learning, adaptability, and entrepreneurial self are no longer presented simply as opportunities but as binding imperatives for survival in conditions of precarity. As critical scholarship has shown, the injunction to "learn continuously" functions as a disciplinary mechanism that naturalizes insecurity and reconfigures structural risks into matters of individual responsibility (Biesta, 2019). Jessop (2002) captures this dynamic in his analysis of neoliberal governance as operating less through direct state control than through a dispersed proliferation of strategic sites of coordination—such as schools, workplaces and digital platforms—where subjects are induced to align their conduct with market logics. Within such frameworks, the learner is not recognized primarily as a democratic agent, cultural participant, or bearer of rights, but as a responsibilized entrepreneur of the self, compelled to manage uncertainty through the vigilant optimization of their own capacities.

This reframing reveals the central paradox of the knowledge society discourse. While it celebrates learning as the pathway to opportunity and empowerment, it simultaneously places individuals more deeply within circuits of competition, evaluation, and control. The subject is not oriented toward critical judgment or collective renewal but toward continual adaptation. It is measured by employability and the capacity to remain perpetually flexible in response to shifting economic demands. What was initially heralded as a rupture—a new social order grounded in knowledge—thus appears less as a departure from capitalist rationalities than as their intensification, with education no longer emancipated from the economy but increasingly subsumed by it. Under these conditions, education ceases to operate as a domain where structural inequalities are exposed or alternative imaginaries cultivated (Simons & Masschelein, 2008) and instead functions as a symbolic and practical apparatus for managing inequality by translating systemic dispossession into individual responsibility. Lifelong learning, upskilling, and flexibility are promoted as adequate responses to precarious conditions, while the deeper causes of those conditions remain unaddressed. As a result, inequality is no longer understood as the outcome of broader structures of capital, class, or power, but reframed as a matter of competence, motivation, or personal failure. Governance here relies less on coercion than on the circulation of policy discourses and managerial instruments that normalize precariousness and responsibilize learners for their own survival. By presenting education as the individualized solution to structural problems, these discourses legitimize the withdrawal of collective guarantees and solidarity so that the promise of empowerment through knowledge becomes itself a technique of control, binding individuals to the very economic and political order that produces their vulnerability.

The abstract narratives of the knowledge society and technological modernization found concrete expression in a series of digitalization programs launched in Central and Eastern Europe during the 1990s and 2000s. In Poland, one of the earliest initiatives was the *Komputer dla ucznia (Computer for a student)* program, which aimed to equip schools with basic desktop computers through partnerships with local governments and private donors. Although limited and uneven, these efforts established a new horizon in which digital literacy was framed as a marker of modernization and European convergence. By the late 1990s, digitalization had become a cornerstone of national educational strategies, exemplified by the Ministry of National Education's flagship *Interkl@sa* (*Intercl@ss*) program (1998), which aimed to connect schools to the Internet, train teachers, and promote using digital tools. While often described as pioneering, it exposed structural inequalities, as wealthier urban schools gained broadband access and multimedia labs while rural schools often relied on outdated hardware and unstable connections. This led to what was described as a "digital divide" within Poland itself. The discourse around these projects present digital tools as neutral instruments of progress, but their implementation often reinforced dependency patterns. The as equipment and software were purchased from multinational corporations. Training materials were translated from Anglo-American sources with limited adaptation to local contexts. The 2000s institutionalized these trends further. Poland's *Pracownie komputerowe dla szkół* (*Computer labs for schools*) program financed computer labs across thousands of schools, accompanied by EU-supported teacher training. Initiatives like the *Szkoła z klasą* campaign popularized the notion that ICT integration was a hallmark of "good teaching". By mid-decade, digitalization had become part of the normative expectations of educational quality, aligned with EU frameworks such as the Lisbon Strategy

(2000), which positioned schools as central to producing digitally competent citizens. At the same time, tensions remained. While official discourse presented digitalization as democratizing, empirical studies pointed to enduring disparities in pedagogical use, as teachers often received only basic technical training (Instytut Badań Edukacyjnych, 2014, pp. 6–19). Computers and Internet connections were frequently used more for administrative or presentational purposes than for collaborative or critical learning. In many schools ICT resources were confined to locked labs accessible only under supervision, reinforcing their perception as inaccessible instruments.

The cumulative effect of these programs led to the deeper integration of digital infrastructures into the governance of education. Schools became increasingly accountable for demonstrating progress in ICT integration, while students were expected to acquire "digital competences" codified in curricular frameworks. Beneath this layer of modernization, the structural conditions of inequality, dependency on foreign technologies, and the persistence of transmissive pedagogy remained intact. In this sense, the digitalization programs of the 1990s and 2000s exemplify the ambivalence of post-socialist educational reform. They succeeded in inscribing the digital into the symbolic order of schooling, but they did so in ways that reinforced rather than transformed the hierarchies of knowledge, authority, and access. What follows is a mode of governance in which education becomes inseparable from its technical mediations. The very act of learning is reframed through the categories that sustain digital capitalism. Far from being neutral supports, these infrastructures reconfigure the conditions of knowledge, embedding power into the mundane operations of platforms and systems that increasingly define the everyday life of schools.

His transformation is structurally aligned with neoliberal rationalities rather than incidental to surveillance and performativity become constitutive features of education, positioning students as perpetual subjects of measurement. The subjects are calculable and continuously responsible for their own optimization, while teachers are responsibilized to translate educational encounters into outputs that can be audited and compared. In this way, the postdigital infrastructure enacts a double governance: of knowledge, by reducing it to circulations of data, and of subjectivity, by rendering learners accountable to those circulations. Postdigitality is therefore not merely a descriptive condition of technological saturation but a mode of governance that organizes relations between learners, institutions, and infrastructures, aligning education with the economization of life and embedding market logics into everyday pedagogical practices. Learning, associated with critical encounter or democratic possibility, is increasingly reconfigured as a site of market-oriented self-regulation, while subjectivity itself is shaped through practices of self-optimization that internalize the imperatives of competitiveness and adaptability. In this configuration, education no longer cultivates civic, cultural, or ethical capacities as its primary horizon but instead manufactures governable actors calibrated to the rhythms and rationalities of data-driven capitalism.

The promise of digital democratization has frequently served as the legitimizing discourse for the contemporary reconfiguration of education Technologies are presented as instruments of inclusion and participation, ostensibly widening access and strenghtening student voice. Such narratives obscure the ways these infrastructures reproduce—and in many cases intensify—epistemic injustice (Fricker, 2007). Students at the margins of dominant cultural and institutional frameworks find their contributions devalued in curricular design, erased in platform architectures, and pre-empted by algorithmic systems that constrain the very conditions of recognition and mobility. Learning analytics and performance dashboards illustrate this paradox. Marketed under the rhetoric of personalization and learner support, they translate education into metrics of efficiency, conformity, and behavioral predictability, reducing learning to data points. As Williamson (2017) shows, such systems do more than measure engagement; they existing inequalities by operationalizing activity data in ways that systematically advantage those already aligned with normative expectations. Far from functioning as neutral mediators, these technologies enact classificatory regimes that privilege dominant epistemologies while rendering experiential, cultural, and affective forms of knowledge as marginal or illegible. In this context, digital infrastructures do not democratize education. But function as mechanisms of stratification, normalizing asymmetries of voice and value while legitimizing exclusion under the veneer of objectivity. The rhetoric of empowerment thus conceals a more fundamental transformation: the embedding of inequality into the technical and epistemic fabric of education itself, where what counts as valid knowledge and who counts as a credible knower are increasingly determined by the logics of datafication and algorithmic governance.

Education, therefore, occupies a paradoxical position within the postdigital condition. While still considered a vehicle of emancipation, it increasingly functions as an apparatus that allocates opportunity along stratified and technologized lines. The rhetoric of democratization conceals the realities of dispossession. The infrastructures of datafication transform learning into an arena where recognition is unevenly distributed, and subjectivities are governed in accordance with the logics of neoliberal rationality (Szkudlarek, 2007, 2016).

Szkudlarek (2016) critiques the metaphor of the knowledge society precisely for its ideological function. It transforms education into a market-oriented pursuit of self-investment, demanding from individuals a continuous process of upskilling to maintain economic relevance. This logic aligns with broader neoliberal frameworks that displace responsibility for social inequality onto individual learners, framing learning as a private responsibility and rendering knowledge exchange into a transactional relation. Within this paradigm, human capital becomes measurable and fungible, subject to the same calculative rationalities as any other economic asset. Social capital, understood in Bourdieu and Passeron's (1990) sense as networks, dispositions, and inherited advantages, operates as a parallel currency of mobility, further stratifying access to opportunities. Education thus ceases to be primarily about cultural formation or democratic participation. Instead, it configures individuals as entrepreneurial actors who must align their subjectivities with fluctuating market demands.

It is within this entanglement of knowledge, governance, and digital infrastructure that the postdigital condition of learning must be situated. Postdigitality does not merely mark the ubiquity of digital tools but names a deeper reconfiguration in which technological systems, neoliberal rationalities, and educational practices converge. Learning is no longer framed as a collective good or a dialogical process of meaning-making. It is increasingly cast as a form of self-regulation, mediated by data-driven infrastructures that normalize precarity, responsibilization, and the economization of subjectivity. The knowledge society's emancipatory promise of democratized access is thus rearticulated as a disciplinary regime, where learners are simultaneously empowered to "take control" of their futures and compelled to conform to the imperatives of datafied capitalism.

The growing integration of technologies such as AI, robotics, and big data is reshaping the structures of labor, education, and social interaction on a global scale, though not in uniform ways. While some sectors benefit from automation and enhanced efficiency, others experience intensified precarity, the erosion of professional skills, and escalating demands for continual reskilling (Caruso, 2018). Within this shifting landscape, the discourses of the knowledge society and economy function less as neutral descriptors than as ideological tools. They rationalize the restructuring of education systems under the banner of innovation and flexibility, while legitimizing the retreat of the state from collective responsibilities in the name of individual adaptability and economic relevance (Castells, 1996; Drucker, 1993). Education is increasingly positioned at the intersection of market logic and social regulation, reinforcing a model of the learner as an entrepreneurial subject tasked with optimizing their human capital. These dynamics are intensified as digital infrastructures saturate everyday life, with AI operating as part of a wider socio-technical apparatus that shapes subjectivity. In education, this manifests in surveillance, personalization, and predictive analytics embedded directly into pedagogical practices (Selwyn, 2019; Williamson, 2017). The boundary between learning and data extraction grows porous, as routine activities—searching for information, correcting, writing emails, summarizing, completing assignments, even interacting with a chatbot—feed machine-learning systems and position students and teachers simultaneously as users and data sources. As generative AI takes on cognitive functions once reserved for learners and scholars, questions of educational purpose become increasingly unsettled, emphasizing the extent to which education has been recast within infrastructures of governance and accumulation.

What emerges is a reconfiguration of education as a contested field in which authority, agency, and justice are negotiated through technological infrastructures. Postdigital education is not simply the incorporation of new tools into existing models of instruction but a terrain shaped by algorithmic systems, platform dynamics, and data economies that reconstitute the learner as a digitally rendered subject, constantly monitored and assessed. Drawing on Jessop's (2002) strategic-relational approach, this moment exemplifies a mode of governance in which institutions perform alignment with digital innovation while underlying hierarchies and exclusions remain intact. The platformization of learning intensifies these dynamics. Rather than fulfilling the emancipatory promise associated with digital transformation, the postdigital condition embeds inequality within systems that appear neutral, efficient, and inevitable (Fraser, 2009). In Central and Eastern Europe, these pressures intersect with distinct post-socialist trajectories. Producing not a mere echo of global neoliberalism but a layered formation of educational governance. The residues of authoritarian statecraft preserve habits of centralization and bureaucratic surveillance. The institutional logic of market reform inserts competition, privatization, and efficiency as default principles of organization. Resurgent ethno-nationalism recasts education as a moral project and a vehicle of nation-building. Together, these strands create a hybrid order in which schools are simultaneously tasked with producing economically competitive subjects, politically compliant citizens, and culturally homogenous communities.

In Poland, this convergence is especially visible. Policy discourses speak the language of modernization and global competitiveness, however reforms are saturated with nationalist appeals to tradition and historical continuity. Schools are therefore tasked with three simultaneous mandates—to prepare students for the demands of knowledge economies, to instill civic obedience within an increasingly polarized polity, and to reproduce a culturally homogeneous national identity. These dynamics highlight the need for a situated critique of educational reform in Central and Eastern Europe, one that resists universalizing accounts of neoliberal globalization and instead attends to the historical, political, and cultural logics of post-transitional societies. Postdigital infrastructures of education should thus be read not merely as technical systems but as political assemblages that crystallize the region's hybrid rationalities: the managerial language of neoliberal efficiency, the disciplinary residues of authoritarian control, and the cultural imperatives of nationalist identity. In this sense, Central and Eastern Europe is not a marginal case but a vantage point from which to interrogate how digital rationalities are refracted through context, producing configurations of governance that both echo and diverge from those prevalent in Western liberal democracies.

The ongoing realignment of education in the region cannot be separated from the digital infrastructures through which it now takes shape. These infrastructures do not merely facilitate instruction. They actively structure it. In the postdigital condition—where data flows, algorithmic evaluation, and platform-based environments organize the daily life of schools—education is increasingly produced through its technological mediations. Pedagogical relationships, institutional priorities, and curricular values are reconfigured in ways that often remain outside public debate, justified by the language of innovation and efficiency. Against this backdrop, a pressing question emerges—one that this book now confronts empirically and analytically: has artificial intelligence transformed what it means to learn in school, and if so, for whom, under what conditions, and at what cost?

2.2 Educational Media in the Postdigital Reality. Has AI Changed School Learning?

Recent scholarship that digital technologies are no longer peripheral to educational life but embedded in its very structure. They shape how schools operate, how knowledge is mediated, and how learning is understood (Jandrić et al., 2018; Macgilchrist et al., 2024). The proliferation of AI-driven tools and infrastructures has sparked renewed interest in rethinking the future of education. Empirical work in this area has been steadily expanding, from ethnographic accounts of classrooms shaped by mobile media, inequality, and reform discourses (Garcia, 2017; Livingstone & Sefton-Green, 2016; Rafalow, 2020; Sims, 2017) to more recent studies tracing how platforms and AI reorganize pedagogical practices across diverse contexts (Bhatia et al., 2024; Cone, 2023; González López & Büchner, 2024; Hangartner et al., 2024; Wagener-Böck et al., 2023). These studies show that what is often presented as technological innovation in fact reconfigures the temporal rhythms, hierarchies, and epistemic boundaries of schooling. Promoted under the banners of personalization and efficiency, platform logics and algorithmic systems entrench particular forms of authority while narrowing horizons of knowledge and extending practices of surveillance.

Although education under neoliberalism has long served to align subject formation with labor market demands (Biesta, 2006; Jandrić & Hayes, 2020; Selwyn, 2013), the rise of AI introduces a new order. Here, learning is no longer understood only as the acquisition of knowledge or skills, but as the continuous production of data—inputs that enable systems to monitor, predict, and optimize behavior. At the same time, it involves new forms of participation and co-creation, where students are drawn into shaping, as well as being shaped by, the digital infrastructures of education. The student becomes both a learner and a data source, subject to feedback loops that often escape interpretation or contestation. As algorithmic systems quietly reorganize the norms and rhythms of schooling, students and teachers navigate a landscape increasingly governed by opaque logics, without adequate frameworks for reflection or resistance. It is this disjuncture—between the pace of technological integration and the absence of critical institutional response—that defines the urgency of the inquiry undertaken in the chapters that follow.

Postdigital education has as a response to the uncritical embrace of technological advancement, pushing back against digital determinism and foregrounding the entanglement of technology with pedagogy, governance, and political economy (Knox, 2019; Jandrić & Hayes, 2020). It does not reject technology as such, but resists the assumption that innovation inherently improves educational practice. Instead, it asks how digital systems shape social relations in the classroom, reinforce institutional hierarchies, and condition what counts as legitimate knowledge (Selwyn, 2019). From this perspective, attention shifts from functionality to ethics. Educational technologies must be assessed in relation to values such as inclusion, participation, and critical inquiry—not simply efficiency or scale. As Jandrić (2019) warns, the ongoing commodification of learning risks reducing education to a transactional logic, where value is measured through metrics and outputs. In the postdigital condition, the transformation of learning has become a central concern in educational research, pointing to wider changes in how knowledge is produced. Technological developments reshape everyday practices and blur the boundaries between communication, thought, and social interaction. The smartphone illustrates this shift particularly well. By enabling constant connectivity and instant access to information, it integrates learning into daily routines (Twenge, 2017). Its presence has not only extended education beyond the classroom but also redefined its temporal and spatial dimensions, making learning more informal, mobile, and entangled with social relations.

Emerging technologies such as AI, big data, and immersive environments occupy a central place in this postdigital landscape, which require careful and critical analysis. AI, for instance, is often celebrated for its capacity to personalize learning, but its reliance on surveillance, data extraction, and opaque algorithms raises profound concerns (Selwyn, 2019). Deployed in predictive analytics or automated assessment, such systems risk entrenching inequalities by embedding existing biases into processes that remain difficult to question or audit (Williamson, 2017). These technologies are never neutral. They are produced within specific social, economic, and ideological contexts that shape both their functionality and their consequences.

The COVID-19 pandemic further showed the limits of thinking about technology as a simple solution. Mere access to devices proved insufficient without coherent pedagogical strategies, and equitable institutional frameworks. As Selwyn (2013) argues, digital inequality is not reducible to questions of hardware. It also encompasses disparities in the ability to interpret, manage, and act upon information. Cultivating digital literacy, then, requires more than the acquisition of technical skills. It calls for a critical awareness of how digital systems mediate power, shape identities, and govern behavior.

In this context, the integration of AI into education raises questions about autonomy, transparency, and democratic accountability. As these systems increasingly determine evaluation and assessment criteria, notice should be paid to the normative assumptions that are rarely made explicit. Postdigital education calls for a different orientation. Instead of focusing on the technical improvement of tools, it emphasizes reimagining of education as a space for collective agency, ethical reflection, and democratic renewal. As Williamson et al. (2023) note, the future of digital education will be shaped less by innovation itself than by the principles societies choose to uphold, includingequity, intellectual freedom, and the right to learn on just and transparent terms.

Artificial intelligence sharpens these debates. Unlike earlier educational media, it functions as a responsive system that both shapes and is shaped by user behavior. Through continuous data analysis, it generates feedback, sequences content, and simulates interaction. These capacities promise adaptability, but also but also unsettle established notions of epistemic authority and the purposes of education (Jandrić et al., 2020; Knox, 2019; Selwyn, 2013). By embedding metrics of efficiency and prediction into design, AI risks narrowing learning to what can be tracked and optimized (Williamson et al., 2023). Pedagogical practices grounded in human judgment and relationality are increasingly unsettled by algorithmic systems capable of producing content and directing cognitive pathways without human mediation. As Bayne and Ross (2024) argue, the involvement of AI in meaning-making compels a reconsideration of what it means to know, to learn, and to act within technologically mediated environments.

Posthumanist and actor-network approaches help frame this transformation not as a simple displacement of the human but as a redistribution of agency. Braidotti (2019) and Ferrando (2019) conceptualize intelligence as emergent within assemblages of human and non-human actors, foregrounding the entangled character of cognition in digital ecologies. From this perspective, AI is not a neutral tool but an epistemic agent that participates in structuring the conditions of learning. This raises critical questions about learner autonomy, the changing role of the teacher, and the shifting ontologies of knowledge itself. If AI contributes to organizing and validating educational experience, pedagogy must respond not only through technical adaptation but through ethical and political critique. In the postdigital condition, teaching entails more than managing content. It requires examining the infrastructures that shape access, legibility, and authority, asking not only what is learned but through which systems and in whose interest.

The pedagogical potential of AI-enhanced media is often measured through narrow indicators such as engagement, retention, or test scores. At the same time, deeper dimensions of learning—like critical reflection, metacognition, independent judgment—are frequently overlooked. Even well-designed systems that provide personalized support (Alam & Mohanty, 2023) can foster passivity, as students start depending on automated cues rather than developing their own capacities (Selwyn, 2013). Moreover, the data infrastructures on which these technologies rely are not neutral. Personalization algorithms can reproduce structural inequalities, reinforcing exclusion through opaque mechanisms that are difficult to detect or challenge. The integration of AI into education, therefore, cannot be reduced to questions of usability or outcomes. It requires sustained attention to the political, epistemological, and ethical conditions under which technologies shape learning.

These tensions are particularly visible in contexts such as Poland, where the adoption of AI in schools has been marked by ambivalence and concern. Teachers express skepticism, often linked to fears of the erosion of educational integrity (Pyżalski 2025). Such anxieties are articulated in moral terms, portraying AI as a force of decline that undermines authenticity and encourages "intellectual laziness" (Williamson et al., 2023). These narratives echo earlier cycles of technological anxiety in which each new medium was cast as a threat to pedagogical tradition. By maintaining a strict opposition between human-led and machine-assisted instruction, they entrench binary thinking and inhibit the development of more nuanced pedagogical models capable of addressing the complexities of hybrid learning environments.

Despite the proliferation of AI in student practice—especially in everyday tasks like homework and writing—educational policy in many

CEE countries continues to lag behind. Institutional responses have largely emphasized access to tools and basic digital literacy, treating AI as an inevitable feature of modernization. It is not understood as an object of critical pedagogical inquiry. As recent studies indicate (Pyżalski et al., 2025), students are already engaging with AI in sophisticated and often unregulated ways. The rapid normalization of these practices has outpaced the capacity of schools to respond, revealing a growing disjunction between classroom realities and the frameworks designed to govern them. AI is no longer simply a tool for delivering content. It is becoming an active participant in how knowledge is organized, legitimated, and assessed. This shift necessitates not only practical strategies for responsible integration but a broader rethinking of what educational agency might mean in an increasingly automated epistemic landscape.

The integration of AI into education presents far-reaching ethical and socio-political challenges, reshaping how learning is structured and governed. As Schiff (2022) observes, national AI strategies tend to prioritize economic growth and innovation, often at the expense of educational values. In this climate, schools risk becoming laboratories for data-driven governance, where algorithmic efficiency displaces more relational and emancipatory conceptions of pedagogy. The biases embedded in AI systems—particularly those trained on historical data—can amplify existing inequalities, affecting learners along lines of race, class, gender, and neurodiversity. Research by Eubanks (2018) demonstrates how so-called "personalized" systems may in practice reinforce exclusion, codifying structural disadvantage into predictive models that operate without transparency or recourse. Despite claims to tailor learning to individual needs, adaptive platforms frequently promote a narrow educational logic that prioritizes conformity, optimization, and task completion, sidelining critical thinking and reducing the space for both student and teacher agency (Selwyn, 2019; Williamson et al., 2023).

The everyday normalization of AI—marketed as convenience, productivity, or seamless functionality—further obscures these dynamics. Many of the tools now used in educational practice were not designed with pedagogical integrity or ethical accountability in mind. Their integration reflects a broader cultural shift toward automation as a default solution, one that rarely pauses to ask what is lost when inquiry is outsourced or when decisions are delegated to systems whose logics remain opaque. In this context, ensuring human oversight is not merely a safeguard but a pedagogical imperative. Educators must retain authority over the conditions of learning, while students must be equipped with critical digital literacies that allow them to interrogate algorithmic recommendations and understand how data circulates (Jandrić et al., 2020; Selwyn, 2013).

Meeting these challenges requires more than technical safeguards or formal ethics checklists. What is needed are governance frameworks attentive to the social, cultural, and political contexts in which AI is designed and applied. This entails resisting technocratic rationalities that reduce education to inputs and outputs, while strengthening commitments to equity, autonomy, and democratic deliberation (Schiff, 2022). From a posthumanist standpoint, AI also prompts a deeper reconsideration of how learning and knowledge are understood. A relational ontology can be employed here, one that conceives humans, technologies, and environments as co-constitutive (Braidotti, 2019; Haraway, 2013a). Within this view, AI is not a neutral instrument but an active participant in structuring epistemic practices. It shapes what is learned, how knowledge is organized, who is authorized to speak, and how educational subjectivities are formed. Pedagogy, in turn, becomes an ongoing ethical negotiation—attuned to the entanglements of human and algorithmic actors, and committed to keeping education open, critical, and socially accountable.

This ontological shift redefines educational agency. Pedagogies grounded in humanist assumptions and transmission-based models give way to approaches that conceive learning as emergent, relational, and situated within assemblages of human and non-human actors. AI systems become part of extended cognitive networks that blur distinctions between mind, tool, and environment. Concepts such as "cyborg pedagogy" (Garoian & Gaudelius, 2001) describe how technologies mediate and co-produce learning, dissolving binary divisions between educator and medium. In this setting, the teacher is refigured less as a transmitter of knowledge than as a curator of hybrid learning ecologies. Teaching brings ethical discernment, contextual sensitivity, and pedagogical care into environments increasingly shaped by algorithmic logics.

The integration of AI into educational governance is gradually reshaping the distribution of pedagogical authority. Intelligent tutoring systems, predictive analytics, and algorithmically guided learning environments increasingly mediate how education is structured and delivered, introducing layers of decision-making that operate beyond the reach of educators and shifting influence toward data-driven infrastructures whose internal logics remain inaccessible to those responsible for teaching. As these systems orchestrate sequencing and evaluation, teachers are recast as facilitators of pre-scripted instructional pathways, their professional agency tethered to platforms built around optimization and prediction—values that sit uneasily with the ethical, dialogic, and context-sensitive dimensions of pedagogy. This is not a clean rupture with earlier models of educational control. In many Central and Eastern European contexts, as Klus-Stańska (2012) notes, teaching has long been organized around content delivery and behavioral assessment, with autonomy constrained by standardized curricula, external examinations, and institutional cultures that privilege procedural conformity. In this light, the adoption of AI may serve less to disrupt than to intensify existing dynamics. By enhancing administrative efficiency and reinforcing instructional regularity, it may deepen a technocratic model of schooling in which teachers supervise rather than shape learning, and students are trained to meet predefined expectations with increasing precision. What emerges is a vision of education reframed through behavioral metrics and data flows—one that privileges predictability over complexity and standardization over uncertainty (Williamson et al., 2023). In this configuration, traditional instructional models and AI-based systems converge, not through technological innovation alone but through a shared tendency to delimit what counts as legitimate educational action, subordinating teacher judgment and student subjectivity to logics of control and reducing the space for critical awareness.

What is diminished in this configuration are the uncertain, affective, and speculative dimensions of education—those practices that require time, attentiveness, and tolerance for ambiguity. The capacity to reflect ethically, to venture into unfamiliar intellectual terrain, or to encounter difference without predetermined outcomes becomes difficult to sustain in environments governed by metrics and predictive control. The question, then, is not whether AI enhances or diminishes learning, but what kinds of educational relationships and subjectivities it privileges, and at what cost to pedagogical practices that resist quantification. This issue cannot be separated from AI's entanglement with coloniality. Algorithmic systems are built on data and infrastructures shaped by histories of domination and extraction. Many rely on datasets that privilege Western, affluent, and Anglophone contexts, reproducing normative assumptions about intelligence, success, and behavior (Nemorin, 2024). Alternative epistemologies—Indigenous worldviews, Global South traditions, and pluriversal ways of knowing—are not simply excluded but systematically marginalized (Visvanathan, 1997). Such asymmetries are embedded in technologies presented as neutral, which in practice filter and rank learners according to culturally narrow criteria. Decolonial scholarship stresses that these are manifestations of epistemic violence. As Quijano (2000) argues, the coloniality of power endures through systems that organize knowledge, value, and personhood hierarchically. In AI, these hierarchies are recast in the language of optimization and efficiency, masking the reproduction of inequities within code and infrastructure. Addressing this requires more than inclusive design. It demands a rethinking of whose knowledge counts and how it becomes legible in digital systems. Critical race and decolonial studies call for epistemic pluralism not as a token of diversity but as a constitutive principle for reimagining the architectures of AI and education (Mohamed et al., 2020). Within educational settings, such pluralism reorients human–machine relations around historical accountability, dialogic learning, and relational epistemology. Technology here is not a neutral mediator or disruptive force but part of a broader ethical and political terrain in which educators, students, and systems must negotiate the conditions of learning. This perspective resists the standardizing effects of algorithmic governance and affirms education as a practice rooted in multiplicity, shaped by lived histories, and oriented toward justice.

Posthumanist scholarship offers a lens to look into these dynamics, exposing the political and epistemological assumptions embedded within AI systems. Haraway's (2013b) notion of "situated knowledges" emphasizes that all knowledge—including that operationalized through algorithms—is historically and culturally situated, shaped by institutional contexts and distributions of power. AI technologies are therefore not neutral instruments but products of particular social imaginaries that encode and reproduce hierarchies of race, gender, language, class, and geography, often invisibly, through patterns of optimization presented as objective, but carrying normative weight. As AI platforms become part of educational practice, their claims to neutrality demand questioning. Systems trained on predominantly Euro-American datasets or aligned with commercial imperatives privilege particular conceptions of intelligence, learning, and success. They may diminish or erase other epistemic traditions. In transnational and post-socialist contexts such as Central and Eastern Europe, this dynamic can deepen existing asymmetries by marginalizing local pedagogical forms and subordinating educational priorities to external models of "best practice". Furthermore they can produce subtle forms of epistemic dependency where modernization coincides with the erasure of plurality. Addressing these challenges requires a commitment to epistemic justice, understood not only as access to information but as the recognition and legitimation of diverse knowledge traditions. This entails asking whose knowledge is encoded in algorithmic systems, how it is structured and represented, and which voices are elevated or excluded in automated decision-making. It also requires rethinking educational technologies as systems that embody assumptions about learning.

Posthumanist ethics offer an alternative orientation to these issues. It shifts attention from individualist notions of autonomy toward a relational understanding of subjectivity and agency. Braidotti (2019) develops an ethical sensibility grounded in sustainability, interconnectedness, and shared accountability, reframing educational technologies not as neutral tools to be optimized but as participants in socio-technical ecologies. From this perspective, AI is part of broader assemblages of learning in which care, equity, and responsiveness are integral to pedagogy. The focus of ethical debate therefore extends beyond concerns about privacy or bias. It includes the historical, cultural, and political conditions that shape how AI systems operate in particular educational contexts. Learning environments shaped by such an orientation treat complexity as inherent to education rather than a problem to be solved, and remain open to multiple ways of knowing attentive to the uneven distribution of epistemic authority. They create space for dialogue between human and mechanic agents without collapsing differences or surrendering judgment to automation. In this sense, the ethical integration of AI in education involves rethinking the purposes of education itself and clarifying whose knowledges, lives, and futures it is intended to serve. Reconsidered in light of these debates, De Corte's (1994) paradigm of "learning with media" becomes particularly relevant. Technologies, especially those driven by AI, are not passive carriers of content but active in shaping how knowledge is structured and valued. Adaptive systems may generate personalized learning pathways, offering support to individual learners, but the predictive logics behind them rest on assumptions about effective and desirable learning. These assumptions, far from neutral, reflect dominant cultural and epistemological norms and in doing so restrict the scope for diverse ways of knowing and learning.

The postdigital context complicates inherited distinctions between human and technological agency in education. AI systems not only deliver content but filter, organize, and prioritize information, shaping the very conditions under which learning unfolds. As they assume central roles in instructional mediation and evaluation, they influence curricular direction and delimit what counts as valid knowledge (Jandrić et al., 2018; Noble, 2018; Williamson et al., 2023). This redistribution of authority challenges established notions of authorship and pedagogical control. Rather than operating as neutral instruments for efficiency or scale, AI systems are embedded in socio-technical assemblages that negotiate power, access, and epistemic legitimacy. Postdigital pedagogy offers a framework for examining how these assemblages structure education—not only through technological affordances but through the values and assumptions encoded in their design.

Alam and Mohanty's (2023) framework develops this discussion by treating educational technology as an ecosystem, not an add-on. They identify four dimensions—mobility, interactivity, AI, and immersive tools—that together shape contemporary learning environments. Mobility extends learning beyond fixed spaces, enabling context-sensitive education but exposing inequities in infrastructure and access. Interactivity can sustain collaboration and inquiry, however when applied superficially, it reduces learning to distraction disguised as engagement. AI and immersive media such as virtual and augmented reality broaden pedagogical possibilities but also intensify concerns about surveillance, bias, and the erosion of relational teaching. While AI enables personalization, Alam and Mohanty (2023) stress that it should complement human judgment. Similarly, immersive tools require thoughtful integration into instructional design if they are to carry educational value. The strength of their model lies in highlighting that the pedagogical significance of emerging technologies cannot be separated from ethics, equity, and support. Realizing this potential depends not only on technical provision but on sustained investment in inclusive policy, teacher development, and critical reflection on the social conditions in which technologies are deployed. In this sense, postdigital pedagogy shifts the focus from choosing tools to designing systems that remain responsive, pluralistic, and attentive to the complexities of both learners and technologies.

These concerns are articulated in the works of Pyżalski (2024) and Stunża (2024), who examine the tension between technological efficiency and pedagogical integrity. Pyżalski (2024) points out that AI systems short-circuit key cognitive and emotional processes—struggle, reflection, productive failure—by providing immediate answers and solutions.

While such acceleration may boost performance on discrete tasks, it risks reducing learning to passive consumption and bypassing the inquiry and resilience that emerge through friction and uncertainty. Stunża (2024), while acknowledging AI's potential for personalization, stresses that its value depends on how it is situated within broader pedagogical aims. Drawing on Freirean traditions, he argues for learning environments in which students critically interrogate the socio-technical assumptions built into technologies they use. In this view, AI is not a neutral authority but a historically and culturally situated actor, interacting with rather than determining processes of meaning-making and subject formation. When educators approach AI as contingent and interpretable infrastructure, pedagogical agency shifts. It becomes responsive to institutional frictions, local constraints, and the lived experiences of teachers and students. Instead of framing human and machine in opposition, this perspective shows how algorithmic outputs circulate within everyday school routines—sometimes accepted, sometimes modified, sometimes resisted. Students also engage with these systems from different starting points. For some, AI provides support; for others, it introduces misrecognition or exclusion. Learner agency is uneven, shaped by prior literacies, socioeconomic position, and institutional narratives about success and ability. Critical digital literacy in this setting cannot be equated with technical fluency alone. It requires the capacity to interrogate the epistemic and institutional logics that underpin AI—how systems classify knowledge, structure authority, and define what is visible or valuable (Dixon-Román et al., 2020; Selwyn, 2013). AI functions as a regulatory device based in wider cultural imaginaries and institutional practices, reconfiguring not only how knowledge circulates but whose knowledge is legitimized, how learning is made legible, and what forms of participation are recognized or, sometimes, excluded. Understanding AI in these terms shifts attention from its novelty or technical promise to its entanglement with school governance, and the shaping of educational subjectivities.

When AI systems are introduced into education without institutional reflection or participatory deliberation, their adoption often reinforces technocratic logics of efficiency, prediction, and control. Classrooms shaped by these priorities shift away from interpretive engagement and relational pedagogy, becoming environments where compliance, performance, and quantification dominate (Noble, 2018; Williamson et al., 2023). Ambiguity and disagreement—vital dimensions of learning—are displaced by procedural clarity and algorithmic certainty. Students' positions within these systems are not fixed. Postdigital education emerges through the interplay of algorithmic infrastructures and institutional constraints, producing conditions in which learners are neither wholly determined by technology nor fully autonomous. Where students are engaged as agents who can question the terms of their interaction with AI, new forms of authorship and agency become possible. These openings are partial but they create space to redirect the normative flows of data. However such interventions cannot resolve the structural asymmetries of schooling. They reorient learning toward context and epistemic plurality. In these moments, education is not reduced to measurable outputs but remains connected to the social and political worlds in which it unfolds. These dynamics are inseparable from the material and institutional conditions of schooling. AI does not enter a vacuum but attaches to terrains already marked by educational policy and long-standing pedagogical tensions, reconfiguring rather than erasing them. Teachers must navigate contradictory demands—balancing algorithmic prompts with professional judgment, and policy imperatives with classroom realities. Students encounter AI not as a neutral support but as part of a wider assemblage that signals which forms of knowledge are valued and which learners are recognized. In this environment, identity is not pre-given but shaped in ongoing encounters with human and non-human actors.

How students are positioned—as capable or deficient, visible or peripheral—emerges through these mediated interactions. Recognition, in this sense, is not only a matter of social affirmation but of epistemic visibility: whose knowledge practices are rendered legible and whose are silenced. From a postdigital perspective, such positioning cannot be separated from the entanglement of technological infrastructures with institutional, cultural, and political forces that shape what counts as legitimate learning. From a posthuman angle, recognition extends beyond human actors, as algorithmic systems themselves participate in structuring the conditions of visibility and invisibility, embedding assumptions about value and authority into the architectures of education. The next chapter turns to this terrain, examining how AI functions within postdigital peripheries, particularly in Central and Eastern Europe, as a site where questions of cultural legibility, recognition, and epistemic inclusion become especially acute.

2.3 Identity, Exclusion, and Epistemic Pluralism in the Postdigital Periphery

In the postdigital landscape of Central and Eastern Europe, education plays a central role in shaping identities within contexts marked by unstable infrastructures and politicized cultural narratives. Modernization efforts, nationalist projects, and neoliberal restructuring continue to shape how education is organized and experienced across the region (Silova, 2010). Within uneven digital environments, where disparities in access and literacy persist, identity emerges as a contingent process shaped by social and spatial inequalities (Bayne, 2015). In Poland and neighboring countries, curricula often emphasize national history and moral education, reinforcing epistemic hierarchies that are further legitimized by market-driven priorities of competitiveness and digital competency. These intertwined logics sustain dominant narratives of development and belonging while sidelining alternative ways of knowing and being. Hybrid postdigital identities often come into conflict with these normative structures. Although student populations are increasingly diverse—socially, linguistically, and digitally—schools in countries such as Poland, Czechia, and Lithuania frequently lack the capacity to engage meaningfully with this complexity. The response to the arrival of Ukrainian refugee students after 2022 illustrates these tensions. Under-resourced digital infrastructures and rigid curricula left many schools unable to provide adequate language instruction or culturally responsive pedagogy. These shortcomings reveal more than logistical limits. They expose a deeper failure to extend epistemic hospitality. As Fricker (2007) notes, hermeneutical injustice occurs when dominant frameworks render certain experiences unintelligible. In education, this is compounded by digital platforms whose algorithmic design reinforces prevailing norms while marginalizing others (Noble, 2018), contributing to the silencing of subaltern perspectives both within and beyond the classroom.

Formal schooling in Poland has struggled to recognize or support the hybrid and often precarious identities of students who fall outside normative expectations. The experience of Ukrainian refugees entering the system after the Russian invasion of 2022 illustrates this gap. Many schools, already operating with limited resources, were unprepared to provide sustained language support or culturally responsive teaching. They also lacked the pedagogical orientation and institutional flexibility to address educational needs, psychological trauma, or different forms of knowledge and experience (Popow, 2023). This failure must be situated within the broader trajectory of neoliberal education reform in Poland, where performance metrics has been prioritized over equity and social cohesion. The mechanisms through which this reform agenda is realized are most visible in the evaluative culture of schools, where quality is increasingly measured through narrow indicators that privilege standardization over inclusion (Gromkowska-Melosik, 2018).

The growing reliance on test results and institutional rankings as proxies for quality makes these tensions especially visible. Although these measures appear objective, they frequently obscure the structural disadvantages faced by newly arrived or marginalized students. As Szkudlarek (2016) observes, this model reduces education to an instrumental pursuit of employability, sidelining humanistic values such as empathy, ethical engagement, and collective responsibility. The case of Ukrainian emphasizes the urgency of a pedagogical shift—away from narrow content delivery and assessment, and toward an ethic of care, responsiveness, and epistemic justice suited to the complexities of a postdigital, pluralist society. Current reform efforts, such as the draft resolution on the Digital Transformation of Education Policy, show how neoliberal priorities remain intact even when framed in the language of innovation. Although the policy signals support for technological modernization, the integration of digital tools in classrooms has rarely led to meaningful pedagogical change. Instead, technologies are layered onto traditional models, reinforcing hierarchies and rote routines rather than fostering collaboration, interactivity, or student agency, a dynamic that reflects the broader post-socialist pattern of combining the appearance of innovation with the persistence of conventional authority structures (Silova, 2010). In this setting, digital platforms often reproduce epistemic hierarchies instead of challenging them. National heritage and neoliberal performance metrics continue to dominate curricular and institutional priorities, leaving little room for critical engagement with diverse or contested knowledge systems. Identity is therefore not simply a matter of individual expression but is co-constructed through institutional practices, technological mediation, and infrastructural limitations. Students must navigate complex intersections of class, gender, ethnicity, geography, and digital competence within systems that frequently withhold recognition from post-socialist, refugee, feminist, or queer perspectives. The inadequate response to Ukrainian refugee students after 2022 was not only a question of limited resources but revealed a deeper refusal to accommodate epistemic difference.

Addressing the exclusions and asymmetries embedded in post-socialist education systems requires a decolonial and postdigital pedagogy grounded in epistemic pluralism—one that values multiple ways of knowing and understands identity as relational and negotiated. In Central and Eastern Europe, the transformation of education since 1989 has been driven by broader geopolitical and epistemological realignments. The collapse of state-socialist institutions opened the way for neoliberal reforms, with repeated invocations of "crisis" used to legitimize market-driven restructuring (Olssen & Peters, 2005). This discourse has cast public education as ineffective and in need of restructuring, justifying the growth of private tutoring, commercial edtech platforms, and individualized learning services. The result is a system increasingly governed by entrepreneurial and self-investment logics (Ball, 2012; Bourdieu & Passeron, 1990), often at the expense of collective, democratic, and locally embedded imaginaries. Curriculum reforms across the region have tended to align schooling with ideals of modernization, privileging efficiency and economic output while marginalizing regional and alternative knowledge traditions (Silova, 2010). In Poland, this trajectory has converged with a broader conservative turn, exemplified by the 2017 re-centralization of the system and the reinstatement of a national curriculum anchored in Catholic doctrine, historical continuity, and patriotic instruction. It shows how, in education in Poland, conservative and neoliberal tendencies operate simultaneously, reinforcing each other's functions (Popow, 2015).

The integration of digital technologies into education has reshaped how young people in Central and Eastern Europe negotiate identity. Digital platforms create openings for engaging with marginalized knowledge traditions, forming connections across borders, and experimenting with subjectivities that exceed official educational scripts. At the same time, they are embedded in algorithmic and commercial infrastructures that reinforce global hierarchies—privileging dominant languages, aesthetics, and cultural norms while obscuring dissenting or minoritized perspectives (Noble, 2018). In the region's post-socialist context, where education remains bound up with unresolved struggles over identity and authority, these contradictions are particularly visible. The legacies of state socialism, overlaid with neoliberal restructuring and renewed nationalist projects, have produced systems in which the question of valid knowledge—what counts, who decides, whose experience is recognized—remains unresolved. As Silova (2010) observes, the interaction of these forces narrows the space for epistemic diversity, reducing education to an instrument of national alignment or economic utility. Under such conditions, identity cannot be treated as fixed or given. It emerges through the intersections of class, gender, ethnicity, geography, and technological access, as well as through young people's shifting positions within global flows of meaning and power.

The growing presence of AI in education adds another layer to these dynamics. In a region where technological infrastructures remain uneven and knowledge production is peripheral to global centers, AI functions not only as a tool but as a structuring force that shapes how learning is defined and practiced. As Pyżalski (2025) observes, generative AI in Polish schools is used largely to streamline administrative tasks—producing quizzes or rewording texts. It is not used for fostering student autonomy or critical engagement with the technology itself. Few teachers address its ethical or social implications in the classroom. This instrumental use reflects a wider pattern in neoliberal schooling, where technical efficiency and automation are valued over dialogue and deeper pedagogical reflection. At the same time, most AI systems are built on Anglophone, Eurocentric datasets, reflecting cultural and linguistic biases that marginalize local knowledges and identities (Noble, 2018). In such settings, the promise of innovation is undermined by the persistence of epistemic exclusions that are digitally mediated but structurally rooted. The adoption of AI in Central and Eastern Europe cannot, therefore, be reduced to innovation or efficiency. It must be examined through the lens of epistemic justice. Pyżalski's findings point not Pyżalski (2025) only to the limited pedagogical use of generative AI but also to teachers' doubts—concerns about dependency, the erosion of trust, and the potential for misuse. More telling is the absence of institutional guidance on how to approach AI ethically and inclusively. This absence signals a broader failure of what Fricker (2007) terms epistemic hospitality: the willingness to recognize and include different ways of knowing. In this vacuum, AI can reinforce hierarchies—privileging dominant languages, embedding extractive data practices, and silencing perspectives that lie outside the prevailing epistemic order.

If schools are to move beyond these exclusions, integrating AI must become part of a wider rethinking of education itself. A decolonial, post-digital pedagogy would not treat identity formation as an isolated or apolitical process but as one shaped by collective struggle, structural conditions, and mediated experience. Here, the dialogical character of AI can become pedagogically significant. When students engage with AI systems not as authoritative sources but as interlocutors, they can begin to treat outputs as starting points for a conversation. Such a perspective resonates with constructivist traditions in which knowledge emerges through questioning, negotiation, and reflection (Vygotsky, 1978; Bruner, 1996; Freire, 1970). Within the Polish context, Klus-Stańska (2012) similarly critiques transmissive models of teaching and calls for pedagogies that recognize learning as an interpretive, dialogical process grounded in the agency of students. Taken together, these perspectives suggest that if framed critically, AI could serve not as an instrument of automation but as a support for inquiry—posing alternative formulations, exposing contradictions, or simulating perspectives that students and teachers interrogate together.

Realizing this potential requires curricula that foreground epistemic pluralism, digital literacy as a practice of critique, and pedagogies that emphasize equity, reflection, and shared authorship of knowledge. Rather than positioning students as passive recipients of predefined content, schools could cultivate conditions in which learners co-construct knowledge, reflect on the cultural and political assumptions embedded in AI systems, and practice the ethical discernment necessary for dialogical engagement. In this framework, AI becomes less a mechanism of efficiency than a catalyst for reflective practice—a means of enabling students to encounter difference, test interpretations, and expand the horizons of what counts as legitimate knowledge. By embedding these practices institutionally—through participatory governance, inclusive curricular design, and teacher development—education systems in Central and Eastern Europe could begin to transform schools into spaces that not only absorb postdigital identities but actively cultivate them. Spaces where epistemic justice, critical thinking, and relational responsibility define what it means to learn.

The transformations of education systems in Central and Eastern Europe—driven by neoliberal governance, nationalist agendas, and uneven processes of digital development—demonstrate that learning in the postdigital knowledge society is a situated and contested practice.

Schools cannot be understood as neutral sites of technological implementation but as institutional arenas in which struggles over knowledge, identity, and authority are negotiated through curricular frameworks, infrastructural arrangements, and administrative regimes. The growing presence of AI, the dominance of standardized metrics, as well as the marginalization of alternative epistemologies expose hierarchies that are structural and enduring. At stake is not merely the question of how students learn, but whose knowledge is recognized, whose experiences are rendered intelligible, and whose futures are envisaged within the sphere of education.

2.4 Methodological Considerations

This study is based on a critical ethnography (Carspecken, 2013) conducted between 2022 and 2024 in two state-funded secondary schools in the Tricity region of Poland. The research sought to examine how learning is discursively constructed in everyday educational life—across classroom interactions, institutional routines, educational media, and national policy discourse. The fieldwork was undertaken in a period marked by profound disruption: the COVID-19 pandemic continued to affect school routines and access, while the Russian invasion of Ukraine in 2022 brought new populations of refugee students into Polish schools and created additional pressures on teachers and institutions. These conditions made sustained ethnographic presence difficult, as schools operated under shifting regulations. I visited several schools and conducted exploratory conversations with teachers before selecting two sites where access was possible and where I was able to gather the most substantial body of material. My aim was not to establish a comparative design. Observations quickly revealed that the most salient differences between schools were intersectional—shaped by local demographics, institutional cultures, and resource allocations—rather than formal distinctions between institutions. For this reason, the study focuses on these two schools as sites through which to explore the broader dynamics of postdigital education in the Polish context. To situate the analysis, it is first important to outline the institutional and regional contexts in which the research took place and to clarify the methods through which the material was generated.

Before turning to the methodological framework, it is necessary to contextualize the two schools in which the study was conducted. Both institutions are located in the Tricity region, a metropolitan area in northern Poland with a population exceeding 760,000. The research employed participant observation, individual interviews with teachers, and informal conversations with students. Additionally, educational media in both schools were examined, alongside official documents and curricular materials issued by the Polish Ministry of Education.

The first school, a large educational complex in a central district serving both primary and secondary levels, enrolls students from across the socio-economic spectrum. While many pupils come from lower- and lower-middle-income households, the school also includes students from well-educated and affluent families, making its intake socially mixed. The institution has at times contended with incidents linked to far-right affiliations, behavioral challenges, and student mental-health crises. Despite this complexity, it is widely recognized for pedagogical creativity and a rich extracurricular offer. Teachers are noted for motivating learners and building an interest-driven environment that supports students from both advantaged and disadvantaged backgrounds.

The second school, likewise centrally located and known for a long-standing academic traditions (including pathways into medicine and architecture), also brings together students from varied social backgrounds. Compared with School 1, however, it enrolls a relatively higher share of students from privileged, middle- and upper-middle-class families, and parents more often hold higher education degrees. The teaching staff includes several doctoral degree holders, and the school sustains a competitive academic ethos. Students frequently articulate liberal worldviews, with some support for neoliberal economic ideas also present. Emphasizing conventional academic excellence, the school continues to function as a route into elite professional and academic trajectories while still educating a socially diverse student body.

The contrast between these institutional environments provides an entry point for examining how configurations of prestige and everyday school culture shape students' orientations toward knowledge and learning. Rather than treating the schools as fixed categories, the study approaches them as situated contexts in which broader social patterns are negotiated in practice. This comparative framing makes it possible to trace how similar policy frameworks are interpreted differently across settings. At the same time, it draws attention to how institutional positioning intersects with students' trajectories and expectations, creating distinct yet overlapping conditions for the production and recognition of knowledge within contemporary secondary education.

Access was obtained through formal procedures, including institutional consent, data protection agreements, and district-level notification. Separate written consent was collected from interviewees. Participation was strictly voluntary, and respondents were informed that they could withdraw at any point without consequence. In the case of students, informal conversations were conducted only after securing the approval of school authorities and, when necessary, parental consent, in order to comply with child protection standards. These steps ensured that the research adhered to both institutional regulations and broader ethical principles of qualitative inquiry, with particular attention to minimizing risk and safeguarding the dignity of participants.

Participants included classroom teachers of humanities and social science subjects (Polish, history, geography, and civic education—HiT/WOS), as well as students in junior-year classes. The fieldwork employed a multi-method qualitative design: participant observation in schools and digital learning environments, semi-structured interviews with teachers (eight in School 1 and six in School 2), and a series of informal conversations with students conducted in hallways, staffrooms, and other everyday settings. A total of 14 individual interviews were conducted with teachers (11 women, 3 men) and approximately 30 informal conversations with students. Over the course of two years, 43 observations were conducted of lessons regularly held at both schools, primarily in the humanities and social sciences. Conducting individual interviews with students proved difficult due to the requirement of obtaining parental consent in each case and the limited time available to students, many of whom reported being occupied with extracurricular or after-school commitments. For this reason, individual interviews were replaced with informal conversations, which allowed for more spontaneous exchanges while still offering valuable insights into students' perspectives. Observations concentrated on classroom practices, the pedagogical uses (or absences) of technology, and the ways in which both students and teachers navigated institutional norms, expectations, and tensions related to learning and digital media. Field notes were recorded on a daily basis, and analytic memos were composed at the end of each week to capture emerging patterns and reflexive insights.

All participants were anonymized, with schools and individuals referred to using coding systems designed to protect confidentiality. Reflexive memos were kept throughout the fieldwork to document the researcher's position as an academic outsider who nonetheless maintained prior professional ties to regional teacher networks, and to trace how these positionalities shifted over time as relationships within the schools developed. The purpose of the study is not to achieve statistical generalizability. The focus lies on understanding how learning practices and meanings are negotiated within particular institutional and discursive contexts, shaped by broader tensions between technological automation, procedural compliance, and the formative, humanistic role of education.

School ethnography offers a robust qualitative methodology for investigating the complex social, institutional, and cultural dimensions of educational settings (Spindler & Spindler, 1987). Within this framework, my inquiry focuses on how learning is enacted, understood, interpreted, and contested in diverse school contexts. I pay particular attention to the spatial and discursive configurations of learning—both formal and informal—as they unfold in institutional settings and through educational media. Situated within the postdigital condition, this analysis understands learning as a distributed, socio-material practice mediated by both analog and digital technologies. The interplay between official curricular materials and digital platforms constitutes a dynamic landscape in which educational subjectivities and meanings of learning are continuously negotiated. By attending to these entanglements, the ethnographic approach adopted here seeks to illuminate the shifting logics of learning in a knowledge society.

Following Carspecken's (2013) critical ethnographic methodology, this study was initiated without predefining a media focus, allowing the inquiry to evolve organically in response to the dynamics observed within the research sites. Viewing methodology as a rigorous and reflective process of problem formulation and question refinement (Palka, 2006), I sought a framework that would enable the reconstruction of learning discourses while situating them within broader socio-political, cultural, and educational contexts. Carspecken's approach emphasizes uncovering the often-unspoken assumptions and power dynamics that underlie everyday educational practices by interpreting interaction patterns and examining how meaning is co-constructed in institutional settings. The analysis was guided by a reconstructive lens that aimed to understand how students and teachers ascribe meaning to different modes and spaces of learning—particularly in relation to educational media and classroom practice—while reflexively connecting these micro-level insights to macro-level structures of governance and epistemic power.

Incorporating autoethnographic reflections into my field notes allowed me to critically examine my own subjectivity and positionality within the school system, acknowledging the ambiguity of boundaries between researcher and participant inherent in participant observation. Immersed in the everyday life of the schools, my interpretations were shaped by the roles ascribed to me by both students and teachers, revealing how research is embedded within relational and affective dynamics. Drawing on Ellis and Bochner (2006), who frame the autoethnographer as a storyteller and communicator, I viewed the challenge not merely as a question of analysis, but of narrative construction—how to ethically and effectively tell the story of my encounters. The research took place against the backdrop of an intense national debate over educational reform in Poland, marked by curriculum revisions, the introduction of controversial new subjects, and proposed measures such as the abolition of homework and reductions to the obligatory reading list—changes frequently framed as corrective responses to earlier ideologically driven policies. These public discourses of the crisis echoed within the school, shaping participants' perceptions and producing a dynamic in which some teachers and students frequently sought reassurance or interpretive clarity from me, positioning the researcher as a quasi-therapeutic figure. This emphasizes the emergence of what could be termed a "therapeutic culture" in educational research contexts during periods of institutional instability. As Wajszczyk (2018) notes, participant observation in schools presents unique methodological challenges, particularly in negotiating trust and access. My presence as an academic was sometimes met with skepticism or anxiety, rooted in a perceived divide between theoretical and practical expertise. These tensions resulted in selective access, as some teachers declined participation—particularly in science and language subjects—prompting a strategic focus on the social sciences and humanities, including geography, social studies, history, and Polish language classes.

My positionality as an adult academic researcher—external to the everyday life of the schools I studied—shaped both the form and content of my ethnographic engagement. Introduced through formal channels and institutional correspondence, I carried the symbolic weight of academic authority, but my presence was interpreted in contradictory ways. While some teachers acknowledged my theoretical expertise and pedagogical training, others dismissed or misunderstood my role, at times mistaking me for an undergraduate conducting a student project. These divergent perceptions reflected broader hierarchies within the school and society, where practical teaching experience is often privileged over theoretical knowledge. Despite this ambiguity, I was regularly drawn into informal roles that exceeded my intended observer status. Teachers, particularly in moments of institutional need, began to treat me as a proxy educator—leaving me alone with students under the assumption that I could maintain order. Although I refrained from assuming pedagogical control, I found myself navigating the implicit expectations placed upon me, stepping in when necessary to ensure student safety. This blurring of roles exemplifies the methodological tension between participant and observer, raising critical questions about the ethical and epistemological implications of being positioned as both insider and outsider within the field.

I was aware that my presence in the classroom altered the social ecology of the space—even if only subtly. My notetaking, occasional questions, and general behavior marked me as a figure of surveillance and inquiry. Initially, students responded with distance or curiosity, referring to me vaguely as "the lady who sits with us." My earliest interactions were often with students on the social periphery—those less engaged with mainstream peer networks and more willing to interact with an outsider. Over time, more central students began to approach me, seeking an ally in negotiating school routines or airing grievances. However, even when I shared reflections on my observations, students interpreted them through the lens of school discourse, engaging with me as if I were another teacher. This highlighted the institutional conditions under which critical engagement becomes muted, even in the presence of a researcher. My temporary presence, followed by my departure, emphasizes the extractive potential of research. Despite my efforts to build relationships and foster mutual understanding, I remained a transient figure—ultimately reinforcing my own academic positionality within the hierarchical structures of schooling and research. This recognition guided my ethical commitment to represent student voices with care and to foreground the situatedness and partiality of the knowledge I produced.

In my study on learning within the postdigital knowledge society, I grounded my methodological approach in the recognition of the discursive construction of learning. Rather than treating learning as a self-evident or universal process, I investigated how it is constituted through language, institutional practices, and power relations. To capture this complexity, I combined school ethnography with critical discourse analysis (CDA), focusing not only on classroom practices but also on the broader rhetorical landscape in which these practices are embedded. This methodological integration allowed me to explore how dominant narratives of learning and educational media are discursively constructed and maintained in the school context. Drawing on CDA traditions (Green & Dixon, 1993; Duff, 2002; Gottlieb, 1989; Shepherd, 2014), I analyzed how language functions as a vehicle for power, shaping what counts as legitimate knowledge and who is authorized to learn or teach. I also followed emphasis on uncovering the ideologies embedded in discourse and used the frameworks of Gee (2014) and Laclau (2005) to identify and interpret the dominant discourses, particularly by attending to the use of "empty signifiers"—symbols that play a central role in hegemonizing the discourse of learning.

Ernesto Laclau's discourse theory provided the conceptual framework for this analysis. According to Laclau (2005), discourse is not limited to speech or writing but encompasses any relational system in which meaning is constituted through the interplay of elements. Objectivity itself, he argues, is produced within discourses, meaning that entities do not preexist their relational positioning but are defined by it. This theoretical stance has critical implications for education: curricula, pedagogies, and policies are not neutral instruments for delivering knowledge, but discursive formations that construct subject positions for both students and teachers. Within this terrain, dominant discourses operate by marginalizing alternative perspectives and naturalizing their own logic as common sense. Central to this process is the role of the empty signifier—a symbol or term that, while lacking fixed meaning, becomes a focal point for diverse ideological investments. In education, such signifiers (e.g., "*innovation*," "*excellence*," or "*digital competence*") function as nodal points around which educational reforms and identity claims are articulated. These signifiers gain significance not through their semantic clarity but through their capacity to unify disparate demands and mask structural contradictions, thus reproducing hegemonic understandings of learning and its social function.

To structure my critical discourse analysis (CDA), I employed the framework developed by Gee and Green (1998), which outlines four interrelated discursive dimensions—world building, activity building, identity building, and connection building—that illuminate how learning is socially and discursively constructed within institutional contexts. These dimensions enabled a nuanced analysis of learning as a situated, socio-cultural practice rather than a purely cognitive or individual process. World building captures the attribution of meaning to both tangible and abstract realities. Activity building maps how discursive interactions organize actions and practices. Identity building examines how subjectivities—inflected by emotion, belief, and epistemic stance—are constructed. Connection building links discourse temporally, situating interactions within broader narratives. Rooted in Bakhtin's (1981) concept of "social languages," this framework views language as a fluid, hybrid medium through which diverse worldviews and modes of participation are expressed. It highlights how educational discourses do not merely reflect but actively constitute the institutional logics, power relations, and epistemic hierarchies that shape who learns, what counts as knowledge, and how legitimacy is conferred in the postdigital knowledge society.

To contextualize school-level practices within broader discursive frameworks, the study also examined a range of curricular and policy documents. These included digital materials available on the Integrated Education Platform (Zintegrowana Platforma Edukacyjna, ZPE), and three national policy documents: the *Digital Transformation Policy for Education 2024–2035* (MEiN, 2024), the *Amendment to the National Core Curriculum* (MNEa, 2024), and the *Draft Core Curriculum for Civic Education* (MNEb, 2024). These materials were analyzed alongside field data to identify alignments and dissonances between official policy framings and lived school experience.

This analysis was supplemented by a close reading of textbooks, worksheets, and classroom materials, as well as the digital platforms actually used by students in classroom practice. In today's educational landscape, traditional textbooks have lost their monopolistic role as primary sources of knowledge, supplanted by an ecosystem of digital resources that facilitate multi-layered, experiential learning. Students navigate assignments by strategically tailoring responses to meet teachers' expectations while simultaneously using smartphones to pursue personalized learning journeys that contribute to identity formation. This dual modality, accelerated by the COVID-19 pandemic and the subsequent transition to online education at a formative age, has blurred the boundaries between formal and informal learning. Ethnographic observations revealed that students often regard traditional pedagogy as outdated and misaligned with contemporary technological, psychological, and civilizational realities. Instead, platforms like YouTube and TikTok emerged as primary knowledge sources, where algorithmically curated content and specific influencers shaped students' world view. However, the personalized nature of these platforms—mediated through algorithms that adapt to users' behaviors—posed methodological challenges, as my research accounts could not replicate students' individualized feeds, emphasizing the deep entanglement of personalization and learning in the digital age.

While designing the ethnographic study, I assumed that at the very beginning I would let the students guide me through the world of learning. At first by observing, then by interacting with them directly, I learned about their school learning and their world saturated with the constant presence of the phone and connection to the Internet. I was curious to see how their generation is becoming part of the knowledge society with constant access to it. However in attempting to understand the educational preferences and practices of youth, my interactions with online platforms are inherently biased, differing significantly from the organic, personalized experiences of the students themselves. Despite this challenge, I collaborated closely with students to identify and analyze the most significant sources of information they valued. This approach allowed me to capture and interpret their perspectives more effectively, bridging the gap between my research-oriented interactions with digital platforms and their lived experiences within these online learning environments.

In contrast to traditional methodologies, I employed critical discourse analysis (CDA) not only on written educational media but also on interviews, classroom speech, and online content, recognizing discourse as a space where objectivity is constructed (Laclau, 2005). Although this expanded application may be seen as unconventional, it is essential for capturing the multifaceted dynamics of learning discourse across the diverse domains in which it manifests (Gee & Green, 1998). Learning is thus conceptualized as a discursive practice—a socially situated product of group activities over time (Gee & Green, 1998, p. 148)—enabling an analysis of how social practices, and discursive forms shape educational engagement. Integrating discourse analysis with ethnographic methods provides a nuanced understanding of how learning is defined and distributed within classroom interactions, institutional rituals, and mediated environments such as assessments and AI-driven platforms. This approach, grounded in the distinct "logics-of-inquiry" articulated by Birdwhistell (1977), informs how research questions are shaped and findings represented. While I acknowledge that learning discourse extends beyond school settings (Biesta, 2006), my focus on educational discourse—including AI-based media—offers insight into the cultural and technological realities shaping how young people conceptualize learning today.

To ensure both anonymity and analytical clarity, a coding system was employed throughout the text. Teachers are indicated with the code *T*, students with *S*, and *IC* designates informal conversations. The participating schools are anonymized as *School 1* and *School 2*. In instances where reference to a specific individual or institutional context is analytically significant, excerpts are accompanied by the relevant school code. In cases of recurring situations or general observations, however, such coding is omitted, as the institutional attribution does not add interpretive value.

The chapters that follow examine the contradictions of education under the combined pressures of systemic reform and postdigital change. Schools are treated not as sites where technology is simply adopted, but as institutions where conflicting logics converge: the demands of automation and measurement, the persistence of bureaucratic regulation, and the claims of pedagogy grounded in professional judgment, care, and local circumstance. Within this terrain, teachers and students appear as active participants who interpret, mediate, adapt, and sometimes subvert the directives and technologies that organize their daily routines. Athough algorithmic systems and standardized assessments embed practices that emphasize compliance and efficiency, these practices are rarely implemented in a uniform way. They are redefined, creating spaces in which authority and legitimacy are contested. At times this contestation takes the form of silence or withdrawal. At others it produces inventive uses of digital tools that enable collaboration or extend learning beyond intended frameworks. Such practices are central to understanding postdigital schooling. They reveal how educational subjectivities are constituted not only through conformity but also through negotiation and resistance. The analysis therefore seeks to clarify the conditions in which alternative understandings of learning take shape and to assess how far these alternatives succeed in challenging, or end up reinforcing, the hierarchies that continue to define educational life in Central and Eastern Europe.

References

Alam, A., & Mohanty, A. (2023). Educational technology: Exploring the convergence of technology and pedagogy through mobility, interactivity, AI, and learning tools. *Cogent Engineering, 10*(2), 2283282. https://doi.org/10.1080/23311916.2023.2283282

Bakhtin, M. M. (1981). *The dialogic imagination: Four essays* (M. Holquist, Ed., C. Emerson & M. Holquist, Trans.). Austin and London: University of Texas Press.

Ball, S. J. (2003). The teacher's soul and the terrors of performativity. *Journal of Education Policy, 18*(2), 215–228. https://doi.org/10.1080/0268093022000043065

Ball, S. J. (2012). *Global education Inc.: New Policy Networks and the Neo-Liberal Imaginary.* Routledge.

Bayne, S. (2015). What's the matter with 'technology-enhanced learning'? *Learning, Media and Technology, 40*(1), 5–20. https://doi.org/10.1080/17439884.2014.915851

Bayne, S., & Ross, J. (2024). Speculative futures for higher education. *International Journal of Educational Technology in Higher Education, 21*(1), 39. https://doi.org/10.1186/s41239-024-00469-y

Bell, D. (1973). *The coming of Post-Industrial Society: A Venture in Social Forecasting.* Basic Books.

Bhatia, K. V., Arora, P., & Gupta, S. (2024). Edtech platforms from below: a family ethnography of marginalized communities and their digital learning post-pandemic. *Learning, Media and Technology*, 1–15. https://doi.org/10.1080/17439884.2024.2328693

Biesta, G. (2006). *Beyond learning. Democratic Education for a Human Future.* Routledge.https://doi.org/10.4324/9781315635811

Biesta, G. (2019). Should teaching be re (dis) covered? Introduction to a symposium. *Studies in Philosophy and Education, 38*(5), 549–553.

Birdwhistell, R. (1977). Some discussion of ethnography, theory and method. *About Bateson: Essays on Gregory Bateson*, 103–144.

Bourdieu, P., & Passeron, J.-C. (1990). *Reproduction in education, society and culture* (R. Nice, Trans.; 2nd ed., Vol. 4). Sage.

Braidotti, R. (2019). *Posthuman knowledge* (Vol. 2). Polity Press.

Bruner, J. (1996). *The culture of education.* Harvard University Press.

Buchowski, M. (2006). The specter of Orientalism in Europe: From exotic other to stigmatized brother. *Anthropological Quarterly, 79*(3), 463–482.

Carspecken, F. P. (2013). *Critical ethnography in educational research: A theoretical and practical guide.* Routledge.

Caruso, L. (2018). The Fourth Industrial Revolution and the role of digital innovation. *European Journal of Social Theory, 21*(3), 389–408. https://doi.org/10.1007/s00146-017-0736-1

Castells, M. (1996). *The rise of the network society.* Blackwell. https://doi.org/10.1002/9781444319514

Chelcea, L., & Druţă, O. (2016). Zombie socialism and the rise of neoliberalism in post-socialist Central and Eastern Europe. Eurasian Geography and Economics, 57(4–5), 521–544. https://doi.org/10.1080/15387216.2016.1266273

Cervinkova, H., & Rudnicki, P. (2019). Neoliberalism, neoconservatism, authoritarianism. The politics of public education in Poland. *Journal for Critical Education Policy Studies, 17*(2).

Cone, L. (2023). The platform classroom: Troubling student configurations in a Danish primary school. *Learning, Media & Technology, 48*(1), 52–64. https://doi.org/10.1080/17439884.2021.2010093

Dale, R. (2007). Specifying globalization effects on national policy: a focus on the mechanisms. In *the Routledge Falmer reader in education policy and politics* (pp. 58–74). Routledge.

De Corte, E. (1994). Toward the integration of computers in powerful learning environments. In *Technology-based Learning Environments: Psychological and Educational Foundations* (pp. 19–25). Springer Berlin Heidelberg. https://doi.org/10.1007/978-3-642-79149-9_3

Dewey, J. (1916). *Democracy and education.* Macmillan.

Dixon-Román, E., Nichols, T. P., & Nyame-Mensah, A. (2020). The racializing forces of/in AI educational technologies. *Learning, Media and Technology, 45*(3), 236–250. https://doi.org/10.1080/17439884.2020.1667825

Drucker, P. (1993). *Post-capitalist society.* HarperBusiness.

Duff, P. A. (2002). The discursive co-construction of knowledge, identity, and difference: An ethnography of communication in the high school mainstream. *Applied Linguistics, 23*(3), 289–322.

Ellis, C. S., & Bochner, A. P. (2006). Analyzing analytic autoethnography: An autopsy. *Journal of Contemporary Ethnography, 35*(4), 429–449. https://doi.org/10.1177/0891241606286979

Eubanks, V. (2018). *Automating inequality: How high-tech tools profile, police, and punish the poor.* Martin's Press.

Fraser, N. (2009). *Scales of justice: Reimagining political space in a globalizing world* (Vol. 31). Columbia University Press.

Freire, P. (2000). *Pedagogy of the oppressed* (30th anniversary ed., M. B. Ramos, Trans.). Continuum.

Fricker, M. (2007). *Epistemic injustice: Power and the ethics of knowing.* Oxford University Press.

Francesca Ferrando. (2019). *Philosophical posthumanism.* Bloomsbury Academic.

Garcia, A. (2017). *Good reception: Teens, teachers, and mobile media in a Los Angeles high school.* MIT Press.

Garoian, C. R., & Gaudelius, Y. M. (2001). Cyborg pedagogy: Performing resistance in the digital age. *Studies in Art Education, 42*(4), 333–347. https://doi.org/10.1080/00393541.2001.11651708

González López, A. E., & Büchner, F. (2024). EdTech in a broken world: Breaking and repairing in Argentinian and German schools. *Postdigital Science and Education*. https://doi.org/10.1007/s42438-024-00490-4

Gee, J. P., & Green, J. L. (1998). Discourse analysis, learning, and social practice: A methodological study. *Review of Research in Education, 23*(1), 119–169. https://doi.org/10.3102/0091732X023001119

Gee, J. P. (2014). An Introduction to Discourse Analysis: Theory and Method (4th ed.). Routledge. https://doi.org/10.4324/9781315819679

Gottlieb, E. E. (1989). The discursive construction of knowledge: The case of radical education discourse. *International Journal of Qualitative Studies in Education, 2*(2), 131–144.

Green, J. L., & Dixon, C. N. (1993). Talking knowledge into being: Discursive and social practices in classrooms. *Linguistics and Education, 5*(3–4), 231–239.

Grek, S. (2009). Governing by numbers: the PISA 'effect' in Europe. *Journal of Education Policy, 24*(1), 23–37. https://doi.org/10.1080/02680930802412669

Gromkowska-Melosik, A. A. (2018). *Testy szkolne i rekonstrukcja edukacyjnej rzeczywistości. Horyzonty Wychowania, 17*(41), 59–73.

Haraway, D. (2013a). A cyborg manifesto: Science, technology, and socialist-feminism in the late twentieth century. In *The transgender studies reader* (pp. 103–118). Routledge.

Haraway, D. (2013b). Situated knowledges: The science question in feminism and the privilege of partial perspective 1. In *Women, science, and technology* (pp. 455–472). Routledge.

Hangartner, J., Hürzeler, D., & Aebli, N. (2024). Everyday approaches to platform-mediated personalized learning in secondary schools. *Learning, Media & Technology*. https://doi.org/10.1080/17439884.2024.2367051

Herder, J. G. (2002). *Philosophical writings* (M. Forster, Ed.). Cambridge University Press.

Instytut Badań Edukacyjnych. (2014). *Kompetencje komputerowe i informacyjne młodzieży w Polsce: Raport z międzynarodowego badania kompetencji komputerowych i informacyjnych ICILS* 2013.

Jandrić, P., Knox, J., Besley, T., Ryberg, T., Suoranta, J., & Hayes, S. (2018). Postdigital science and education. *Educational Philosophy and Theory, 50*(10), 893–899. https://doi.org/10.1080/00131857.2018.1454000

Jandrić, P. (2019). We-think, we-learn, we-act: The trialectic of postdigital collective intelligence. *Postdigital Science and Education, 1*(2), 275–279. https://doi.org/10.1007/s42438-019-00055-w

Jandrić, P., & Hayes, S. (2020). Postdigital we-learn. *Studies in Philosophy and Education, 39*(3), 285–297. https://doi.org/10.1007/s11217-020-09711-2

Jandrić, P., Hayes, D., Truelove, I., Levinson, P., Mayo, P., Ryberg, T., & Hayes, S. (2020). Teaching in the age of Covid-19. *Postdigital Science and Education, 2*(3), 1069–1230. https://doi.org/10.1007/s42438-020-00169-6

Jessop, B. (2002). *The future of the capitalist state.* Polity Press.

Jessop, B. (2018). Valid construals and/or correct readings? On the symptomatology of crises. In *The pedagogy of economic, political and social crises* (pp. 49–72). Routledge.

Jessop, B. (2020). *Putting civil society in its place: Governance, metagovernance and subjectivity.* Polity Press

Klus-Stańska, D. (2012). Wiedza, która zniewala–transmisyjne tradycje w szkolnej edukacji. In *Forum oświatowe* (Vol. 24, No. 1 (46), pp. 21–40).

Knox, J. (2019). What does the 'postdigital' mean for education? *Postdigital Science and Education, 1*(2), 357–370. https://doi.org/10.1007/s42438-019-00045-y

Laclau, E. (2005). *On populist reason.* Verso.

Livingstone, S., & Sefton-Green, J. (2016). *The class: Living and learning in the digital age.* NYU Press.

Macgilchrist, F., Allert, H., Cerratto Pargman, T., & Jarke, J. (2024). Designing postdigital futures: Which designs? Whose futures? *Postdigital Science and Education, 6*(1), 13–24. https://doi.org/10.1007/s42438-023-00424-y

Mohamed, S., Png, M.-T., & Isaac, W. (2020). Decolonial AI: Decolonial theory as sociotechnical foresight in artificial intelligence. *Philosophy & Technology, 33*, 659–684. https://doi.org/10.1007/s13347-020-00405-8

Montessori, M. (1964). *The Montessori method.* Schocken.

Nemorin, S. (2024). Towards decolonising the ethics of AI in education. *International Journal of Inclusive Education.* https://doi.org/10.1080/14767724.2024.2333821

Noble, S. U. (2018). *Algorithms of oppression: How search engines reinforce racism.* NYU Press.

Novotný, P., Dvořák, D., Dvořáková, M. (2023). Czech School Reforms: Between East and West. In: Krejsler, J.B., Moos, L. (eds) School Policy Reform in Europe. Educational Governance Research, vol 22. Springer, Cham. https://doi.org/10.1007/978-3-031-35434-2_10

Olssen, M., & Peters, M. A. (2005). Neoliberalism, higher education and the knowledge economy: From the free market to knowledge capitalism. *Journal of Education Policy, 20*(3), 313–345. https://doi.org/10.1080/02680930500108718

Organisation for Economic Co-operation and Development. (1996). *Lifelong learning for all.* OECD.

Organisation for Economic Co-operation and Development. (1989). *Education and the economy in a changing society*. Paris: OECD.
Piattoeva, N. (2015). Elastic numbers: National examinations data as a technology of government. *Journal of Education Policy, 30*(3), 316–334.
Palka, S. (2006). Metodologia. *Badania. Praktyka pedagogiczna. Gdańsk.*
Popow, M. (2015). *Kategoria narodu w dyskursie edukacyjnym. Analiza procesów konstruowania tożsamości w podręcznikach szkolnych*. Wydawnictwo Naukowe Uniwersytetu im. Adama Mickiewicza w Poznaniu.
Popow, M. (2023). Międzykulturowe uczenie się w doświadczeniu polskich nauczycieli po wybuchu wojny w Ukrainie w 2022 r. *Teraźniejszość–Człowiek–Edukacja, 25*(2) (94), 65–87. https://orcid.org/0000-0002-6763-7474
Pyżalski, J. (2024). Co generatywna sztuczna inteligencja może zrobić z edukacją i od czego to zależy? In J. Pyżalski & A. Łuczyńska (Eds.), *Sztuczna inteligencja: prawdziwe zmiany w edukacji?* Fundacja Szkoła z Klasą.
Pyżalski, J. (Ed.). (2025). *Generatywna sztuczna inteligencja w polskiej szkole: Przecieranie szlaków. Badania ilościowe i jakościowe nauczycieli klas 4–8 szkół podstawowych*. NASK – Państwowy Instytut Badawczy.
Rafalow, M. H. (2020). *Digital divisions. How schools create inequality in the tech era*. University of Chicago Press.
Quijano, A. (2000). Coloniality of power, Eurocentrism, and Latin America. *International Sociology, 15*(2), 215–232. https://doi.org/10.1177/0268580900015002005
Schiff, D. (2022). Education for AI, not AI for education: The role of education and ethics in national AI policy strategies. *International Journal of Artificial Intelligence in Education, 32*(3), 527–563. https://doi.org/10.1007/s40593-021-00270-2
Selwyn, N. (2013). *Distrusting educational technology: Critical questions for changing times*. Routledge.
Semjén, A., Le, M., & Hermann, Z. (2018). The goals and consequences of the centralization of public education in Hungary. *Acta Educationis Generalis, 8*(3), 9–34.
Selwyn, N. (2019). *Should robots replace teachers? AI and the future of education*. Polity Press.
Silova, I. (2010). Rediscovering post-socialism in comparative education. In I. Silova (Ed.), *Post-socialism is not dead: (Re)reading the global in comparative education* (pp. 1–24). Emerald Group Publishing.
Simons, M., & Masschelein, J. (2008). The governmentalization of learning and the assemblage of a learning apparatus. *Educational Theory, 58*(4), 391–415. https://doi.org/10.1111/j.1741-5446.2008.00296.x
Sims, C. (2017). *Disruptive Fixation: School reform and the pitfalls of techno-idealism*. Princeton University Press.

Shepherd, M. A. (2014). The discursive construction of knowledge and equity in classroom interactions. *Linguistics and Education, 28*, 79–91.

Spindler, G., & Spindler, L. (1987). *Interpretive ethnography of education: At home and abroad*. Lawrence Erlbaum Associates.

Stunża, G. (2024). Adaptacyjne uczenie wspomagane sztuczną inteligencją dla emancypacji i refleksji. In J. Pyżalski & A. Łuczyńska (Eds.), *Sztuczna inteligencja: prawdziwe zmiany w edukacji?* (p. 93). Fundacja Szkoła z Klasą.

Szkudlarek, T. (2007). Empty signifiers, education and politics. *Studies in Philosophy and Education, 26*(3), 237–252. https://doi.org/10.1007/s11217-007-9033-7

Szkudlarek, T. (2016). *On the politics of educational theory: Rhetoric, theoretical ambiguity, and the construction of society*. Routledge. https://doi.org/10.4324/9781315712505

Twenge, J. M. (2017). *IGen: Why today's super-connected kids are growing up less rebellious, more tolerant*. Atria Books.

Wagener-Böck, N., Macgilchrist, F., Rabenstein, K., & Bock, A. (2023). From automation to symmation: Ethnographic perspectives on what happens in front of the screen. *Postdigital Science and Education, 5*, 136–151. https://doi.org/10.1007/s42438-022-00350-z

Wajszczyk, K. (2018). Meandry badań etnograficznych w szkole. *Jakościowe Badania Pedagogiczne, 2*, 132–155.

Visvanathan, S. (1997). *A carnival for science: Essays on science*. Oxford University Press.

Vygotsky, L. S. (1978). *Mind in society: The development of higher psychological processes*. Harvard University Press.

World Bank. (1994). Higher education: *The lessons of experience*. Washington, DC: World Bank.

World Bank. (1995). *Priorities and strategies for education: A World Bank review*. Washington, DC: World Bank.

Williamson, B. (2017). *Big data in education: The digital future of learning, policy, and practice*. SAGE.

Williamson, B., Eynon, R., Knox, J., & Davies, H. (2023). Critical perspectives on AI in education: Political economy, discrimination, commercialization, governance and ethics. In *Handbook of artificial intelligence in education* (pp. 553–570). Edward Elgar Publishing. https://doi.org/10.4337/9781800375413.00037

CHAPTER 3

Discursive Constructions of Learning at School

This chapter investigates the ways in which learning is discursively constituted within educational policy, educational media and school-based discourse, set against the broader backdrop of the postdigital knowledge society. It focuses on the tensions between institutionalized frameworks of schooling and more personalized, student-centered modes of learning.

The analysis proceeds through three interrelated dimensions: the discourse *about* learning, the discourse *of* learning, and learning as a discursive *space*. The first refers to public, expert, and media-generated narratives that define legitimate strategies and outcomes of learning, both within formal education and in broader societal contexts. The second dimension—*the discourse of learning*—concerns how learning is articulated and operationalized in educational practice, frequently shaped by didactic norms such as predefined goals, learning outcomes, and curriculum structures. This dimension lends itself to socio-cultural analysis, particularly in terms of how meaning is constructed through classroom interaction. As Mercer (2004) emphasizes, dialogue and communicative exchange are central to the co-construction of shared understanding, reflecting, and reproducing broader institutional and cultural logics. Similarly, Wickman and Östman (2001) demonstrate that classroom discourse not only mediates learning but actively structures the interpretive possibilities available to students, enabling the collaborative construction of meaning. These processes form part of what Evans

M. Popow, *Learning in the Postdigital Knowledge Society*, Palgrave Studies in Educational Media,
https://doi.org/10.1007/978-3-032-21956-5_3

and Kurantowicz (2009) and Evans (2013) describe as dynamic *landscapes of learning* or *knowledge ecologies*—fluid spaces in which social and cultural experiences intersect with discursive practices to produce situated knowledge.

Subsequent sections of the chapter analyze how learning is represented and framed in official curricular documents, educational media, and the lived narratives of students and teachers. The inquiry is situated within the conceptual frameworks of Gee and Green (1998), which allow for a nuanced understanding of how discourse shapes social roles, practices, and epistemologies within educational contexts. Within these frameworks, I examine several recurring discursive constructs: learning as rewarding labor, learning as survival, learning as a form of intellectual development and necessity, and autonomous learning. The analysis itself will foreground students' and teachers' voices, integrating interpretation directly into the narrative.

Prior to this, I provide an account of the socio-cultural environments of the two schools under investigation, foregrounding the contextual specificities that shape the production and reception of learning discourses.

3.1 What Did I Learn About Postdigital Learning at School?

In analyzing the ethnographic material gathered in schools, my attention focused on both the everyday enactments of learning and the discursive frameworks through which learning is understood—particularly in relation to the schooling and postdigital condition shaped by the iGen generation's constant connectivity and incidental engagement with knowledge (Twenge, 2017). Although I initially approached the field expecting to observe meaningful transformations in pedagogical practice prompted by technological development, what emerged instead was a striking persistence of established educational structures. Digital tools were certainly present, but their role remained largely supplemental. Instead of changing the institutional logic of schooling, they were assimilated into existing routines with minimal impact on core practices.

This observation stands in tension with more optimistic accounts of educational transformation driven by digital media (Muzata et al., 2024). In contrast to such narratives, the findings indicate that postdigitality has not substantially disrupted the normative frameworks or hierarchies embedded in school life. It functions primarily as a surface adaptation—an adjustment that signals continuity rather than transformation, and highlights the resilience of inherited pedagogical forms. Learning, moreover, is never determined by technology alone. It is mediated through the interaction of individual dispositions, institutional cultures, and historically sedimented educational expectations (Filipiak, 2009). The persistence of these frameworks becomes particularly visible when examining how students and teachers confront the expanding role of algorithmically mediated information in everyday learning.

Students now encounter knowledge within ubiquitous, often curated environments where information is available immediately. This immersion, however, does not translate automatically into critical engagement. Instead, it raises fundamental pedagogical questions about the role of schools in a context where factual content can be retrieved with ease but not always carefully interpreted. As one teacher noted, the task is no longer simply to transmit knowledge but to identify which forms of knowledge remain vital and irreplaceable in a world increasingly shaped by automated information flows (T_1_School_2). What emerges, therefore, is less a digitally transformed pedagogy than a set of unresolved tensions: between availability and interpretation, access and relevance, automation and educational judgment.

At the onset of my fieldwork, I noticed a pronounced discrepancy emerged between students' everyday digital fluency and the digital competencies required in academic contexts. Some students lacked access to desktop computers at home and relied exclusively on smartphones or tablets. They navigated smartphone interfaces with ease and displayed intuitive familiarity with generative AI tools—ranging from translation apps and content generators to social media filters—but they often struggled with structured academic tasks such as formatting documents or using spreadsheets. The digital literacies developed informally outside of school did not readily transfer into the expectations of schoolwork. It exposed a disconnect between everyday digital practices and institutional norms. For teachers, this mismatch often generated frustration, as fluency in desktop applications was assumed to be universal. For students, it created a sense of inadequacy, as their competencies were perceived as irrelevant or even illegitimate in formal educational settings.

Other students, however, had more consistent access to desktop and laptop computers, earlier exposure to formal digital tools, and greater confidence in navigating academic software. This contrast highlights not simply differences in resources but the intersection of cultural expectations and pedagogical assumptions, emphasizing how digital literacies are socially distributed and institutionally validated in uneven ways. This divergence also reflects a broader trend identified in educational research. Operational digital skills developed in everyday life do not necessarily translate into the higher-order literacies demanded by schools or labor markets (Murray & Pérez, 2014). The Polish case mirrors this gap. While digital devices are widely available, inequalities in digital capital—understood as the combination of skills, access, and institutional support—remain pronounced (Szostak & Kenc, 2021). These disparities became particularly visible during the COVID-19 pandemic, when the shift to remote education exposed not only uneven infrastructural provision but also the limits of pedagogical and institutional readiness to address them (Kruszewska et al., 2022).

The digital repertoires developed by students with fewer technical skills—though no less creative or resourceful—often fall outside what counts as legitimate within school contexts. The hierarchy is not located in the tool itself but in the cultural framing of its use. What is recognized as academic in one context may be dismissed as inadequate or even suspicious in another. In this sense, technology functions less as a bridge to opportunity than as a mirror that reflects and reproduces the inequalities structuring students' educational lives (Bourdieu & Passeron, 1990). The result is not simply a difference in competence but a difference in positioning, where students are variously legitimized or marginalized depending on their alignment with institutional expectations. What appears as a deficit of ability is more accurately a manifestation of unequal access to the technological environments schools implicitly demand. As Fraser (2009) argues, this is not merely inequality but maldistribution—a systemic privileging of some students' starting points over others, sustained under the guise of institutional neutrality.

The primary use of technology among students was the retrieval of information directly related to school assignments, homework, and exam preparation. Online activity was closely aligned with the logic of test-based assessment, which shaped the school context. Because knowledge was predominantly measured through tests, students tend to use digital resources that reproduced this format. Ready-made tests with answer keys and repositories of past exam papers became common points of reference, while Messenger groups functioned as informal networks for circulating completed assignments and materials from previous years.

Within this environment, tests were not regarded as obstacles but as predictable tasks that could be strategically managed. Several students described them as the simplest form of evaluation, since correct answers could often be located online with minimal effort. Technology, in this sense, functioned less as a means of expanding understanding than as a mechanism for aligning responses with anticipated examination patterns, with platforms such as Scribd—hosting answer keys and prepared solutions—particularly valued for narrowing the gap between student work and institutional expectations. What emerged was a mode of learning oriented not toward inquiry or critical engagement but toward the reproduction of assessment logics, where digital tools reinforced the proceduralism of schooling. In both schools, the use of generative AI followed this instrumental orientation and was marked by secrecy and distance from formal pedagogical aims. Students rarely disclosed their reliance on AI to teachers, instead using it covertly to generate works that would satisfy institutional requirements. While the extent of infrastructure and experimentation varied, the institutional framing of AI was consistent. Classrooms neither provided space for dialogue about its implications nor encouraged reflection on its consequences. The issue was not merely one of access but of culture, as what counted as legitimate technology use was governed less by material conditions than by curricular hierarchies and the exam-oriented rhythms of school life.

Within this broader pattern, differences emerged not as absolute contrasts between schools but as variations in the purpose, and social framing of students' practices. In the more selective, academically prestigious setting—such as gaining entry into groups of high-achieving students—many demonstrated fluency with digital environments and a disposition toward experimenting with AI. Routine tasks, such as document formatting, multimedia preparation, tasks lists, data management, were seamlessly integrated into school life, supported by stable home access to computers and Internet, as well as parental endorsement of "productive" digital activity. Some students, particularly boys, described iterative engagements with generative AI that bordered on meta-cognitive experimentation. One student explained that he was "*teaching the machine to think like me*" (S_IC_2_School_2), framing his practice as an exploration of the technology's affordances. Such practices were cultivated not only by access to resources but by a socio-technical environment in which school demands, home expectations, and digital culture reinforced an ethos of technological engagement.

By contrast, other students across both schools described digital routines that were less reflective and more pragmatic. Phones rather than computers were their main point of access. AI use was largely task-oriented, used for finding quick answers, copying from open-access sites, or generating material to fulfill assignments. In these cases, technology was deployed as a strategy of compliance. It was used for exploration, producing a disjunction between everyday practices and the normative expectations of school. Here, the issue was not a lack of fluency but the absence of alignment between informal literacies and the forms of digital competence recognized by the institution.

This divergence became particularly visible in out-of-school contexts. Among students with higher levels of cultural and social capital, AI practices extended into areas of curiosity and self-education. Some trained small models, compared generative systems, or debated the risks of AI by referencing public intellectuals encountered on YouTube or in podcasts. Among their peers, both in the same school and in the other, AI was used for more playful or expressive purposes, like generating images for TikTok, or enhancing the circulation of Messenger group content. While these practices may appear divergent, they reveal a shared pattern. AI use is situated within the cultural ecologies students inhabit, whether those emphasize exploratory engagement or social exchange.

What united both contexts was the instrumental logic of AI use in relation to formal schooling. Students frequently described ChatGPT and similar systems as "*silly*" or producing content that "*made no sense*," but they continued to employ them. "*Chat GPT is stupid, but it's good enough for school*," (S_IC_2_School_1) one of the students told me.

These criticisms functioned less as outright rejections of the technology than as acknowledgements of its limitations, accompanied by a pragmatic acceptance of its usefulness. As one student remarked, "*Nobody checks whether the assignment was written with ChatGPT; in fact, if someone does it on their own, they usually get a 3 [satisfactory grade], so what's the point of not doing it with ChatGPT?*" (S_IC_2_School_2). This observation illustrates how students calibrate their expectations of AI to the perceived thresholds of school evaluation. They do not turn to AI for deeper understanding or original insight, but for its capacity to meet procedural demands efficiently. Taken together, these practices point not to a simple divide between privileged and disadvantaged learners, but to a spectrum shaped by the interplay of habitus and institutional culture. Across both schools, students engaged with AI in ways that combined skepticism with utility and pragmatism with experimentation. The critical issue lies not in whether AI is used, but in how social conditions and educational environments structure what counts as legitimate learning practice, and what remains relegated to the realm of expedient but unofficial workarounds.

The differences in how students described their digital practices were not organized simply by the school they attended, but by the resources and dispositions they brought with them. Students from families with higher levels of education often presented formal digital tasks as routine. "*Making a presentation is just part of school now, everyone does it,*" (S_IC_School_1) one student explained, treating competence with institutional tools as obvious and universal. This apparent ease shows how certain digital practices, when aligned with curricular norms, are naturalized as part of being a "good student" and converted into educational advantage (Bourdieu, 1984; Ragnedda & Ruiu, 2020).

Others, however, described the same tasks with hesitation. "*I always worry I'll do something wrong and lose the file (...) It just happens to me, and I always have to ask dad for help*" (S_IC_School_1) a student admitted, recalling the frustration of redoing work that disappeared from the computer. For her, digital practices were not routine but precarious, marked by the risk of failure and embarrassment. This contrast highlights how informal competencies developed through smartphones or social media, though creative and resourceful, were rarely recognized in school.

The consequences were not only practical but affective. "*We don't do things like others do, ours is more basic,*" (S_IC_School_1) another girl concluded, speaking with resignation about the difference between her skills and the polished standards teachers valued. Such remarks show how hierarchies of recognition become internalized. Students whose capitals matched school expectations approached tasks with confidence, while others felt inadequate or hesitant. In this way, schools sustain uneven trajectories by validating certain repertoires and dismissing others, reproducing inequalities under the guise of neutrality (Bourdieu & Passeron, 1990, p. 59; Fraser, 2009). This tension highlights a wider contradiction. While students' practices reveal how digital skills are unevenly recognized, institutional and policy frameworks present digital competence as a universal, standardized ideal detached from these lived inequalities.

Building on the discussion of how digital technologies shape social learning practices outside of formal education, it is necessary to examine the institutional frameworks that regulate their integration in schools. The European Commission's *Digital Competence Framework for Educators*

(DigCompEdu) exemplifies contemporary policy discourse, positioning technology as a central measure of pedagogical effectiveness. It identifies six domains of competence—ranging from the design of digital resources to the empowerment of learners—mapped onto twenty two competencies that together establish a normative vision of what it means to be an effective educator in the digital age. Viewed through Gee and Green's concept of *discourse*, the framework operates as more than a technical guide. It prescribes a socially sanctioned way of being a teacher, linking digital fluency into the very definition of professionalism. In this reading, teaching is not described as a generic practice but as one that must be mediated, evaluated, and legitimized through technology. DigCompEdu thus reshapes professional identity by stipulating which forms of action and values are recognized as belonging to the role of the "digitally competent" teacher.

The classroom evidence complicates this narrative. While the framework prescribes empowerment and reflexivity, students' experiences of technology were largely procedural, tied to testing and compliance. Digital tools were mostly used to meet assessment requirements. From Gee and Green's perspective, this reveals a dissonance between the institutional *Discourse* promoted by policy and the everyday discourses enacted by students, who calibrate their use of technology to the narrow demands of exams and evaluation. From Laclau's perspective, the framework functions less as a practical instrument than as a symbolic articulation. It secures legitimacy for the idea of digital transformation while pedagogical practices remain deeply anchored in older logics of standardization and control. DigCompEdu, in this sense, illustrates how policy constructs powerful imaginaries of learning and teacher identity that circulate at the discursive level but translate unevenly—and often superficially—into practice.

This contradiction is not merely theoretical. It is vividly reflected in classroom life. Scholars such as Selwyn (2014) and Castañeda and Williamson (2021) have shown that digital tools are typically deployed as supplements to traditional methods rather than as catalysts for pedagogical innovation. Smartboards or tablets often serve to make conventional content delivery appear more engaging, without altering underlying power relations or epistemic assumptions (Wilkin et al., 2017). Teachers frequently frame technology as a way of bridging generational divides, and rarely look at it as integral to their pedagogical ethos (Suárez-Guerrero & Rivera-Vargas, 2023). This approach sustains a behaviorist paradigm in which knowledge transmission is prioritized over co-construction. My own observations confirmed this model. In one history lesson on Polish rescuers during the Second World War, the teacher read aloud from a text while students listened passively, then answered predefined factual questions. The static nature of this instruction inhibited critical thinking and provoked disengagement, with students responding through boredom.

Immersing myself in the daily environment, I too felt the pervasive lethargy of the classroom. It was felt in widespread lack of stimulation and continual escape to smartphones. Students repeatedly described their classes as monotonous and psychologically draining. They were turning instead to digital content as a coping mechanism. Their accounts, echoing my embodied experience, show how technologically equipped and pedagogically stagnant environments generate a culture of disengagement where boredom becomes the dominant affect. Mobile devices, far from being mere distractions, functioned as portals through which students sought cognitive and emotional stimulation absent from formal lessons. This behavioral pattern aligns with research findings. Bergdahl et al. (2020) note how mobile device use frequently compensates for uninspiring instruction, while Macklem (2015) links it to broader motivational deficits. Such disengagement is not simply passive but performative, as students curate their own fleeting and fragmented learning environments through digital media. In this way, the contradiction at the heart of the classroom becomes apparent. While policy promotes digital tools as instruments of empowerment, their everyday use by students signifies both a rejection of formal pedagogical authority and an attempt to reconfigure learning through alternative, self-directed forms of engagement.

The accounts of boredom voiced by students can be read through Gee and Green's (1998) analytic matrix, which highlights how classroom life is structured through discoursive world, activity, identity, and connection building. Students described lessons as "*repetitive sequences*," a state of "*lethargy*," or as being "*dead*" with exhaustion, constructing a shared reality in which school was imagined less as discovery than as endurance. The metaphors of tunnels, cycles, and survival show how testing and waiting dominate the temporal order of schooling. Within this world, distraction and coping practices—scrolling TikTok, sharing answer keys, using AI to finish assignments—were not simply rule-breaking but ways of reconfiguring participation. Students performed the official activity of lesson attendance while simultaneously engaging in hidden micro-practices of endurance, which made the school day bearable but still reinforced its procedural character.

These practices also shaped students' identities and connections. "*I can't remember anything from this, I can't concentrate, I feel sleepy the moment I enter here*," (S_IC_School_1) one boy explained. He positioned himself as incapable within the environment of school, even as he displayed fluency with digital tools outside it. Messenger groups, TikTok, and AI formed connections that extended learning beyond the classroom, but these networks were calibrated toward satisfying minimal institutional thresholds. Taken together, boredom was not simply an affective state but a discursive position that organized how learning was lived in school. The postdigital classroom thus appeared as a layered space. Official discourses of testing and compliance coexisted with counter-discourses of survival and coping. These counter-discourses revealed the fragility of pedagogical authority but also reproduced its logics, leaving students suspended between critique and compliance.

In both schools I observed, the integration of digital technologies did little to disrupt the prevailing pedagogical order and boredom. Devices such as tablets, laptops, and interactive software were present, sometimes even encouraged, but their use rarely extended beyond surface-level enhancements. They were used for brightening PowerPoint slides, or animating quizzes. In these contexts, digital tools were not mobilized to foster critical dialogue, inquiry-based learning, or democratic participation. Instead, they were absorbed into the existing hierarchical and assesment-driven grammar of schooling. The image of the student as a digitally fluent, reflexive learner remained largely aspirational. In practice, what technologies enabled was the gamification of repetition. Platforms like Kahoot or Quizlet encouraged speed and recall rather than conceptual depth or interpretive nuance.

Moreover, the integration of technology in classrooms, while outwardly modernizing education, often leaves intact the traditional epistemological frameworks it seeks to reform. A detailed review of digital instructional tools—such as those found on the national Integrated Educational Platform (PZE)—reveals that interactivity is often limited to surface-level enhancements of didactic models. For example, in a history lesson on the fall of the Carolingian dynasty, the stated objectives required students to: explain what happened to Charlemagne's empire after his death; identify its division on a map; assess how the fall of the Carolingian dynasty affected the significance of imperial institutions; and explain who the Normans were and what role they played in shifting the power dynamics of contemporary Europe. In the methods and techniques section, the lesson was described as "teaching through discussion" using interactive exercises, with students directed to consult materials on the PZE website, including texts, an electronic map, and online tasks.

When reviewing the lesson structure and instructions, it becomes apparent that interactive tools serve primarily to diversify the lesson without assuming a significant didactic role. The improvement in history teaching is framed as the addition of so-called interactive methods, like presentations, digital texts, web-based illustrations, and online tests, but the underlying pedagogy remains unchanged. The lesson focuses on locating answers in provided maps and texts and then responding to test-style questions, reproducing a textbook logic under a digital guise. Such digital "lures" mask the continuity of transmissive pedagogy beneath a veneer of innovation. PowerPoint slides, interactive quizzes, and AI-assisted tools do not challenge the teacher-centered model, however they make it more visually appealing and easier to accept. Lovin's (2011, as cited in Selwyn, 2014) notion of the "digital ether" captures this paradox. Technological sophistication may depoliticize educational discourse by naturalizing digital engagement as inherently progressive. In reality, the postdigital classroom often reaffirms existing power relations under the guise of innovation. Despite the proliferation of digital tools, the dominant instructional paradigm remains largely unaltered. The promise of transformative education through technology continues to prove elusive.

My fieldwork revealed a profound dissonance between the ambitious rhetoric of digital transformation promoted by policy frameworks and the actual pedagogical practices observed in schools. I frequently encountered didactic practices that reflected minimal pedagogical innovation, particularly in subjects like history, geography, and social studies, where traditional tools—such as maps—were often replaced with jpg images projected onto screens, accompanied by teacher-led pointing or annotations. Similarly, instruction commonly relied on passive formats like educational films or YouTube videos supplemented by multiple-choice or comprehension questions. Despite official mandates to enhance digital competencies and promote technologically enriched learning environments, digital tools such as PowerPoint, and platforms like Microsoft Teams were predominantly used to replicate existing didactic structures. This was particularly visible during remote lessons in School No. 1, where low levels of student engagement, and logistical barriers—such as the inability to access a laptop or stable Internet connection—were normalized as inevitable. Teachers frequently expressed skepticism about the educational value of remote learning, and this skepticism was coupled with an acceptance of exclusion as a matter of individual responsibility. Students without access to proper devices or sufficient mobile data were framed as personally unprepared, what illustrates the neoliberal tendency to shift the burden of inequality onto the individual through discourses of self-management and resilience.

The gap between the rhetoric of transformation and classroom practices was not incidental but structurally produced. Schools, confronted with external reform pressures, did not fundamentally alter their pedagogical logics but selectively adapted in ways that preserved continuity. Digital tools became incorporated into the performance of modernization, signaling alignment with policy expectations while leaving epistemic and organizational routines untouched. In Laclau's terms, "*digital transformation*" functions as an empty signifier. It condensed diverse and often contradictory demands—innovation, competitiveness, equality, modernisation, development, future—into a symbolically powerful but materially underdetermined promise. This is characteristic of how institutions absorb reforms through selective adaptation. They may maintain the recognizability of routines while staging responsiveness (Jessop, 2002, 2008). What appeared as innovation was, in practice, a managed spectacle: a demonstration of modernity that safeguarded the institutional order rather than transforming it.

This tendency to equate digital access with educational equality remains one of the most persistent illusions in contemporary discourse around school modernization. As Kopciewicz (2020) observes, the presence of technology in classrooms is frequently mistaken for pedagogical progress, even as it conceals deep disparities in how students actually engage with digital tools. From Gee and Green's perspective, what is at stake is not merely access to devices but the alignment—or misalignment—between institutional discourses of "competence" and the everyday discourses through which students navigate their learning. The assumption that students are naturally motivated by digital enhancements ignores both the saturation of their everyday media environments and the exhaustion produced by repetitive instructional formats. For many students, these digital add-ons no longer carry novelty or meaning, but appear as extensions of the same procedural logics that govern standardized testing and assessment. The promise of transformation, therefore, remains suspended between policy discourse and pedagogical reality. It invoked as a legitimating symbol while classrooms continue to reproduce established hierarchies of knowledge and participation.

This critique came through most clearly in a conversation with one student, who described her experience of digital learning with striking clarity: "*What seems attractive and new to you is obvious to us because we've grown up with it. It might be something novel for older-generation teachers, but for us, quizzes, colorful pictures, YouTube videos—none of that is extraordinary. We know how it works. What we need is a space for quiet reflection, and turning school into one big social media hub doesn't help. It's a constant trigger. It's either boring or too much. It's not that we don't understand what we're watching; we can critique it*" (S_IC_2_School_2). Her words expose a fundamental misalignment between adult assumptions about digital engagement and students' lived realities. From Gee and Green's perspective, her statement performs a boundary-drawing between competing discourses. The institutional discourse of "*digital innovation*" that positions color, spectacle, and interactivity as inherently engaging, and the students' situated discourse that redefines engagement in terms of depth, quiet, and reflection. By declaring that they "*can critique it*," the student reclaims epistemic authority, resisting the deficit framing that casts young people as passive consumers of digital content.

In Laclau's terms, the signifier "*engagement*" becomes contested terrain. For teachers and policymakers, it condenses aspirations of modernization and interactivity; for students, it risks becoming an empty promise that masks a lack of intellectual stimulation. The antagonism here is not simply about technology but about the symbolic order of schooling: who defines what counts as meaningful learning, and whose experiences of engagement are recognized as legitimate.

The discourse articulated in this student's critique unsettles the assumption that digital tools naturally bridge generational divides. Instead, it reveals a structural irony. What institutions present as innovation, students experience as either banal repetition of familiar media practices or intrusive overstimulation. The problem, therefore, is not technology itself but the superficial, stimulus-driven ways it is used within the classroom. Rather than deepening inquiry or fostering reflection, these practices reinforce a model of schooling where students are positioned as audiences to be entertained, not subjects invited into dialogue.

At the same time, students' capacity to critique and navigate digital content is deeply inflected by their social position. In both schools, I encountered students whose early digital exposure had been carefully regulated by parents—some of whom delayed giving their children smartphones, imposed strict limits on screen time, or encouraged structured extracurricular activities as a counterweight to digital immersion. These students often voiced critical views of social media, describing online content as manipulative, shallow, or addictive, and chose books, music, or sports as more intentional alternatives. Such orientations were not merely matters of individual preference but cultural performances that positioned them within identities coded as intellectually legitimate. Their narratives resonated with broader middle-class discourses of self-management and delayed gratification, discourses that invest non-digital practices with symbolic capital and frame digital abstinence or moderation as signs of distinction (Bourdieu, 1984).

By contrast, students from less privileged backgrounds tended to describe their digital habits as largely unregulated, structured more by entertainment, habit, or pragmatic necessity. During informal conversations in school corridors—when I managed to divert their attention away from their phones—I would ask about the function of smartphones in their lives. Most often, they struggled to respond, appearing surprised by the very question. When they did attempt to articulate an answer, they typically concluded that "*phones were simply things one had.*" Their everyday practices in school, especially during breaks, confirmed this. Phones functioned as central devices, indispensable for both communication, and distraction. These uses carried little of the reflexive distancing valorized in middle-class accounts. They were narrated in terms of immediacy, entertainment, emotions and necessity.

This lack of reflexive framing also extended into classroom practices. On several occasions, students were unable to use their smartphones effectively to find information or support formal learning tasks, especially when ChatGPT provided incorrect answers. This disjuncture illustrates the paradoxical relationship between access and epistemic agency. Possession of digital devices did not translate automatically into critical or educationally valued practices. In this way, the differences between students did not map neatly onto a generational divide—an idea central to discourses of "digital natives"—but rather onto what might be described as differentiated digital subjectivities. These subjectivities encompass the dispositions and interpretive frameworks through which students inhabit and make sense of digital culture (Bourdieu, 1984). Crucially, they are not evenly distributed but stratified across lines of class, habitus, and cultural capital. For some, digital moderation became a marker of distinction and intellectual legitimacy. For others, immersion in digital culture emerged as a taken-for-granted condition of life, valuable for its immediacy but difficult to reframe as an epistemic resource.

Seen through this lens, the student's critique of school-based digital tools is more than a rejection of school pedagogy. It is also a disclosure of how cultural hierarchies shape what is recognized as meaningful engagement. Student's plea for "quiet reflection" unsettles the assumption that the path to learning necessarily lies through constant interactivity. Instead, she articulates a counter-discourse that revalues depth, slowness, and ambiguity—qualities increasingly displaced in algorithmically structured environments. Far from disengaged, students like her are highly attuned to the absence of such conditions, and in naming this absence, they lay bare the epistemic limits of a schooling model that too often confuses access with equality and novelty with substance.

In contrast to students whose digital habits were shaped by deliberate parental regulation, those without such guidance, often from less advantaged backgrounds, described a markedly different relationship with technology. For many of these students, access to a smartphone was never framed as something to be managed or discussed. It was simply part of daily life, often introduced early and used without clear boundaries. Several mentioned that their phones were only taken away as a form of punishment, not as part of a broader pedagogical effort to shape media literacy or critical awareness. This absence of guided digital socialization contributed to a more unbounded use of social media. Unlike their peers who approached platforms with a degree of reflexivity, these students often saw no reason to limit their engagement. They described their digital routines as obvious and unproblematic habits. Social media, they explained, offered content that was interesting and relevant to their everyday experiences, something they actively wanted to spend time with, not something from which they needed a break.

These findings complicate common narratives about the "digital generation" by revealing a stratified landscape of technological engagement. They also challenge any simplistic assumption that the presence of digital tools alone ensures meaningful participation in contemporary knowledge cultures. The potential of digital technology to support learning is not evenly distributed. It is mediated by family background, school context, and broader socio-cultural resources. In this sense, what appears as technological fluency on the surface often masks deeper forms of cultural disadvantage. What we see instead is a stratified digital literacy landscape in which the capacity to use technology as a tool of inquiry itself becomes a form of distinction. For students in more advanced educational environments, digital practices are supported by teachers and families in ways that encourage exploration and critical reflection, placing technology into broader repertoires of epistemic agency. For students from disadvantaged backgrounds, by contrast, digital practices are fragmented and instrumental, shaped by algorithmic ecosystems that amplify precarity.

In School 1, two distinct trajectories of digital learning practices became visible. One of the top-performing students in the class presented on his phone three artificial intelligence applications. He carefully explained how he constructed prompts for each of them, compared the outputs, and—using his own terms—"taught" the language models, approaching each as a distinct system that required its own method of interaction. This type of metareflective engagement exemplifies the ability to operate across multiple semiotic domains simultaneously, what Gee (2003) describes as learning to recognize and act within different symbolic systems and their associated practices. The student was not a passive consumer of AI tools but positioned himself as a designer. He established his own rules of interaction and managing the process of learning.

Another student, by contrast, was engaged in strategy games. His involvement extended beyond playing. He streamed his sessions live and commented on strategies for an online audience. This practice corresponds closely to what Gee terms active and critical learning. In this process the player does not merely reproduce existing patterns but develops the capacity to recognize the underlying design principles of the game and to deploy them flexibly in new situations (Gee, 2003, pp. 45–47). Here, strategy games functioned as more than entertainment. They became resources for knowledge-building, reflection, and dissemination, situating the student within a wider affinity group of gamers and commentators (Gee, 2003, pp. 26–27).

Strategy games, in particular, illustrate what Gee identifies as transfer of learning. Players continually confront new challenges, transferring previously mastered strategies while testing their validity under altered conditions. When familiar strategies fail, innovation becomes necessary. In such moments, the activity aligns with the most robust sense of learning—experimental and reflective—though one rarely available in traditional classroom contexts (Gee, 2003, pp. 123–124). For the student producing live commentary, play thus became a form of pedagogical practice, combining analysis, experimentation, and communication. Taken together, these observations resonate with Gee's argument that video games are sites where players "*learn to think about semiotic domains as design spaces*" (2003, p. 43). One student experimented with different AI models, interrogating their rules and boundaries. The other engaged with the mechanics of strategic play, treating them as a laboratory of prediction and problem-solving. Both cases emphasize that digital games and AI technologies can serve not merely as diversions but as arenas of critical and reflective learning.

The context of postdigital learning is complemented by the digital surveillance to which students are constantly subjected by adults. With apps like Librus—widely used in Poland—as well as platforms like WhatsApp, Messenger, and email, parents are not only more connected to their children's academic lives but are also more directly involved in monitoring and controlling their progress. Librus, in particular, allows parents to track attendance, view achievements, and check schedules, granting a level of access that was previously unavailable without in-person engagement. The use of digital tools allows parents to stay continuously connected with their children's education. In fact, parents sometimes receive updates on their child's grades even before the students themselves, as they get instant notifications on their phones whenever a new grade is recorded in the system. Therefore, the electronic journal serves as a vital means of sharing information, while also enabling parents to closely monitor their child's academic progress, strengthening parental control. Access to real-time updates on grades and attendance encourages parents to monitor and engage in their child's education more frequently. Technology makes it easier for parents to track their child's development and respond quickly if needed.

The integration of platforms into school communication illustrates how learning is increasingly governed through digital infrastructures of surveillance and accountability. These tools extend pedagogical labor beyond the classroom, positioning teachers as community managers while delegating monitoring functions to parents (Selwyn et al., 2017). This co-management of student performance, structured by platform affordances, aligns with neoliberal logics of responsibilization and outcome-based governance. Rather than fostering trust, parental involvement is reframed around control, with platforms offering real-time data that supplants relational engagement (Zuboff, 2019). The result is a shift in the teacher-parent-student dynamic. Schools outsource emotional and cognitive oversight to families, while students internalize performance pressures under continuous observation. Despite these transformations, instructional practices remain largely traditional, This reinforces, what Bernstein (1996) calls the total pedagogization of society and places educational control within the family life (Beck-Gernsheim, 1998; Selwyn, 2014).

The use of platforms puts students in a continuous loop of parental oversight that exemplifies Zuboff's (2019) surveillance capitalism, where behavioral data—grades, attendance, assignments—are extracted and circulated in real time. This feedback infrastructure restructures the home–school relationship around performance, eroding temporal distance and students' sense of autonomy. As Jessop (2002) notes, such systems reflect neoliberal reflexive governance, offloading accountability onto families while reinforcing institutional hierarchies. Students increasingly resist these dynamics through acts of postdigital rebellion, such as sharing Librus content on TikTok, reappropriating institutional metrics through irony and peer-based reinterpretation. These gestures, while symbolic, mark informal sites of agency and negotiation within a tightly surveilled environment. What Jessop terms symbolic compliance is clearly at play. Students outwardly conform to the routines of digital schooling, while at the same time undermining them through parody and tactical reuse. Zuboff's analysis of surveillance capitalism helps situate this dynamic, showing how infrastructures built to commodify behavior are simultaneously used by students as tools for humor resistance.

Librus, the electronic school management system, makes this tension tangible. In its official function, it condenses school life into calculable traces—marks, weighted averages, and attendance records. In this institutional framing, grades operate as empty signifiers. They stand in for "learning," "progress," or "quality," condensing heterogeneous practices into a single measure of performance (Laclau, 2005). Once circulated among peers, these same artifacts begin to function as floating signifiers, their meaning pulled between competing discourses. For schools and parents, they signify accountability and discipline. For students, they can be reframed as memes or objects of parody. On TikTok, the dramatized deletion of Microsoft Teams re-signifies one of the central infrastructures of digital governance as a symbol of closure and emancipation, further emphasizing how institutional signifiers of modernization and efficiency are re-signified as burdensome or absurd. These acts of circulation and reinterpretation do not abolish the hierarchies encoded in digital schooling, but they destabilize their fixity, showing how even the most tightly managed infrastructures remain open to subversion and alternative articulations (Gee & Green, 1998; Selwyn, 2014; Zuboff, 2019).

The ethnographic observations suggest that postdigital learning in schools is shaped less by technological innovation than by the persistence of institutional routines. While digital tools are present, their use tends to reinforce rather than disrupt existing pedagogical hierarchies and governance structures. Students engage with these environments in adaptive and at times resistant ways, but the epistemic and relational foundations of schooling remain largely unchanged. Understanding the dynamics of postdigital learning, therefore, requires a shift in focus—from devices and platforms to the discursive formations that determine what counts as learning, how it is evaluated, and whose knowledge is legitimized. The following section draws on critical discourse analysis (Gee & Green, 1998; Laclau, 2005) to examine how learning is constructed within educational discourse.

3.2 Learning as a Rewarding Labor

Conceptualizing learning as a form of labor enables a critical examination of how educational discourse positions learners, defines learning practices, and attributes value to knowledge. Within this framework, learning is not an autonomous or intrinsically rewarding activity but a socially and economically regulated process aligned with the logics of productivity and measurable output. It is structured by institutional expectations that demand discipline and self-monitoring. This perspective challenges the traditional separation between intellectual and manual labor, emphasizing that knowledge production involves intensive, regulated work governed by norms of efficiency and performative success.

On the level of discursive world building, a representative example of this logic is found in official educational materials, such as Integrated Educational Platform (PZE), which instructs students: "*You already know the conditions under which learning becomes difficult: avoid hunger, noise, and fatigue. Keeping things in order, eating well, and sleeping enough will help. But that's not all. Do you know how to organize your study space to work longer and more enjoyably? Did you know you can influence how easily you grasp new and sometimes difficult material? Learn some effective learning strategies and test them during self-study. See how it works*" (ZPE, 2023).

Framing learning as labor embeds it within the postdigital knowledge economy, where education is organized around productivity rather than open inquiry or intellectual autonomy. Within this framework, learning is redefined as a structured activity aligned with neoliberal imperatives of human capital development, transforming students into "*cognitive workers*" whose worth is assessed through outputs such as grades and credentials (Szkudlarek, 2010; Szkudlarek & Zamojski, 2020). As students internalize norms of constant improvement, schooling becomes a disciplinary regime that governs through normalization rather than coercion (Foucault, 1972). This logic is materialized in the organization of learning spaces and daily habits: "*Effective learning depends on optimizing both physical space and bodily needs: a properly positioned desk, good lighting, an ergonomic chair, and appropriate screen distance all contribute to reducing fatigue. (…) Organization of study time—regular breaks, consistent routines, sufficient sleep, and proper nutrition—enhance focus and memory. (…) Attention and physical well-being are thus framed as prerequisites for academic success*" (We learn quickly and effectively, 2023). These seemingly neutral recommendations reinforce the coupling of learning with discipline, making educational performance contingent on the rational management of one's body, space, and time.

Disciplinary mechanisms in education are deeply entwined with the logic of neoliberal governance, positioning learners as self-regulating actors tasked with managing their own success through continuous assessment. Within this framework, learning is instrumentalized—no longer centered on critical inquiry or intellectual formation but oriented toward measurable outcomes. Students internalize institutional expectations, monitoring their performance and aligning their behavior with standardized metrics, while educational policies recast learning as a lifelong obligation linked to economic relevance. Simons and Masschelein (2008) describe this transformation as the governmentalization of learning, where individuals are governed through the imperative to constantly update and optimize their skills. Curricular documents reflect this shift, emphasizing the need to "upgrade and expand one's qualifications" and to make informed decisions about education and employment in the service of lifelong learning (Curriculum Framework, 2022). In this regime, failure is framed as a personal deficit rather than structural exclusion, and the school emerges not as a space for collective development or emancipation but as a site of preparatory conditioning—where learners are molded into entrepreneurial subjects, navigating an economy that demands continuous intellectual labor under conditions of institutional control and socio-economic pressure.

Zamojski (2022, p. 59) identifies a transformation in education from holistic pedagogical engagement to individualized, commodified learning strategies shaped by neoliberal rationality. This shift centers education around the acquisition of measurable competencies, reinforcing meritocratic narratives that portray learning as a matter of personal responsibility. Such framings obscure the structural inequalities that shape educational outcomes, presenting the education system as a neutral arena of equal opportunity. Success appears as a function of effort and adaptability, when in fact it reflects the reproduction of social privilege (Bourdieu & Passeron, 1990). Learning becomes a labor process, quantified through certifiable skills and outcomes rather than cultivated through dialogical engagement (Zamojski, 2015). This neoliberal logic permeates policy documents that emphasize intellectual effort as a condition for adulthood. For instance, a methodological guide for high school history teachers from the Integrated Educational Platform promotes student activity and asserts that a successful lesson leaves the student "*intellectually exhausted*" (Płonka, 2022). This metaphor of productive exhaustion mirrors the ideological construction of the learner as an entrepreneur of intellectual capital, evaluated through measurable performance and self-discipline. In this framing, education is reduced to preparation for labor markets, marginalizing inquiry and reinforcing market-oriented values in everyday pedagogy.

The restructuring of educational categories such as learning goals and outcomes into instruments of economic management reflects a shift in how learning is understood and valued. What was once grounded in pedagogical dialogue and formative engagement now serves frameworks of productivity and measurement. Zamojski (2015, p. 83) notes that this redefinition narrows learning to an individual task, detaching it from its social and relational foundations. This discourse gained prominence in Central and Eastern Europe—particularly in Poland—through the implementation of the National Qualifications Framework (Krajowa Rama Kwalifikacji), which reorganized educational aims around standardized learning outcomes. In the introductory report we read: "*The*

Integrated Qualifications System (ZSK) supports the motivation of individuals to learn and to acquire qualifications in two ways. First, it introduces solutions that ensure the transparency and credibility of available qualifications. It provides tools that facilitate planning one's development and making rational choices. Second, the implementation of the ZSK in Poland contributes to intensifying discussions about the need for continuous learning. The ability to learn constantly, to think critically, and to remain open to change is gaining crucial importance today. This development aligns with the forecasts of Alvin Toffler, who in the 1970s wrote: 'Knowledge will increasingly take on a transitory character. What is considered fact today may already tomorrow prove to be false information. This is by no means an argument against learning facts or acquiring data. The point is that a society in which individuals constantly change jobs, place of residence, sever social ties, and so on, must place enormous emphasis on the very process of learning'" (Ministry of National Education [MEN], 2019).

The report situates the Integrated Qualifications System (ZSK) within a broader narrative that frames learning as a lifelong obligation, directly tied to employability and adaptability. By invoking Alvin Toffler's forecasts from the 1970s, the document legitimizes its vision of continuous learning through a discourse of inevitability. Knowledge is transient, the labor market unstable, and therefore the individual must assume responsibility for perpetual reskilling. This framing exemplifies what Olssen and Peters (2005, p. 336) describe as the neoliberal recasting of education as an investment in human capital, where the value of learning lies less in collective or civic development than in the individual's capacity to remain competitive. Critical thinking and openness to change—named in the report as key competencies—thus function not as emancipatory aims but as adaptive strategies within a volatile economy.

Learning is no longer framed as a process of inquiry or ethical development, but as a means of acquiring credentials for economic participation. The promise of meritocracy conceals the fact that access to such competencies is shaped by structural advantage. By presenting learning outcomes as universal and neutral, this system masks disparities rooted in social structure. It recasts responsibility for educational failure onto the individual, removing attention from the conditions that constrain learning. In this context, education becomes less about formation and more about compliance with systems that prioritize efficiency and output over meaning.

Framing learning as labor fundamentally reshapes the role of educational institutions by placing mechanisms of control, responsibility, standardization, and surveillance within the learning process. Competency-based assessment models enforce rigid structures that prioritize measurable outcomes over intellectual experimentation or failure, transforming education into a mechanized system that molds students into self-monitoring subjects. These structures align with labor market expectations, where productivity and efficiency define value. The learner is redefined as an economic agent, and learning becomes a means of self-management and optimization. While this model promotes effort and individual achievement, it narrows the purpose of education to market readiness, displacing its critical and relational dimensions. Technologies often reinforce this shift. As Selwyn (2014, p. 33) observes, educational tools function as a "Trojan Mouse"—ostensibly progressive but introducing efficiency-driven logics into the school environment. Digital platforms that promote personalization and continuous self-assessment further this agenda by casting students as entrepreneurial subjects managing their own development. In this logic, learners are expected to produce intellectual capital, continuously reskill, and remain competitive—transforming education into a regime of labor.

If we take a broader view of the discourse of learning as work, as it appears in educational documents, reports, and teaching materials, several distinct layers can be identified. On the level of activity building, this transformation reconfigures the teacher-learner relationship by repositioning educators as facilitators of individualized data-driven learning paths. While this model suggests autonomy, it reflects neoliberal logics of self-management that shift responsibility for learning entirely onto the student. The teacher's role is reduced to efficient content delivery and monitoring progress through quantifiable metrics. At the same time, framing learning as labor marginalizes the emotional and ethical dimensions of education. Discipline, effort, and performance become dominant values, while critical inquiry is subordinated to task-oriented productivity. Digital technologies, often celebrated as inclusive and innovative, reinforce this trajectory by embedding performance metrics and behavioral optimization into everyday educational practice. As knowledge is commodified and schools function increasingly as preparatory sites for labor markets, the civic and ethical purpose of education erodes (Zamojski, 2022, p. 61). This shift is mirrored in curriculum frameworks and policy discourse, which emphasize abstract notions such as "*future competencies*" or "*creativity*" while obscuring the actual learning processes centered on memorization and compliance. Such terms function, in Laclau's (2005) sense, as empty signifiers—floating ideals that mask the instrumental rationality underpinning them. As Jessop (2008) argues, policy thus becomes a vehicle for economic competitiveness, privileging market adaptability while marginalizing education's democratic and intellectual functions.

The prominence of competencies must be situated within the political economy of post-Fordist capitalism, where education is restructured to meet the demands of flexible labor markets. These competencies, although presented as universally essential, are pedagogically ambiguous and ideologically loaded as they reflect a selective privileging of forms of learning that enhance economic responsiveness (Jessop, 2002, p.52). This convergence of corporate and international institutional discourse reinforces the repositioning of education as a mechanism for producing agile, self-governing individuals who can adapt continuously to labor market volatility. In this rearticulated framework, lifelong learning becomes not a right or emancipatory process but a mandate for self-optimization. It aligns public education with neoliberal governance. The shift displaces education's democratic and civic functions, redefining its purpose as the cultivation of economic actors capable of managing their own productivity and value in uncertain global economies (Jessop, 2008).

The elevation of "critical thinking" in the report *Critical Thinking, Evaluation of Information Credibility: Conclusions from International Educational Research and a Literature Review* by the Educational Research Institute (IBE) as a central educational objective exemplifies how postdigital educational discourse appropriates pedagogical ideals while stripping them of their epistemological complexity. Frequently defined through cognitive operations such as logical reasoning (Ennis, 2016; Facione, 2015), critical thinking is framed as a universal and context-independent skill, detached from the relational and material conditions of its enactment. This abstraction turns critical thinking into an empty signifier—promoted as universally attainable but pedagogically vague, masking the institutional constraints that limit its actual cultivation in formal schooling. Such framing aligns with the broader discourse of "*future competencies*," another empty signifier, which, as Zamojski (2022, p. 57) argues, often misaligns with the civic and ethical purposes of education. Drawing on Biesta's critique of outcome-driven education, Zamojski contends that the commodification of learning transforms students into consumers of educational services, redefining the state's role from guarantor of democratic education to provider of skill-oriented training. The European Qualifications Framework illustrates this shift by translating classical pedagogical categories—knowledge, skills, and social competencies—into economic outcomes measured by their utility in the knowledge economy. Within this framework, learning is no longer situated as a transformative or collective process but as an individualized accumulation of human capital, regulated by neoliberal governance and directed toward labor market adaptability. The institutionalization of competencies like critical thinking thus functions less as a commitment to intellectual emancipation as a strategy of depoliticized social reproduction under the guise of economic modernization.

The discourse of future competencies has reconfigured learning into a process of continuous self-optimization, where the absence of a defined educational endpoint traps individuals in a permanent cycle of adaptation to unstable market demands. Framed rhetorically as empowerment, this temporal open-endedness becomes, in practice, a disciplinary imperative—a manifestation of neoliberal subjectivity in which learners internalize chronic insufficiency and pursue upskilling as a condition of economic survival. As formal education gives way to fragmented, decentralized modalities—micro-credentials, platform-based certifications, workplace training—the boundary between learning and labor changes. Competency development is no longer a pedagogical aim but a lifelong economic obligation. It places educational activity into regimes of productivity and behavioral performance. This restructuring reflects Foucault's (1972) concept of governmentality. Learners become self-monitoring subjects governed through internalized norms of responsiveness and adaptability. They do not even need direct institutional coercion. In parallel, Fraser's (2013) critique of the commodification of social goods shows how learning, once a public entitlement, is recast as a privatized asset. It becomes disconnected from civic, ethical, and relational commitments. At the level of discursive connection building, this transformation detaches learning from its social embeddedness. It is no longer experienced as a collective or public good but as an individual pursuit, deeply connected with meritocratic assumptions. Competency discourse naturalizes the idea that success stems from effort and that competencies are universally attainable, which hides the structural inequities that shape access, participation, and recognition. Lifelong learning, while framed in the vocabulary of growth and autonomy, functions as a mode of economic governance—pushing individuals to remain in a constant state of productive becoming, never complete, never secure, always ready for the next demand.

In the everyday reality of school, the discourse of *learning as rewarding labour* is not mediated through policy ideals such as the European Qualifications Framework or visions of future competencies. But rather through the immediate and tangible incentives embedded in school structures. Drawing on Gee and Green's (1998) notion of connection building, it becomes evident that students do not engage with learning as a process of future-oriented competence development. For them it is a means of securing short-term validation—passing a test, obtaining a grade, or eventually receiving a certificate. "*In the end, it will pay off for them—they have to study now so that later they can make decisions about their own lives, to have any possibility of choice. Sometimes they're not even fully aware yet of what they can achieve, but at this stage, the matura is the gateway. They have to put in the effort. I don't like this form of testing either, all the cramming—I know it's tedious and boring—but in the end, there's the freedom to choose their own life path*" (T_3_school_2). Learning is discursively tied to achievement in the narrowest procedural sense. It reduces education to a succession of hurdles to overcome. Within this frame, the value of knowledge lies not in its dialogical or transformative capacity, but in its capacity to be exchanged for quantifiable results. What matters is the grade rather than the insight. The exam score is more important than the intellectual process. This logic aligns closely with the discourse of *learning as rewarding labour*. Study is framed as tedious effort that will eventually "pay off" through the promise of future autonomy symbolized by the high school final exam. Here, learning is not valued for its immediacy or ethical significance but for its deferred exchange value within institutional and labor market systems. Gee and Green's (1998) notion of *connection building* is visible in the way students are asked to link monotonous tasks of memorization and testing to imagined futures, while Laclau's (2005) concept of the *empty signifier* shows how the high school final exam condenses heterogeneous aspirations into a single object that legitimizes present sacrifice.

This disjunction between policy discourse and everyday educational practice is particularly visible in the Polish school system, where neither students nor teachers meaningfully refer to the language of "lifelong learning," "critical competencies," or "adaptive knowledge economies" that dominates strategic documents and reform agendas. These frameworks, while rhetorically powerful at the level of policy, remain abstract, decontextualized, and pedagogically irrelevant within the daily life of school. Instead, students inhabit an environment structured by relentless assessment, where knowledge is rendered instrumental, stripped of depth, and reconstituted as input for performance systems. The experience of learning is thus shaped not by reflective engagement or shared inquiry but by the urgency of "passing," enacted through rituals of reproducing model answers and strategically navigating requirements. In this sense, the everyday practices of students simultaneously reproduce and destabilize the discourse of rewarding labor. They comply with its demands while re-signifying its instruments through pragmatic shortcuts.

This regime implicitly conditions students to internalize a logic of transactional learning that mirrors the broader neoliberal configuration of education as individualized labor. Within this framing, learning is reconstituted as a form of productivity, measured by quantifiable outputs and reduced to its exchange value within assessment systems. Success is narrowly defined, while the ethical and dialogical dimensions of education are marginalized, and epistemic agency is subordinated to compliance. What emerges is a paradox at the heart of contemporary schooling. Institutions are charged with preparing young people for futures marked by uncertainty and adaptability, however the everyday pedagogical practices cultivate dispositions of short-term pragmatism.

This contradiction emphasizes the fragility of official reform agendas. The language of adaptability, lifelong learning, and critical competencies circulates powerfully in policy discourse. However it remains detached from the lived realities of classrooms, where assessment rituals and exam preparation dominate. In Laclau's (2005) terms, these aspirational ideals function as empty signifiers, unifying disparate goals under the veneer of progress while masking the persistence of proceduralist practices. The symbolic economies of schooling—where marks constitute the main currency of value—ensure that learning is performed and rewarded within narrow, predefined parameters, leaving little room for alternative imaginaries. In this sense, the promise of education as a space of critical formation is continually undermined by the structural imperatives of standardization and accountability, which bind students to cycles of compliance and foreclose the very capacities that policy rhetoric celebrates.

3.3 Learning as Survival

This subchapter explores how the survival metaphor reshapes students' perceptions of learning, revealing a broader shift toward instrumentalism, bureaucratic compliance, and emotional detachment from the educational process. Within this logic, learning is navigated strategically, with success defined less by meaningful engagement and more by one's capacity to endure standardized demands and perform efficiently. The metaphor of survival suggests that students do not see school as a place for personal or intellectual development but as a bureaucratic and disciplinary institution in which their primary task is to endure boredom and accumulate the necessary knowledge to pass standardized exams. *At school, we learn what the teachers require us to. Otherwise, we won't pass. I don't know what else to say. Nothing else is really happening here. You just have to get through it until the final exams* (S_IC_1_school_1). Their focus on examinations as the endpoint of education—rather than seeing learning as valuable in itself—reveals how the logic of schooling has become transactional. Knowledge is not something to be engaged with, but rather something to be memorized and reproduced in service of institutional requirements. The emphasis on "*learning all the necessary information to pass the exam*" signals that the value of knowledge is increasingly defined by external validation and quantification, rather than by its transformative or empowering potential: "*We just have to get through it somehow. We study to move forward, to get into university. It's all about exchanging this information for grades. Our real goals lie elsewhere. It's always been that way. Was it any different when you were in school?*" (S_IC_2_school_2).

The framing of school learning as a survival strategy discloses a more profound disquiet at the core of contemporary education. For a significant number of students, the school no longer constitutes a space of intellectual exploration or personal formation. Rather, it is experienced as a bureaucratic apparatus to be navigated. Its value is measured by the acquisition of credentials rather than the cultivation of understanding. When students describe schooling as simply "part of our fate," such statements articulate not aspiration but resignation. They articulate an acceptance of institutional demands devoid of meaningful engagement. As Dudzikowa (2001, pp. 132–133) argues, the enduring myth of the school as a site of holistic human development collapses under the weight of routinization, decontextualized content, and an everyday rhythm that detaches learning from lived experience and relational depth. The classroom, under these conditions, becomes a space of detachment. This pedagogical hollowness is not incidental. It is structurally embedded in a system that increasingly subordinates education to economic rationalities and performance metrics (Jessop, 2002, p. 241). Within such a framework, learning is redefined not as an open-ended pursuit of meaning or participation in a knowledge community, but as an exercise in endurance—marked by procedural output.

The conceptualization of school learning as *survival* fundamentally shifts the discourse on education from one centered on intellectual and personal development to one characterized by endurance. Within this framework, *survival* functions as what Laclau (2005) describes as an empty signifier—a term that holds significant emotional and ideological weight, but remains open to multiple interpretations. While students and teachers alike invoke the language of *surviving school*, there is no precise articulation of what exactly must be survived, suggesting that the term captures a diffuse but deeply felt condition of struggle.

This use of *survival* as an empty signifier reveals a profound dissonance between the structure of schooling and the lived experiences of students. It is clear that school is experienced as a space of endurance rather than one of empowerment, but the lack of a clear object of struggle suggests that the oppressive forces shaping students' experiences are so embedded in the system that they are difficult to name directly. This absence of specificity points to a structural crisis in education—one that is not tied to individual teachers, subjects, or policies, but rather to the broader logic of schooling itself.: "*It is what it is here—you have to sit here because we're supposed to go to school, and no one asks whether we want to or whether anything interesting happens for us here. I get really sleepy at school; in general, I go to bed late, and in the morning it's hard for me, and somehow you just have to survive. And you have to be at school by eight—I don't know who decided that for us. My mom says school isn't supposed to be interesting, and, well, it isn'*t [laughs – MP]" (S_IC_school_1).

The construction of learning as survival, voiced in student narratives and enacted through their embodied practices, points to a deeper crisis of engagement. The crisis surpasses mere cognitive disinterest and extends into the domain of psychosomatic withdrawal. The physical postures and behaviors frequently observed in classrooms—yawning, head-lowering, disconnection, compulsive engagement with mobile devices—should not be hastily dismissed as inattentiveness. Rather, they may be read as tacit forms of resistance. They suggest refusals to participate in pedagogical routines perceived as irrelevant or affectively vacant. These disengagements reflect not a rejection of learning per se, but of the forms through which it is institutionalized. Digital platforms such as TikTok or YouTube, offering immediate responsiveness, stand in stark contrast to the unidirectional and non-responsive nature of much classroom instruction. The affective appeal of these platforms should not be interpreted as escapism alone but as symptomatic of an educational system that fails to create meaningful conditions for engagement. Crucially, students' re-engagement during dialogic moments and participatory formats suggests that the problem lies less with their motivation and more with the structural rigidity of pedagogical design. When the classroom allows for recognition students demonstrate a sustained capacity and desire to engage. What is commonly pathologized as apathy may thus be better understood as a response to the systemic misalignment between institutional forms of schooling and the relational realities of learners.

The figuration of the learning subject through the prism of survival foregrounds a deep-seated crisis in the function and ethos of contemporary schooling. When students' educational trajectories are marked by chronic fatigue, anxiety, and a pervasive sense of institutional estrangement, schooling no longer operates as a site of cognitive emancipation. Instead it becomes a mechanism for the normalization of psychosocial strain and bureaucratic submission. In such a context, the cultivation of reflexivity and agency is displaced by the habituation to discomfort, rendering endurance, but not understanding. This phenomenon resonates with critical accounts of neoliberal education, which highlight how the logics of performativity systematically erode conditions for relational learning.

The dual articulation of survival—as both coping strategy and aspirational goal—reveals a structural contradiction within the normative discourse of learning. While official pedagogical narratives position schooling as a transformative journey toward autonomy and civic participation, the lived experience increasingly privileges compliance. In this configuration, education ceases to function as a space of inquiry and becomes an obstacle course. Students are interpellated not to learn because knowledge is intrinsically valuable, but to persist because exhaustion is an expected condition of institutional passage. This reconfiguration of purpose induces not resistance but resignation. Students internalize boredom as endemic to schooling rather than symptoms of its dysfunction. Such dynamics echo Foucault's (1972) analysis of disciplinary power, wherein institutions govern not through overt coercion but by embedding normative expectations into the very sensorium of the subject. Within this regime, the struggle itself becomes depoliticized. It is treated as natural and inevitable.

One of the most revealing features of the survival discourse among students is their apparent inability to envision alternatives to the existing educational model. The absence of articulated demands for reform or the imagination of different pedagogical possibilities points to a profound internalization of the school as an immutable, totalizing institution. Students do not critique or propose change because they have come to see schooling not as a transformable space, but as a fixed existential reality to be endured: (“*this is school*,” “*it has always been like that*”; “*it is what it is*”). This normalization signals a deep ideological saturation in which the logic of survival is not merely a coping strategy but a defining frame through which education is experienced and understood. The internalization of survival as a normative mode of engagement fosters compliance, discourages resistance, and conditions individuals to accept exhaustion and precarity as unavoidable. In this way, education does not merely prepare individuals for participation in society. It actively configures their subjectivity to align with the demands and tolerances of capitalist economies, reinforcing broader systems of discipline and control.

The analysis of digital practices cited by students in discussions of learning and the Internet suggests that the discourse of survival is not confined to the physical space of the classroom but extends into the digital domain, It reveals a systemic logic of engagement structured by tactical compliance. Here, survival operates less as an affective disposition than as a strategic modality, through which students manage the procedural and outcome-oriented demands of schooling. Within this framework, the value of knowledge is subordinated to the imperatives of efficiency and expediency. Students’ use of digital tools—ranging from generative AI and online solution databases to homework support platforms—does not simply reflect avoidance or disengagement. It signifies a pragmatic response to institutional pressures that reward completion over understanding.

This instrumentalization of technology marks a profound epistemological shift. Learning is no longer experienced as a dialogic or interpretive process, but as a navigational task aimed at fulfilling preset requirements with minimal cognitive friction. In this context, the metrics of success are task fulfillment and procedural compliance, not conceptual depth or intellectual autonomy. The delegation of cognitive labor to algorithmic systems signals a rearticulation of the learning process in postdigital conditions, wherein machine intelligence increasingly mediates, structures, and in many cases displaces human inquiry. What emerges is a model of learning-as-output—one that mirrors and reinforces broader shifts toward automation and affective detachment in knowledge economies (Jessop, 2008).

The strategic deployment of artificial intelligence and digital resources by students to circumvent traditional pedagogical demands foregrounds a growing disjunction between institutional expectations and emergent forms of student agency. Within a system in which learning is experienced as a mode of endurance, students do not passively absorb instruction but instead engage in forms of digitally mediated negotiation that contest the legitimacy of prevailing educational norms. These practices should not be read as rejections of learning per se, but as situated responses to a model of schooling increasingly perceived as misaligned with the epistemic conditions of contemporary life. The recourse to AI-generated outputs, including entire assignments, reflects not a moral failing but the erosion of pedagogical relevance in a system structured around assessment metrics and formal compliance rather than inquiry, dialogue, or intellectual risk.

In this context, AI functions not as an external disruption but as a systemic artifact. This is an extension of educational regimes that privilege quantifiable results over critical reflection. Students' gravitation toward algorithmically enhanced tools emphasizes the widening gap between inherited pedagogical forms and the logics of a postdigital knowledge economy in which cognition is increasingly technologized. This epistemic shift destabilizes long-standing assumptions about the humanistic aspirations of education. As core cognitive practices such as writing, problem-solving, and synthesis are outsourced to machines, the normative foundations of education—as a site for cultivating critical subjectivity and democratic agency—are thrown into question.

The instrumental use of AI thus operates as both a survival strategy and an implicit critique. It signals a pragmatic adaptation to institutional pressures. Simultaneously it is a symptom of an education system that has failed to render learning meaningful or resonant. To dismiss such practices merely as academic dishonesty is to overlook the structural conditions that make them both rational and, in some cases, necessary. What is required is not stricter enforcement but a rethinking of pedagogical purpose—an effort to reimagine learning as a relational and ethically situated practice within a digital milieu defined by abundance, automation, and epistemic flux.

The normalization of survival as an educational orientation reveals a deeper transformation in how subjectivity is governed within contemporary schooling. What may appear as individual resignation—students enduring rather than engaging with school—is in fact symptomatic of a broader restructuring of educational experience under late capitalist conditions. The convergence of neoliberal rationality and therapeutic governance has redefined what it means to be a learner: no longer an intellectually curious subject engaged in shared inquiry, but an emotionally self-regulating individual, compelled to manage the psychological consequences of systemic strain. This reconfiguration reflects what Jessop (2016) describes as a strategic-relational selectivity, whereby educational institutions are recalibrated to align with dominant economic rationalities. Within such a configuration, performance and continuous self-optimization become normative imperatives, shaping both institutional practice and individual aspiration.

Education, in this context, no longer functions as a site of collective emancipation but is subsumed into a regime of affective and economic control. Therapeutic discourses—emphasizing resilience—are mobilized not to confront the structural causes of student distress but to manage its symptoms of student distress, and to stabilize the very systems that generate psychic strain. Brunila's (2014) analysis of the therapisation of education emphasizes how emotional well-being is repurposed into an individualized project of self-management. It is aimed at masking the displacement of institutional responsibility onto the learner. Rather than challenging the conditions that produce alienation, exhaustion, and disengagement, Within this system schools increasingly configure emotional regulation as a moral obligation. In this regard, survival becomes psychopolitical. It is both the price of institutional participation and the precondition for recognition as a competent student-subject.

This dual logic—care intertwined with control—produces a contradictory affective economy in which students are simultaneously pathologized and held responsible. While institutions nominally attend to student well-being, they continue to enforce high-stakes accountability regimes and performance metrics that exacerbate stress and erode relational depth.

In Fraser's (2013) terms, such arrangements exemplify a mode of "progressive neoliberalism," wherein emancipatory language is co-opted to legitimize market-driven structures. The promise of care, when decoupled from structural critique, functions less as support and more as pacification—redirecting political affect into therapeutically managed forms of compliance.

Under these conditions, survival is no longer a deviation from educational norms but a logical outcome of their restructuring. Students internalize endurance not as a contested condition but as a normalized disposition. They are expected not only to produce but to remain composed, to persist affectively within a system that continually undermines their psychic and epistemic agency. As Jessop (2016) and Brunila (2014) both warn, the alignment of economic rationality with therapeutic governance risks depoliticizing educational suffering, transforming a structural condition into an individualized burden. The survivalist posture, in this light, should not be interpreted as resistance or failure, but as a rational adaptation to an education system that has ceased to make learning meaningful—and a tacit critique of the very conditions it demands students endure.

The discourse of *learning as survival* emerges not only from students' narratives but is also reflected—although in a refracted, often pathologizing form—in teachers' commentaries. Interviews with educators reveal a dual perspective. They express concern for students' fragility, coupled with a diagnosis of generational inadequacy. As one teacher states, "*These children are fragile, they're like snowflakes—anything can hurt them. They struggle to find their place in secondary school. They memorize, they guess, they're only interested in what will be on the test. I'm frightened by how delicate they are and how pragmatic they've become*" (T_5_school_2); "*It's the snowflake generation. I always have to think during lessons whether I might say something that offends them. How will they manage in upper school? Will they even make it to the final exams? How will they survive in adult life? I honestly don't know*" (T_1_school_2). These statements echo the discourse of survival articulated by students, but they also repurpose it through the lens of cultural diagnosis, producing what Bakhtin (1994) would describe as a *double-voiced discourse*—a mode of speech that both reflects genuine experience and simultaneously aligns with hegemonic ideologies that neutralize critique by reframing it as personal deficiency.

This dual function of the survival discourse reveals its complex, polysemic character, which can be analytically disaggregated into two interwoven registers. On one level, *learning as survival* reflects students' lived reality within an education system that is increasingly instrumentalized, as well as assessment-driven. Here, survival is not merely a metaphor but a concrete, embodied response to institutional pressures. Students experience schooling less as a site of personal or intellectual transformation and more as a system to be navigated tactically in order to secure credentials. Within this logic, the pursuit of understanding gives way to strategic adaptation. Superficial learning strategies and recourse to digital tools such as generative AI become rational responses to a regime that prioritizes output over depth. As Jessop (2008) has argued, such educational systems are selectively shaped to reinforce broader socio-economic logics, privileging market-oriented performance over democratic or emancipatory aims. Survival, under these conditions, is not a failure of effort or character—it is the mode through which students endure the structural violence of schooling, which disciplines rather than liberates, and exhausts rather than animates.

However, when refracted through adult perspectives—particularly those shaped by dominant cultural narratives about generational change—the same survival discourse becomes a site of moral judgment. Students' strategies for coping with educational stress are reinterpreted as evidence of emotional fragility and lack of resilience. What may be expressions of alienation, anxiety, or institutional critique are recoded through the culturally saturated trope of the *snowflake generation*, reducing systemic distress to individual inadequacy. In this reading, survival is not acknowledged as the cost of navigating a hostile system but is instead weaponized as a rhetorical device to delegitimize student voices and reaffirm adult authority. As Fraser (2013) notes, neoliberal formations are adept at co-opting emancipatory discourses and rearticulating them in ways that reinforce, rather than challenge, structural inequities. Emotional distress is framed not as a consequence of exploitative educational arrangements but as a personal failing to be corrected through resilience training, therapeutic discipline, or better emotional management. Affective self-regulation becomes the norm, displacing collective political responses with individualized forms of adaptation (Brunila, 2014).

The ideological function of this double-voiced discourse lies precisely in its capacity to convert critique into pathology. While students may articulate survival as a way of naming their educational condition, the same language is appropriated to foreclose its critical edge. Institutional actors—teachers, administrators, policymakers—acknowledge that students are struggling, but the response is often not structural transformation but affective governance. Students are taught how to endure rather than empowered to resist. In this configuration, the very notion of survival is depoliticized. It is no longer a call for reimagining education but a background condition to be absorbed, managed, and normalized.

This distinction—between survival as a condition produced by structural contradiction and survival as a symptom of personal fragility—signals a broader ideological contest over the meaning of education. If survival is understood exclusively as a matter of individual deficiency, then the educational response will remain within the domain of behavioral and affective correction. It means more psychological programs, more emphasis on grit and self-care, and more attempts to teach students how to adjust. Such interventions leave untouched the institutional logics that make survival necessary in the first place. If, however, survival is recognized as a rational response to a system that erodes curiosity and dampens subjectivity, and even instrumentalizes learning, then it compels a different set of questions—ones that demand pedagogical, ethical, and structural reconfiguration. The survivalist discourse—when taken as a form of situated knowledge—reveals the extent to which contemporary schooling functions not as a site of possibility but as a mechanism of endurance. Its regulatory force lies in its ambivalence. It names harm while simultaneously neutralizing it. To move beyond this impasse requires not only listening to what survival signifies for students but interrogating the institutional arrangements that have rendered it the prevailing grammar of education.

The survivalist discourse explored throughout this subchapter reveals a profound disjunction between the institutional form of education and its lived experience by students. Learning, far from being experienced as a process of intellectual growth or curiosity-driven exploration, is increasingly reduced to a matter of endurance—a bureaucratic challenge to be navigated and survived. The normalization of exhaustionand instrumental learning reflects a systemic failure to align educational practices with meaningful engagement. However, survival does not exhaust the possibilities of learning. The next subchapter—*Learning as Necessity and Intellectual Development*—shifts focus from the logic of endurance to the conditions under which learning is experienced as a meaningful, necessary, and intellectually formative activity.

3.4 Learning as Necessity and Intellectual Development

The following part examines how students and teachers articulate the meaning of learning, revealing tensions between institutional demands, pedagogical ideals, and student agency. Teachers tend to frame learning both as a necessity—driven by exam requirements and formal benchmarks—and as a pathway to intellectual and cultural development. These aspirations often clash with students' perceptions of relevance and engagement, particularly when traditional cultural forms such as literature or history fail to resonate. This friction emphasizes the complexity of teaching in an environment where the instrumental and intrinsic purposes of education frequently collide, leading to frustration when students appear unmoved by the forms of cultural capital teachers value. One teacher expressed this dissonance explicitly: "*Sure, it would be nice if they wanted to read Tokarczuk, but they are not interested in that. They are not going to learn it. They're interested in being a YouTuber. This is an interesting career. And books, theater—it's no longer fashionable*" (T_2_school_1).

This passage demonstrates how hierarchical distinctions between forms of knowledge are explicitly articulated by teachers and tacitly reinforced through institutional materials. A teacher's remark that "*it's no longer fashionable*" to engage with literature or theater reflects more than cultural nostalgia. It reveals an epistemological anxiety about the waning authority of traditional cultural capital in an age shaped by digital media. Within this framing, student aspirations—particularly those directed toward newer, digitally mediated domains—are subtly dismissed as lacking depth or enduring value. Such a valuation hierarchy does not only reside in teacher discourse but is embedded in curricular structures, especially in textbooks that standardize what counts as legitimate knowledge. For example, a prompt in a history textbook—"*What important information is contained in the excerpt from Widukind of Corvey's Chronicle?*" (Understanding the Past 1, p. 323)—frames the student's task not as interpretive or analytical but as extractive. There is a correct, institutionally sanctioned answer to be found. The phrasing presumes that the "important" content is already determined by the textbook's epistemic framework, reducing learning to the retrieval of predefined facts rather than the cultivation of critical or dialogical engagement with historical texts. This approach consolidates a top-down transmission of knowledge, marginalizing student agency and reinforcing a model of education where learning is equated with compliance and reproduction rather than inquiry and intellectual autonomy.

This pedagogical approach frequently leads to student resistance, particularly among those who reject the idea that importance should be dictated to them. During lessons students often argued that textbooks should not determine which knowledge is valuable, asserting their own right to decide what is meaningful in their education:

> "History lesson, Grade 1, school_1
> *T: Find the answer in the textbook to the question: why did Mieszko I convert to Christianity?*
> *S: Can we do a different question?*
> *T: No, you can't.*
> *S: I think it was a political decision that harmed Slavic culture.*
> *T: That's not what I'm asking.*
> *S: But why can't we talk about it?*
> *T: Because you're disrupting the lesson.*"

The student resistance can be understood within a broader struggle over epistemic authority, where students push back against the hierarchical structure of knowledge transmission that dominates traditional schooling. Their reluctance to engage with certain types of academic material is not necessarily a sign of intellectual deficiency or lack of curiosity, as some teachers may perceive it, but rather a rejection of imposed knowledge hierarchies that do not align with their lived experiences or perceived future trajectories. The discourse surrounding "*useful*" and "*useless*" knowledge reflects not just generational differences in cultural priorities but also the ideological underpinnings of the modern educational system, which continues to valorize classical, humanistic learning. Simultaneously the educational system is shaped by neoliberal imperatives that emphasize utility and measurable success. This contradiction places both teachers and students in a conflicted position. Teachers are caught between their desire to cultivate intellectual depth and the pragmatic constraints of preparing students for standardized assessments, while students must navigate between institutional expectations and their own evolving conceptions of relevance and meaning.

The clash between teachers' perspectives and students' agency in knowledge selection reveals deeper ideological tensions within contemporary education. If the goal of education is not only to prepare students for exams but also to shape them into "educated and cultured individuals," then what happens when students resist these definitions of culture? The very fact that students increasingly push back against imposed definitions of "*valuable knowledge*" suggests that the role of education is undergoing a fundamental transformation, that challenges the long-standing top-down model of learning and demands a more participatory, dialogical approach to knowledge production. Whether the system will adapt to these shifts or continue to reinforce rigid epistemological frameworks remains an open question. What is clear is that learning as an institutionally controlled process is being actively negotiated and contested by those who participate in it. The tension between teachers' perspectives on learning and students' attitudes toward what constitutes useful and interesting knowledge highlights a fundamental epistemological divide within contemporary education. Teachers' frustration often stems from students' perceived disengagement from traditional intellectual and cultural forms, such as literature, history, and philosophy, in favor of digital, career-oriented, or entertainment-driven interests. However, this frustration is not merely a reflection of generational differences in intellectual priorities. It is also deeply rooted in an ideological framework that positions certain forms of knowledge as inherently more valuable than others. The discourse of learning expressed by teachers is reinforced in textbooks, which construct and reproduce a specific ethos of the intellectual—one that is historically and culturally linked to the European tradition and serves as the implicit benchmark for legitimate knowledge.

At the center of this discussion lies the concept of "*culture*" and "*being educated*" as empty signifiers—operating as ideological tools that structure the learning discourses of teachers and textbooks, enabling the reproduction of established cultural hierarchies under the guise of objectivity and universality.

This ideological framing is evident in the hierarchical valorization of knowledge within school curricula and textbooks, where classical literature, Western philosophical thought, and canonical narratives are privileged as the standard of education. Such representations construct the ethos of the intellectual as inherently aligned with Eurocentric values, implicitly positioning alternative knowledges as inferior. This disconnect between traditional academic culture and students' lived realities often leads to disengagement and resistance, particularly when the former is presented as intrinsically valuable without contextual relevance. Textbooks, through their structure and evaluative questioning, reinforce this dynamic by presenting knowledge as fixed and authoritative, thereby discouraging students from engaging as active co-constructors of knowledge. This pedagogical approach obscures the socially and historically contingent nature of knowledge itself, limiting the potential for critical and inclusive educational engagement.

Civic identity, for instance, is not introduced as a terrain of pluralistic negotiation or political deliberation but is instead constructed through a historical narrative that equates civilization with Western political traditions and cultural refinement. The history and civics textbooks present citizenship as a product of "civilized" societies, beginning with Ancient Greece and Rome. They are depicted as sources of law, democracy, and infrastructural advancement (roads, aqueduct, sculpture, painting) in contrast to "non-civilized" or peripheral formations. This discourse is then extended to the formation of the great nation-states of France, Germany, and the United Kingdom, which are portrayed as the rightful heirs to classical antiquity and the progenitors of modern democratic culture. Poland, though treated as a distinct subject within the national narrative, is discursively tethered to this Western civilizational arc, thereby legitimizing its place in the continuum of European statehood and civic development. As an example, a passage from the textbook *Understanding the Past 1* (p. 326–327) may serve, which presents civic identity is implicitly shaped through alignment with imperial and Christian structures, especially in the framing of Mieszko I's baptism as a key moment of political and civilizational belonging.

The concept of "*being educated*", as mobilized through this narrative, functions precisely as an empty signifier (Laclau, 2005). It binds together disparate historical references, political ideals, and cultural symbols under a single ideological banner. It appears to denote a universal condition, but its content is historically produced and normatively loaded. The textbook's articulation of the educated, civic subject implicitly requires not only intellectual competence but also alignment with a Eurocentric trajectory of development—measured by proximity to classical antiquity, national sovereignty, and cultural refinement.

In the Polish case, this construction is further reinforced by the explicit coupling of civic and patriotic discourses. Here, the figure of the citizen is not only linked to institutional participation but also framed as the bearer of national tradition and historical continuity. "*Being educated*" in this register entails internalizing a patriotic ethos—valorizing sacrifice and national unity. As Szkudlarek (2007) notes, such uses of empty signifiers enable cultural norms to appear unmarked and objective, when in fact they are selectively assembled to support a dominant vision of social cohesion. What is presented as universal civic culture is, in practice, a narrow synthesis of classical and national ideals.

This mode of representation transforms learning into a form of ideological inscription. Rather than inviting students into critical dialogue about the meaning of culture in diverse or contemporary contexts, the textbook prescribes a model of identity rooted in civilizational lineage and national fidelity. Jessop's (2019) account of how hegemonic social orders are reproduced through consensual ideological forms is particularly relevant here. The signifier "*being educated*" offers the appearance of inclusivity while embedding exclusionary standards of belonging and legitimacy. In this sense, students are not so much educated into citizenship as they are positioned in relation to a normative cultural ideal, which privileges cultural continuity over political contestation, and historical reverence over reflexivity.

The preceding analysis reveals how school-based learning is framed not as an open-ended process of inquiry, but as symbolic alignment with dominant cultural and epistemological norms. Through the mobilization of empty signifiers such as "*culture*" and "*being educated*", textbooks and curricula construct a vision of learning as developmental only insofar as it conforms to pre-established ideals. This constrains not only what counts as legitimate knowledge, but also who is recognized as a legitimate learner. Within and against these constraints, learners carve out spaces of agency.

Social media, particularly TikTok, provides one such space, where school knowledge is not simply reproduced but re-signified. Drawing on Gee and Green's (1998) notion of connection building, these practices link personal frustrations, peer interactions, and institutional expectations into new discursive constellations. The repeated injunction to "*get down to studying*," a phrase that circulates in family and school contexts as a disciplinary command, is recontextualized on TikTok as parody. It becomes a shared cultural resource for students to express both irony and resistance, transforming what was meant as a directive into a marker of identity and solidarity.

Screenshots from electronic gradebooks operate in a similar way. While officially designed as instruments of surveillance and accountability, they are appropriated by students as ironic self-representations. In Laclau's (2005) terms, the gradebook functions here as a nodal point: an artifact around which heterogeneous frustrations—about performance, pressure, or recognition—are condensed and given symbolic form. Its meaning is not fixed. It oscillates between trauma and parody, exposing the instability of institutional authority.

Even the infrastructures of digital schooling themselves, such as Microsoft Teams, are re-signified. The widely shared TikTok clip of deleting Teams is less a technical gesture than an act of symbolic refusal. Within Gee and Green's framework of identity building, such practices allow learners to position themselves against the apparatus of schooling, reclaiming autonomy through playful, but affectively charged acts. The comments under the video reveal the tension between institutional demands and student desires. While some warn that Teams might be useful later, the creator insists on the need to forget school, at least temporarily. This ambivalence illustrates Laclau's insight that empty signifiers—here, "*school*" itself—gain their force not from precise definition but from the affective intensities and identifications they gather.

In these postdigital practices, then, learning is reframed not as the acquisition of sanctioned knowledge but as a process of re-signification, where students mobilize parody and refusal to produce alternative epistemic projects. What emerges is a terrain in which institutional authority is destabilized, and where legitimacy is no longer dictated solely by schools but negotiated across classrooms, peer networks, and algorithmic publics.

3.5 Autonomous Learning

This chapter explores how students engage with learning discourses through digital media, often privileging informal, self-directed learning over formal academic instruction. Students frequently describe their learning—whether constructing a wooden house, mastering culinary techniques, or developing digital skills—as interest-driven and pragmatically aligned with their personal needs, contrasting sharply with the abstract and institutionally constrained nature of school curricula: "*Why can't school teach us how to file taxes in the future or how to navigate public offices? That's something we'll actually need in life, but no one prepares us for it. How will it help me to know what tools were used in Biskupin? I'll never use that—unless I go on Who Wants to Be a Millionaire*" (S_IC_*1_school_1*). "*I learn from YouTubers because they have passion in life, they're specialists, and they show practically how to do something. Right now, I'm watching a creator who builds robots, or sometimes you can watch someone play a game and learn strategy. It's not that school doesn't interest me, but that's the kind of learning I want to do and need, whereas in school I have to*" (S_IC_*2_school_2*). The two student accounts articulate a consistent critique of schooling by juxtaposing everyday, interest-driven learning with the perceived irrelevance of formal curricula. Both statements foreground a discourse of "*needs*", framed as practical, future-oriented, and intrinsically motivating, in contrast to the abstract and compulsory character of school learning. This contrast allows us to analyze how learning itself is discursively constructed in the students' narratives.

From the perspective of Gee and Green's (1998) framework, the first quotation exemplifies world building through the construction of two opposed worlds: one pragmatic and oriented toward future civic participation (taxes, navigating bureaucracies), and the other abstract and disconnected (archaeological details about Biskupin). The activity of learning is thus positioned not as memorization of remote historical facts but as acquiring actionable competences for adulthood. Identity building occurs through the speaker's ironic distance from school knowledge. The reference to *Who Wants to Be a Millionaire* frames curricular content as trivia, valuable only in a game-show context, not in life. The connections drawn are temporal and utilitarian—learning should bridge school with anticipated life tasks. Here, learning is discursively constructed as *use-value knowledge* tied to individual survival and social navigation.

The second quotation similarly enacts a contrast between school-based and informal learning, but the world invoked is mediated by digital platforms and peer culture. YouTubers embody a model of expertise that is passionate, engaging, specialized, and demonstrably practical. The activity of learning is aligned with exploration and imitation, following creators in building robots or developing gaming strategies. This contrasts with the school's demand for compliance—"*whereas in school I have to.*" In terms of identity building, the student positions themselves as an active learner whose curiosity and agency are nurtured outside the classroom, while school constructs them as a passive subject of obligation. Connection building here links learning directly to affect (passion, interest) and to digital networks of knowledge production, situating value in relevance, and authenticity.

In both accounts, learning is discursively defined through a binary opposition: *authentic, interest-driven, needs-based* versus *inauthentic, compulsory, abstract*. This binary itself functions as a discursive construction with ideological weight. Drawing on Laclau (2005), the signifier "*needs*" operates as an empty signifier. It appears universally natural and self-evident, however is filled with particular ideological content. In these accounts, "*needs*" stand for practical utility, and personal alignment. What remains obscured is that such a discourse resonates with neoliberal logics of self-responsibility and self-optimization, in which the learner is cast as an autonomous entrepreneur of the self. The appeal to "*needs*" legitimizes a critique of school but also reproduces an individualized view of education that sidelines collective or civic dimensions of learning.

Thus, a critical discourse analysis reveals that these student narratives are not merely descriptive but performative. They enact learning as a moral and political category. School is positioned as outdated, irrelevant, and authoritarian. Informal digital learning emerges as authentic and relevant. At the same time, through the logic of the empty signifier "*needs*," these discourses contribute to naturalizing the very neoliberal order that constrains possibilities of collective and critical education. Learning, in this sense, is less a neutral process than a contested discursive terrain in which students negotiate identity, authority, and the value of knowledge.

This construction positions autonomy not as relational or socially situated, but as a condition of self-reliance. The appeal of digital media and platforms strengthens this discourse, as they appear to offer open and individualized access to information without the mediation of institutional authority. Here, institutional roles—teachers, curricula, schools—are reframed as obstacles or at best optional supports. Platforms position themselves as guarantors of immediate and personalized learning opportunities. Learning is discursively framed as democratized, because it is accessible to anyone with a device. It is simultaneously market-driven, because learners are cast as consumers navigating a competitive attention economy.

The apparent autonomy offered by this discourse is unstable and ambivalent. Learners are simultaneously empowered to curate and self-direct, while also being subjected to algorithmic governance and cultural logics of productivity. In other words, the *sovereign learner* is less an empirical reality than a discursive construction that legitimizes the displacement of institutional authority by platform capitalism. The promise of autonomy masks the structural inequalities and dependencies that shape actual learning practices. Thus, what appears as the fulfillment of personal needs and interests is also a form of ideological interpellation into neoliberal subjectivity, where individuals take responsibility for systemic limitations and failures.

Digital learning, though often framed as universally empowering, is deeply entangled with algorithmic governance and neoliberal ideologies that obscure persistent structural inequalities. While dominant narratives promote the illusion of equal access to knowledge through digital technologies, such discourse conceals how socio-economic status and opaque algorithmic systems shape educational outcomes and information visibility (Gulson et al., 2022). The seductive aesthetics of platforms, enhanced by AI-mediated representations such as chatbots and virtual influencers, foster a perception of effortless and autonomous learning, while subtly displacing traditional educators and reinforcing platform-defined epistemic hierarchies (Nopas, 2025; Zdravkov, 2025). These AI systems are not neutral tools but active agents of neoliberal rationality, encouraging self-optimization and individualized responsibility while commercializing student attention and engagement (Filgueiras, 2024; Filk, 2025). In this postdigital ecosystem, what appears as learner empowerment is often a choreographed experience that reinforces the commodification of knowledge under digital capitalism (Saltman, 2020).

Autonomous learning in the postdigital era increasingly unfolds through interactions with virtual personas—ranging from real-life influencers to AI-generated figures and bots—on platforms like TikTok and YouTube, where the distinction between human and artificial knowledge providers is frequently collapsed. This epistemological shift reflects a departure from traditional models grounded in institutional authority and expert mediation, replacing them with decentralized, algorithmically curated networks that prioritize affective resonance over credentials or scholarly rigor. The rise of AI-driven influencers and CGI educators signals not just a new mode of information dissemination but a redefinition of epistemic authority, where students assess knowledge based on its digital fluency and emotional impact. As Pawlak (2022) illustrates, these virtual figures possess hyperrealistic features—anthropomorphism, interactivity, emotional responsiveness—that foster parasocial relationships and convey a sense of credibility and authenticity, even while they propagate ideological narratives under the guise of neutrality. While this transformation broadens access and reconfigures how learning is experienced, it also raises urgent concerns about misinformation, ideological manipulation, and the algorithmic structuring of knowledge. The seductive aesthetics of digital learning environments obscure the commercial and ideological forces at play, masking new forms of epistemic dependence under the guise of learner sovereignty. Consequently, postdigital learning both democratizes and destabilizes knowledge, demanding critical scrutiny of how AI-mediated education reshapes the conditions of knowledge production.

The promise of AI-driven learning, embodied in virtual influencers and algorithmically curated educational platforms, rests on a fundamental contradiction. These technologies are often presented as tools for democratizing access to knowledge by offering personalized and engaging learning experiences. In practice, however, they tend to reproduce—and even intensify—existing ideological and structural hierarchies. Far from being neutral, AI-based learning systems privilege certain types of knowledge—typically those aligned with neoliberal values and particular cultural context they were created in Chaka (2022).

Among students with high social capital this tension becomes particularly pronounced. Many of them perform intellectual engagement in public forums—referencing politicians, historians, or public intellectuals on platforms like X—as a way of signaling cultural capital and political awareness. However when it comes to actual academic work, they often rely on algorithmic tools and automated solutions. This does not indicate a rejection of learning but rather a pragmatic adaptation to a system that rewards efficiency and output over sustained reflection. What emerges is a dual engagement with knowledge. It is symbolic and performative in public discourse, and, simoultaneously, instrumental, and task-oriented in educational practice.

This divide points to a broader reconfiguration of learning in the postdigital context. Knowledge is no longer experienced as a coherent domain but is increasingly fragmented and context-dependent, shaped by shifting expectations and modes of participation. Political or intellectual discourse becomes a space for performative rigor, while academic work is approached with a focus on optimization. Even students with considerable cultural capital are not equally positioned within digitally mediated learning environments. Algorithmic systems structure access to information, determine what is made visible, and influence which forms of knowledge are recognized as legitimate. These mechanisms reinforce existing inequalities in participation and recognition, reflecting broader concerns about justice and asymmetries in epistemic authority (Fraser, 1990, 2009).

Within this landscape, traditional markers of expertise no longer carry universal authority. Expertise is invoked when it serves symbolic or strategic purposes, but often bypassed when speed and efficiency are prioritized. AI becomes a way to meet formal educational demands while neglecting more reflective or dialogic forms of engagement. This shift suggests a growing instrumentalization of learning, where knowledge is valued less for its transformative potential and more for its functional utility within institutional routines.

These dynamics challenge common narratives about digital empowerment and learner autonomy. Rather than opening up new epistemic spaces, AI-mediated education often reinforces procedural thinking and narrows the conditions under which learning can take place. As students increasingly contrast the practical relevance of social media content with the abstract or outdated material offered by school curricula, critical questions arise about how knowledge is defined in contemporary education. The issue is not simply whether AI is changing learning, but how educational systems themselves shape what is possible to know—and whose interests those configurations serve.

When asked about the thematic channels they follow on social media, students most often mentioned content related to history, current sociopolitical events, and popular challenge-based YouTubers. The ideological tone of these materials was largely uniform—conservative or nationalist—except in a few cases where students explicitly identified as non-binary. These students reported following left-wing content, linking their media preferences to their psychosexual identity and experiences of marginalization. This suggests that psychosexual identification can shape ideological orientation in digital spaces. For students with non-normative identities, progressive content provides not only political affinity but also forms of symbolic recognition and identity support. As studies have shown, LGBTQ+, youth often turn to online platforms to access affirming content and counter-narratives excluded from mainstream discourse (Craig et al., 2021), making media use a key site of ideological and personal alignment.

The question of whether social media can be a site of knowledge production reveals a deeper epistemological tension within both media theory and educational research. Scholars such as Fisher (2022) and Habgood-Coote (2025) argue that platforms like TikTok, YouTube, and

X represent emerging epistemic environments where knowledge is not anchored in traditional forms of authority but instead takes shape through interaction and algorithmic selection. In this view, social media should not be dismissed as epistemic voids but understood as systems that generate and organize knowledge according to their own internal logics that differ from those of schools.

Some researchers point to the participatory and inclusive nature of these environments, noting their low threshold for contribution and their potential to foster civic engagement (Stewart et al., 2022). This optimism is tempered by growing concerns about the structural features of social media that make them fertile ground for misinformation, ideological enclosure, and epistemic distortion. Burke (2022) describes this as "accelerated epistemic harm"—a process in which engagement-driven algorithms heighten users' exposure to polarizing or radical content, amplifying existing biases and narrowing the field of perceived reality. These systems do not merely distribute information; they organize attention and shape epistemic trajectories.

On platforms like TikTok, nationalist hashtags such as *#polska (#poland)* or *#dumanarodowa (#nationalpride)*—frequently followed by students—function as algorithmically sustained echo chambers. Rather than inviting debate or diversity of perspective, these curated spaces reinforce singular narratives, lending visibility and legitimacy to ideologically charged content while pushing alternative views to the margins. In this sense, learning through social media is not an open-ended or autonomous activity, but a process increasingly shaped by infrastructural conditions that structure what can be known, by whom, and under what terms.

The circulation of images under these hashtags illustrates how learning is discursively constructed through affect, spectacle, and repetition. A paratrooper descending with an oversized Polish flag is framed in the comments as proof of strength and unity: "*Strong Poland*," "*Beautiful, I've got chills*," "*Poles can do it!!*" Such reactions mark not just a reception of knowledge about the nation, but a participation in identity building (Gee & Green, 1998), where learning history or patriotism is enacted as an affective experience, producing belonging through collective admiration and emotional resonance. Similarly, short animations about figures like Tadeusz Kościuszko, described as "*a man ahead of his time*," are accompanied by comments insisting that "*such knowledge should be taught in every textbook*" or lamenting "*I never knew this history*," even though these very elements are explicitly included in every primary and secondary school curriculum. Here, learning becomes an act of world building, in which the past is reconstructed not as a site of uncertainty but as a moral lesson offering clarity about national greatness.

These examples show how TikTok's visual and affective economy sustains what Laclau (2005) terms empty signifiers: "*Poland*," "*nation*," "*honor*," or "*knowledge*" circulate as universally valid reference points, but their precise meaning shifts depending on context—whether attached to Kościuszko's heroism, a sporting victory, or a skydiving stunt. The apparent openness of these signifiers conceals their ideological function. They bind heterogeneous practices and emotions into a singular nationalist narrative, displacing contradictions while reinforcing a sense of sovereign unity.

What is constructed, then, is a version of learning that is less about critical engagement than about affective participation in collective myths. Through activity building (Gee & Green, 1998), liking, sharing, or commenting becomes a mode of pedagogy. To affirm "*Strong Poland*" is already to have learned and repeated the lesson that strength and unity are the nation's defining features. In this configuration, learning is not positioned as the acquisition of contested historical knowledge but as the performance of belonging to an imagined community. TikTok's algorithm amplifies this by privileging content that triggers emotional intensity—pride, indignation, nostalgia—ensuring that learners encounter reiterations of the same discourse rather than alternative perspectives.

This structural dynamic directly challenges the prevailing notion of the autonomous digital learner as the sovereign of knowledge. While the rhetoric of digital education emphasizes learner agency and personalization, research by Krasmann (2020) and Maalsen (2023) reveals how algorithmic systems subtly control epistemic access through logics of surface visibility and affective engagement (Krasmann, 2020; Maalsen, 2023). These systems foster epistemic environments where emotional resonance and entertainment value often eclipse truth or accuracy as benchmarks for knowledge validation. In this context, the "*knowledge of the undereducated student*," as described by Klus-Stańska (2012), emerges not as a failure of intellectual formation but as a consequence of the epistemic structures that dominate contemporary learning spaces. This knowledge is fragmented, algorithmically filtered, and often detached from disciplinary rigor, but it remains central to how students make sense of their world.

The implications of this shift are far-reaching. As Coeckelbergh (2023) points out, digital epistemologies should not be understood merely as technological developments but as deeply political formations, raising important questions about how epistemic agency is distributed and how digital knowledge systems are regulated. Within educational contexts, this suggests a need to reconsider the role of schools. They should be perceived not simply as transmitters of validated knowledge, but as spaces where students might develop the capacity to critically engage with the infrastructures that shape their learning. Rather than positioning the knowledge held by so-called undereducated students as epistemically lacking, it may be more productive to view it as a distinct, though often structurally constrained, form of knowledge production. Pedagogical approaches that make space for this recognition could support the development of reflexive capacities, enabling students to interrogate the ways in which knowledge is constructed in postdigital environments.

Such a perspective invites a re-examination of the institutional hierarchies that have historically determined what counts as educationally valid. Conventional discourse tends to privilege knowledge aligned with expert consensus, often at the expense of insights generated in informal, digitally mediated contexts. This binary opposition overlooks the complex and adaptive strategies through which students make sense of the world online. While the knowledge encountered in these spaces may not conform to academic standards, it frequently demonstrates functional relevance and responsiveness to lived experience. Rather than reflecting a deficit, this kind of epistemic engagement may be seen as operating within a different paradigm—one oriented around multimodal literacy, contextual remixing, and the continuous negotiation of meaning across platforms.

These emerging epistemic formations also introduce notable risks. Algorithmic curation frequently privileges engagement metrics over accuracy or epistemic diversity, contributing to the formation of echo chambers that distort perception and reinforce ideological bias. While it may be tempting to dismiss the knowledge circulating in these environments as illegitimate or to respond by reasserting academic authority, such strategies risk overlooking the complex ways in which digital epistemologies function. A more productive pedagogical approach might involve recognizing these spaces as structurally mediated but meaningful sites of knowledge production. Within this framework, critical literacy becomes less about correction and more about enabling students to understand and navigate the infrastructures that shape their informational landscapes.

Students' practices indicate that engagement with AI is not merely instrumental. It also manages anxiety: "*Sometimes when I get stuck, I just ask ChatGPT or use this AI app to explain it. It sounds silly, but it helps calm me down. I don't always trust the answer completely, but it doesn't make me feel stupid. It's like having a private tutor that doesn't judge you*" (S_IC_school_2). This account complicates dominant narratives of autonomous learning. On the surface, the student appears to embody the ideal of the self-regulating learner. She mobilizes a digital resource to take control of her learning process. However what emerges more strongly is not mastery but the management of affective vulnerability. Autonomy here is less about empowerment than about securing a safe space away from the normative gaze of teachers and peers.

In Gee and Green's (1998) terms, the world being built is one in which learning is closely tied to the risk of judgment, where mistakes carry the possibility of humiliation. The activity of turning to AI is simultaneously cognitive and affective. It resolves a problem but also regulates emotions. In terms of identity building, the learner is positioned less as a "*sovereign of knowledge*" than as a precarious subject negotiating between institutional demands for independence and the fear of inadequacy. Connection building situates this recourse to AI within wider institutional logics, where pressures of performance combine with the affordances of digital tools that offer discretion and non-judgment.

From a discourse-theoretical perspective, the student's practice unsettles the neoliberal articulation of "*autonomous learning*" as an empty signifier of freedom and self-realization (Laclau, 2005). What is framed as independence is deeply mediated by affective precarity and institutional authority. The appeal of AI as a "*private tutor that doesn't judge*" indicates that autonomy is constructed here less as a sign of confidence than as a strategy for managing vulnerability. In this way, AI functions not only as a means of knowledge acquisition but also as a technology of affective containment, insulating the learner from the risks of shame and exposure inherent in the classroom.

This form of autonomy aligns with the neoliberal ideal of the self-reliant subject—one who manages their own learning needs outside institutional structures. However the quote also reveals its fragility. The student does not fully trust the AI's answers but prefers it for the emotional safety it provides. Thus, what emerges is not Deweyan autonomy grounded in inquiry and democratic engagement, but a privatized and affectively insulated autonomy, shaped by postdigital infrastructures that reward self-sufficiency while withdrawing institutional support.

In this light, AI-mediated learning fosters a mode of autonomy that is relationally diminished but operationally functional. The learner is alone, but productive; unsupported, and expected to perform. The student's agency is real, but it is exercised within constrained affective and epistemic conditions, shaped as much by avoidance as by curiosity. This reframes so-called "*autonomous learning*" not as a pedagogical ideal, but as a survival mechanism within environments where institutional recognition is limited, and algorithmic tools offer low-risk alternatives to relational learning.

Taken together, these findings suggest that what is often celebrated as autonomous learning in the postdigital age is, in practice, a deeply ambivalent formation. Students do not reject learning per se, but seek forms of knowledge that feel relevant and accessible—often outside the institutional frame. Their turn to AI and platform-based content reflects both strategic adaptation and affective negotiation within systems that prioritize performance over dialogue. Far from embodying the empowered, self-governing learner idealized in neoliberal discourse, students enact a fragile autonomy shaped by algorithmic infrastructures and epistemic precarity. Postdigital learning, as this chapter has argued, cannot be understood through binary oppositions such as formal/informal or dependent/autonomous. It is a contested terrain in which students navigate institutional distrust and the desire for legitimacy. Recognizing this complexity is essential for reimagining education—not as a corrective apparatus for digital disorder, but as a relational and critical space adapted to the realities of mediated knowledge.

References

Bakhtin, M. (1994). Double-voiced discourse in Dostoevsky. *The Bakhtin reader: Selected writings*, 102–111.

Beck-Gernsheim, E. (1998). On the way to a post-familial family: From a community of need to elective affinities. *Theory, Culture & Society, 15*(3–4), 53–70. https://doi.org/10.1177/0263276498015003004

Bergdahl, N., Nouri, J., Fors, U., & Knutsson, O. (2020). Engagement, disengagement and performance when learning with technologies in upper secondary school. *Computers & Education, 149*, Article 103783. https://doi.org/10.1016/j.compedu.2019.103783

Bernstein, B. (1996). *Pedagogy, symbolic control and identity: Theory, research, critique*. Taylor & Francis.

Bourdieu, P. (1984). *Distinction: A social critique of the judgement of taste*. Harvard University Press.

Bourdieu, P., & Passeron, J.-C. (1990). *Reproduction in education, society and culture* (R. Nice, Trans.; 2nd ed., Vol. 4). Sage.

Brunila, K. (2014). The rise of the survival discourse in an era of therapisation and neoliberalism. *Education Inquiry, 5*(1), 24044. https://doi.org/10.3402/edui.v5.24044

Burke, L. J. M. (2022). *Accelerated epistemic harm: Understanding the role of social media engagement algorithms in online radicalization* (Doctoral dissertation, Carleton University). https://doi.org/10.22215/etd/2022-14961

Castañeda, L., & Williamson, B. (2021). Assembling new toolboxes of methods and theories for innovative critical research on educational technology. *Journal of New Approaches in Educational Research*. https://doi.org/10.7821/naer.2021.1.703

Coeckelbergh, M. (2023). Democracy, epistemic agency, and AI: Political epistemology in times of artificial intelligence. *AI and Ethics, 3*(4), 1341–1350. https://doi.org/10.1007/s43681-022-00239-4

Chaka, C. (2022). Digital marginalization, data marginalization, and algorithmic exclusions: A critical southern decolonial approach to datafication, algorithms, and digital citizenship. *Journal of e-Learning and Knowledge Society, 18*(3).

Craig, S. L., Eaton, A. D., McInroy, L. B., Leung, V. W. Y., & Krishnan, S. (2021). Can social media participation enhance LGBTQ+ youth wellbeing? Development of the social media benefits scale. *Social Media + Society, 7*(1), 1–11 https://doi.org/10.1177/2056305121988931

Dudzikowa, M. (2001). *Mit o szkole jako miejscu wszechstronnego rozwoju: Eseje etnopedagogiczne* (Wyd. 1). Oficyna Wydawnicza "Impuls".

Ennis, R. H. (2016). Critical thinking: Reflection and perspective. *Inquiry: Critical Thinking Across the Disciplines, 31*(3), 16–22. https://doi.org/10.5840/inquiryctnews201126215

Evans, R., & Kurantowicz, E. (2009). Learning in changing educational landscapes: Migration at the margins and biographical narratives of identity in transition. *Between Global and Local*, pp. 65–78.

Evans, R. (2013). Learning and knowing narratives, memory and biographical knowledge in interview interaction. *European Journal for Research on the Education and Learning of Adults, 4*(1), 17–23.

Facione, P. A. (2015). *Critical thinking: What it is and why it counts*. Insight Assessment.

Filk, C. (2025). Ideology critique in the age of algorithmic governance: On the transformative power of critical-reflexive media pedagogy in a platformized society. *Medienimpulse, 63*(2), Article 21. https://doi.org/10.21243/mi-02-25-21

Filipiak, E. (2009). Uczenie się w klasie szkolnej w perspektywie socjokulturowej. *Forum Dydaktyczne*, 5–6.

Filgueiras, F. (2024). Artificial intelligence and education governance. *Education, Citizenship and Social Justice, 19*(3), 349–361. https://doi.org/10.1177/17461979231160674

Fisher, E. (2022). Epistemic media and critical knowledge about the self: Thinking about algorithms with Habermas. *Critical Sociology, 48*(7–8), 1309–1324. https://doi.org/10.1177/08969205211044193

Foucault, M. (1972). *The archaeology of knowledge and the discourse on language*. Pantheon Books.

Fraser, N. (1990). Rethinking the public sphere: A contribution to the critique of actually existing democracy.*Social Text, 25/26*, 56–80.

Fraser, N. (2009). *Scales of justice: Reimagining political space in a globalizing world*. Columbia University Press.

Fraser, N. (2013). *Fortunes of feminism: From state-managed capitalism to neoliberal crisis*. Verso.

Gee, J. P., & Green, J. L. (1998). Chapter 4: Discourse analysis, learning, and social practice: A methodological study. *Review of research in education, 23*(1), 119–169.

Gee, J. P. (2003). *What video games have to teach us about learning and literacy*. Palgrave Macmillan.

Gulson, K. N., Sellar, S., & Webb, P. T. (2022). *Algorithms of education: How datafication and artificial intelligence shape policy*. University of Minnesota Press.

Habgood-Coote, J. (2025). Towards a critical social epistemology of social media. In J. Lackey & A. McGlynn (Eds.), *The Oxford handbook of social epistemology*. Oxford University Press.

Jessop, B. (2002). *The future of the capitalist state*. Polity Press.

Jessop, B. (2008). *State power: A strategic-relational approach*. Polity Press.

Jessop, B. (2016). *The state: Past, present, future*. Polity Press.

Jessop, B. (2019). Critical discourse analysis in Laclau and Mouffe's post-Marxism. *Simbiótica. Revista Eletrônica, 6*(2), 8–30.

Klus-Stańska, D. (2012). Wiedza, która zniewala–transmisyjne tradycje w szkolnej edukacji. In *Forum oświatowe* (Vol. 24, No. 1 (46), pp. 21–40).

Kopciewicz, L. (2020). Oblicza reformy szkolnej–technologiczne praktyki równościowego uczenia się. *Czas Kultury, 36*(01), 39–48.

Krasmann, S. (2020). The logic of the surface: On the epistemology of algorithms in times of big data. *Information, Communication & Society, 23*(14), 2096–2109. https://doi.org/10.1080/1369118X.2020.1726986

Kruszewska, A., Nazaruk, S., & Szewczyk, K. (2022). Polish teachers of early education in the face of distance learning during the COVID-19 pandemic: The difficulties experienced and suggestions for the future. *Education 3–13, 50*(5), 595–609. https://doi.org/10.1080/03004279.2020.1849346

Laclau, E. (2005). *On populist reason.* Verso.

Macklem, G. L. (2015). *Boredom in the classroom: Addressing student motivation, self-regulation, and engagement in learning* (Vol. 1). Springer.

Maalsen, S. (2023). Algorithmic epistemologies and methodologies: Algorithmic harm, algorithmic care and situated algorithmic knowledges. *Progress in Human Geography, 47*(2), 197–214. https://doi.org/10.1177/03091325221149439

Ministerstwo Edukacji i Nauki. (2019). *Ramy kwalifikacji, ECTS i ECVET dla uczenia się przez całe życie.* Warszawa: Ministerstwo Edukacji i Nauki.

Murray, M. C., & Pérez, J. (2014). Unraveling the digital literacy paradox: How higher education fails at the fourth literacy. *Issues in Informing Science and Information Technology, 11*, 85.

Muzata, A. R., Singh, G., Stepanov, M. S., & Musonda, I. (2024, December). Immersive Education: Exploring the Combination of New Technology and Virtual Reality in Real-Time Teaching. In *2024 international conference on electrical and computer engineering researches (ICECER)* (pp. 1–5). IEEE. https://doi.org/10.1109/ICECER62944.2024.10920357

Nopas, D. (2025). Algorithmic learning or learner autonomy? Rethinking AI's role in digital education. *Qualitative Research Journal.* https://doi.org/10.1108/QRJ-11-2024-0282

Olssen, M., & Peters, M. A. (2005). Neoliberalism, higher education and the knowledge economy: From the free market to knowledge capitalism. *Journal of education policy, 20*(3), 313–345.

Pawlak, A. F. (2022). *Ciało w dyskursach transhumanizmu i sztucznej inteligencji. Perspektywa antropologiczna* [The body in discourses of transhumanism and artificial intelligence: An anthropological perspective] (Unpublished doctoral dissertation). University of Łódź, Faculty of Philosophy and History.

Płonka, P. (2022). *Misja: być świadkiem historii. Poradnik metodyczny do programu nauczania historii dla III etapu edukacyjnego (liceum ogólnokształcącego i technikum).* Warszawa: Ośrodek Rozwoju Edukacji.

Ragnedda, M., & Ruiu, M. L. (2020). Digital capital: A Bourdieusian perspective on the digital divide. *Emerald.* https://doi.org/10.1108/978-1-83909-550-420201006

Saltman, K. J. (2020). Artificial intelligence and the technological turn of public education privatization: In defence of democratic education. *London Review of Education, 18*(2), 215–227.

Selwyn, N. (2014). *Education and technology: Key issues and debates.* Routledge.

Selwyn, N., Nemorin, S., & Johnson, N. (2017). High-tech, hard work: An investigation of teachers' work in the digital age. *Learning, Media and Technology, 42*(4), 390–405. https://doi.org/10.1080/17439884.2016.1252770

Simons, M., & Masschelein, J. (2008). The governmentalization of learning and the assemblage of a learning apparatus. *Educational theory, 58*(4), 391–415.

Stewart, H., Cichocki, E., & McLeod, C. (2022). A perfect storm for epistemic injustice: Algorithmic targeting and sorting on social media. *Feminist Philosophy Quarterly, 8*(3/4). https://doi.org/10.5206/fpq/2022.3/4.14291

Suárez-Guerrero, C., & Rivera-Vargas, P. (2023). EdTech myths: Towards a critical digital educational agenda. *Technology, Pedagogy and Education.* https://doi.org/10.1080/1475939X.2023.2240332

Szkudlarek, T. (2007). Empty signifiers, education and politics. *Studies in Philosophy and Education, 26*(5), 393–403. https://doi.org/10.1007/s11217-007-9033-7

Szkudlarek, T. (2010). Inner university, knowledge workers and liminality. In *The Routledge Doctoral Student's Companion* (pp. 374–385). Routledge.

Szkudlarek, T., & Zamojski, P. (2020). Education and ignorance: Between the noun of knowledge and the verb of thinking. *Studies in Philosophy and Education, 39*, 577–590. https://doi.org/10.1007/s11217-020-09718-9

Szostak, E., & Kenc, J. (2021). COVID-19 pandemic vs. digital competences of pupils and teachers in Poland. *European Research Studies Journal.*

Twenge, J. M. (2017). *IGen: Why Today's super-connected kids are growing up less rebellious, more tolerant.* Atria Books.

Wickman, P. O., & Östman, L. (2001). University students during practical work: Can we make the learning process intelligible? *Research in science education-Past, present, and future* (pp. 319–324). Springer, Netherlands.

Wilkin, S., Davies, H., & Eynon, R. (2017). Addressing digital inequalities amongst young people: Conflicting discourses and complex outcomes. *Oxford Review of Education, 43*(3), 332–347. https://doi.org/10.1080/03054985.2017.1305058

Zamojski, P. (2015). Co to znaczy, że szkoła jest „publiczna". *Studia Pedagogiczne, 65.*

Zamojski, P. (2022). *Edukacja jako rzecz publiczna: raport z próby budowania sfery publicznej wokół edukacji w Polsce.* Oficyna Naukowa. Warszawa.

Zdravkov, N. (2025). *Shaping minds, shaping machines: The quiet revolution of AI in UNESCO's educational dream* (Master's thesis). University of Groningen.

Zintegrowana Platforma Edukacyjna. (2023). *Uczymy się szybko i skutecznie.* https://zpe.gov.pl/a/uczymy-sie-szybko-i-skutecznie/DQeh7Tb5F

Zuboff, S. (2019). Surveillance capitalism and the challenge of collective action. In the New labor forum (Vol. 28, No. 1, pp. 10–29). Sage.

CHAPTER 4

The Mechanized Subject and Reversive Knowledge

The figure of the learner in contemporary education is not a neutral or self-evident category but one shaped through discursive operations that reflect deeper ideological commitments. Rather than viewing the student as a passive recipient of instruction, educational discourses actively participate in the production of learner subjectivities, constructed within institutional narratives, pedagogical norms, and socio-political imperatives. These constructions determine not only what it means to learn but also who is recognized as a legitimate learner.

The theory of discourse developed by Ernesto Laclau (2005) offers an analytical lens for unpacking this process. Within their framework, identities do not arise from any essential core but are instead formed through contingent articulations within discursive fields structured by hegemonic struggle. In this light, the term "*learner*" becomes an object of political contestation, not a universal human condition. It is forged within particular regimes of meaning, bound to historically and ideologically situated vocabularies. As Laclau argues, no discourse is free from power. The dominance of neoliberal rationality in educational discourse legitimates certain forms of knowing—those that are productive, individualized, and outcome-oriented—while rendering others invisible or illegitimate.

This dynamic is particularly evident when read through what Gee and Green (1998) describe as identity building, one of the key dimensions through which discourse operates in educational contexts.

M. Popow, *Learning in the Postdigital Knowledge Society*, Palgrave Studies in Educational Media,
https://doi.org/10.1007/978-3-032-21956-5_4

This layer focuses on how learners' identities are shaped and stabilized—or contested—through discursive interactions that are affectively charged and epistemologically consequential. The next sections take this insight further by examining also how students themselves participate in constructing alternative learner identities, often in resistance to the normative scripts imposed by schools. These reversive practices of knowing challenge established educational hierarchies and suggest new ways of being and knowing that remain largely unrecognized within institutional frames.

4.1 The Mechanized Learning Subject

At the policy level, learner identity is increasingly framed through the discourse of competencies, which redefines education in terms of measurable skills and outcomes rather than intellectual exploration or civic engagement. *The European Digital Competence Framework for Educators* (DigCompEdu)—largely unknown to the teachers and students in this study—nonetheless articulates a normative vision of the educator as a digital strategist preparing learners for participation in a data-driven economy. Within this model, education is subsumed into the logic of workforce preparation, privileging adaptability, efficiency, and continuous upskilling in line with Jessop's (2002) account of institutional alignment with market imperatives. While DigCompEdu presents its aims as empowering—urging educators to "*address the concrete learning objective and empower learners*" (p. 17)—empowerment here is defined not as critical engagement with social or epistemic structures but as the capacity to remain employable within volatile knowledge economies.

Teachers in this study largely rejected the managerial and digitally oriented identity implicit in DigCompEdu. They instead positioned themselves as custodians of classical didactics, interpreting technology as a useful supplement but not a pedagogical revolution. As one teacher insisted, "*Technology is interesting, but the essence of teaching remains classic didactics. We're still teaching kids the basics, how to read, write, do math, and get familiar with the world of books. No matter what new tech we bring in, those core skills are still essential. That's what school is really about.*" (T_5_School_2). This refusal demonstrates what Gee and Green (1998) describe as the world-building function of discourse. Teachers construct a professional identity rooted in continuity and the preservation of disciplinary traditions. Through activity building, they legitimate practices centered on traditional didactics distinguishing them from the perceived superficiality of digital tools. The disjuncture between policy rhetoric and classroom discourse is thus not reducible to infrastructural deficits but reflects a deeper identity building struggle over the meaning and purpose of education.

This epistemological conflict extends to the ways teachers conceptualize students' learning. Many expressed frustration, claiming that "*students do not know how to learn*" (e.g., T_4_School_2; T_1_School_1). Learning was depicted as a transactional process devoid of deeper engagement—echoed in remarks such as "*today's generation may have lost the joy of learning*" (T_2_School_2). Such assessments resonate with Britzman's (1998) analysis of surface-level knowledge reproduction, where learning is reduced to procedural compliance, not critical or transformative engagement. Within Gee and Green's matrix, this teacher discourse constitutes connection building that aligns contemporary student practices with a broader narrative of decline, in which generational shifts are perceived as evidence of cultural and intellectual erosion.

The juxtaposition of policy and practice reveals an unresolved contradiction. On the one hand, learners are discursively figured as autonomous managers of their own competencies—flexible "*sovereigns of knowledge*" who must continuously adapt to labor market transformations. On the other, teachers articulate a counter-discourse that devalues students' autonomy, framing their practices as detached from genuine intellectual pursuit. Both discourses, however, are structured by neoliberal grammars of responsibility. Whether framed as insufficiently motivated or insufficiently skilled, learners are cast as accountable for their own educational trajectories. What remains obscured are the infrastructural, cultural, and epistemological conditions that shape both the perceived "loss of joy" and the institutional drive toward competencies.

As it has been already mentioned, the contemporary educational framework in Poland is profoundly structured by a culture of standardized testing, wherein final exams operate not only as instruments for measuring academic performance but also as mechanisms for governance at the system level. As Zalewska (2015) observes, such assessments are designed to enable national benchmarking, encouraging schools to align their pedagogical strategies with test outcomes rather than with the cultivation of higher-order intellectual capacities. This orientation produces a narrowed conception of education that privileges measurable results over the broader aims of personal or civic development. Research by the

Institute for Educational Research (Dolata & Sitek, 2015) further demonstrates that standardized tests inadequately capture the range of students' abilities and disproportionately disadvantage those with non-traditional learning profiles, emphasizing the exclusionary effects of this regime.

Teacher testimonies in this study reinforce these findings. One teacher explained: "*At school, everyone knows from the start that the goal is to pass the final exams, and that's what the students focus on, and that's how we teach them. [...] In Poland, everything is subordinated to the logic of the test, as developed by the Central Examination Board, and everyone knows that for those four years, our job is to specifically prepare them for what will be on the test, and for them to master it well*" (T_1_School_1). This articulation captures the pervasive reach of test-oriented logic, which not only structures classroom practices but also defines the normative expectations of students, teachers, and institutions alike.

From the perspective of Gee and Green (1998), such discourse performs a powerful set of functions. At the level of world building, it establishes a social reality in which exams constitute the ultimate horizon of educational purpose, displacing alternative imaginaries of what schooling might mean. Through activity building, classroom practices are reconfigured into repetitive exercises aimed at reproducing test-compatible knowledge, thereby discouraging forms of engagement that exceed exam requirements. At the level of identity building, both teachers and students position themselves within the same performative frame. Teachers as exam-preparers, students as test-takers. Even connection building is reshaped, as broader links between learning and life are subordinated to the temporality of the exam cycle, reinforcing a narrow instrumentalism.

Within Laclau's (2005) framework, standardized testing emerges as an empty signifier that sutures the field of educational discourse. It appears self-evidently necessary, promising neutrality, fairness, and comparability, while in practice masking its ideological function of subordinating education to quantification and system-level governance. The very indeterminacy of what "*success*" in education means is stabilized by its articulation with test outcomes. The "*test*" thus operates as a hegemonic nodal point. It unifies teachers, students, policymakers, and parents around a common reference, while foreclosing alternative understandings of educational value. As Gobby et al. (2018) argue, such accountability regimes reduce education to compliance with prescribed benchmarks, naturalizing a culture of performance and leaving little space for emancipatory or transformative practices.

Interviews reveal how deeply this logic is internalized. Students overwhelmingly described "*learning for tests*" as the primary goal of schooling, implicitly acknowledging the futility of pursuing knowledge beyond its exam-related utility. In turn, teachers, while often critical of this reductionism, also conceded their complicity. They felt compelled to prepare students for national exams, perpetuating the very system they critiqued (T_4_School_2). In this sense, both groups are locked into a discursive formation that forecloses alternative pedagogical imaginaries, aligning learning with survival and credentialism rather than with autonomy.

The result is a pattern of minimal engagement. Students adapt strategically to the demands of the exam system, while teachers reproduce practices aligned with its logic, despite their recognition of its limitations. What emerges is a profoundly ambivalent subjectivity. Learners and educators simultaneously critique and reproduce the structures that confine them. Within the broader postdigital context, where alternative forms of knowledge circulation thrive in digital spaces, the dominance of testing highlights the persistence of an institutional discourse that resists pluralization, clinging instead to the authority of quantification as the guarantor of educational legitimacy.

This pedagogical orientation situates learning as a process of information acquisition and reproduction, aligning closely with a transmission-based model of education. In this model, curricular materials—textbooks or worksheets—are structured around the recall and repetition of obligatory knowledge. Rather than encouraging critical engagement, students are trained to identify and regurgitate predefined answers. The tendency is especially evident in subjects such as history, where, like in ZPE platform, short source texts are used not as prompts for interpretive analysis but as vehicles for locating the "correct" information. These instructional practices are often accompanied by hints and prompts designed to guide students toward expected responses, reinforcing the belief that knowledge is static, predetermined, and singular (Klus-Stańska, 2012). This model of learning can be likened to assembling a puzzle, where each fact corresponds to a specific place, and deviation from the prescribed solution is penalized. This rigidity is institutionalized through mechanisms such as "the cardinal mistake" on high school exit exams, which can cancel out an otherwise complete answer. The stakes of these assessments—and the cultural weight they carry—embed a high degree of caution and conformity into the learning process. Consequently, students internalize the notion that learning is less about inquiry or exploration and more about avoiding error and meeting predetermined benchmarks.

Teachers' perception that students engage in learning primarily to meet assessment criteria, reproduces a broader cultural narrative of youth as cognitively immature and pedagogically dependent. The recurring figure of the "*young ignorant*" reflects a deficit model of student agency, wherein learners are positioned as lacking the autonomy or reflexivity to navigate their own educational trajectories. Although many educators recognize the formative role of systemic pressures—particularly the dominance of standardized testing and procedural instruction—in shaping instrumental learning habits, they often continue to treat students as deficient in intrinsic motivation and critical capacity: "*They do not even know why they are learning. They come to school because they have to, study only what is necessary, take nothing away for themselves, and make no effort to think critically*" (T_5_school_1). This ambivalence reveals a deeper ideological tension within the profession. While rhetorically committed to learner autonomy, teachers frequently legitimize pedagogical authority through discourses of discipline and correction: "*We have to force them, supervise them, and constantly instruct them. It is not an easy job, because students are like small children who must constantly be watched to make sure they prepare for school, and their parents are reminded to pay for a trip, and so on. This work is constant supervision*" (T_4_school_2). The contradiction emphasizes a structural dilemma—teachers must negotiate between cultivating independent thought and delivering quantifiable outcomes in a performance-oriented system.

Observed classroom practices remain based in transmissive models of instruction, typically structured around teacher-led exposition followed by recitation or control questions. Teachers demonstrated a strong sense of professional legitimacy, often articulating their didactic plans and methods with conviction. Teachers often told me before the start of a lesson what they were going to do and which methods they would use. However, I did not see these declarations reflected in the actual way the lessons were conducted, which relied on the transmission of information and repetition. This continuity reflects Klus-Stańska's (2012) diagnosis of didactics as a routinized cultural practice, executed through procedural directives rather than grounded in reflexive pedagogical inquiry. Within this framework, constructivist learning theories are frequently reduced to methodological slogans. References to students "*sometimes constructing*" and "*sometimes assimilating*" (Klus-Stańska, 2020, p. 12), knowledge function more as rhetorical gestures than as commitments to epistemological co-production. While some educators attempt to design learning environments that support exploration and autonomy, such practices are more often valued for their affective or behavioral impact than for their capacity to disrupt hierarchical knowledge relations. As a result, the dominant instructional imaginary remains anchored in transmission. Knowledge is still to be deliveredand verified, and rarely negotiated through dialogic or experiential processes.

Several systemic and structural factors help explain the persistence of such traditional, teacher-centered pedagogies. In Poland and other CEE national contexts, the rigidity of education systems—characterized by centralized curricula and performance-driven accountability—limits teacher agency and discourages pedagogical experimentation (Gobby et al., 2018). This institutional framework not only encourages didactic teaching focused on exam success but also constrains the implementation of student-centered or constructivist methods. Furthermore, despite exposure to contemporary educational theories, many teachers feel more secure maintaining the authoritative role of lecturer rather than adopting facilitative or dialogical roles that align with learner-centered paradigms. This comfort with traditional methods is reinforced by structural limitations and cultural expectations, fostering a reliance on rote learning and transmissive teaching strategies. As Jerrim et al. (2023) argue, such conditions result in a disjunction between progressive educational rhetoric and the entrenched practices found in everyday classrooms.

This system-driven logic extends into textbooks, worksheets, and assessments, where task construction overwhelmingly emphasizes directive commands—such as "list," "indicate," or "enumerate"—that guide students toward specific, preordained answers. Such formats privilege memorization and factual recall over critical inquiry or interpretive engagement, reinforcing an instrumental model of education in which learning is equated with the passive absorption of standardized content (Özhan et al., 2024). The architecture of these tasks mirrors the mechanics of standardized testing, whereby knowledge is fragmented into quantifiable units and measured according to compliance with fixed benchmarks. As a result, learning is framed as a closed, unidirectional system where information moves from teacher to student or from text to reader with little room for dialogic interaction or critical resistance.

Within this paradigm, the teacher becomes a transmitter of knowledge and manager of assessment-aligned outputs, while students are positioned as passive recipients whose primary role is to reproduce predefined answers (Dole et al., 2016). Consequently, the current system privileges measurable performance over meaningful learning, enacting a pedagogy of compliance that limits the transformative potential of education.

Students, aware that their educational success hinges largely on their ability to gather and memorize information, streamline this process by turning to readily available tools. They often use websites with pre-prepared homework solutions and generative artificial intelligence applications to generate responses and conduct information searches on their behalf. As one student candidly remarked, "*It's just about passing —Chat is enough [laughs]. No one checks it anyway. Besides, if you do it yourself, you get a C, and with Chat, it's always an A, so what's the point?*" (S_IC_school_2). This statement reflects a pragmatic approach: students recognize the limitations of these tools but find them sufficient for meeting the basic demands of their schoolwork.

Students often articulated a pragmatic and utilitarian orientation toward schooling, framing it less as a site of intellectual development and more as a compulsory obligation imposed by external expectations, particularly those of parents. One student reflected: "*The most interested one is my mom. She checks the online gradebook every day and is active in the class group. She really wants me to finish this school and go to university. – And do you care? – I don't know, I don't know what I'll do in life. Will this actually be useful?*" (S_IC_2_School_2). This exchange reveals a disjunction between parental aspirations, tied to credential accumulation and social mobility, and students' own uncertainty about the relevance of formal education to their futures. The student's hesitation—"*I don't know*"—functions as a discursive marker of ambivalence, signaling both a lack of intrinsic motivation and a deeper epistemic skepticism about the value of school-based knowledge.

In informal conversations, students repeatedly emphasized efficiency as their primary criterion in navigating academic requirements. Rather than engaging deeply with curricular content, they mobilized digital tools—websites, AI applications such as ChatGPT, and pre-prepared online resources—as strategies of expedience. These practices reflect a shifting locus of trust in knowledge Away from the authoritative figure of the teacher or the textbook, students move toward accessibility and convenience offered by digital infrastructures. Observational data corroborated these accounts. During lessons, students frequently relied on smartphones to complete worksheets or solve textbook-based tasks by accessing pre-existing online solutions. In doing so, they were able to comply with teacher expectations while bypassing more demanding forms of intellectual engagement.

From the perspective of Gee and Green (1998), these practices reconfigure the discourse of learning across several dimensions. At the level of activity building, the completion of tasks is no longer oriented toward understanding but toward the strategic fulfillment of institutional demands. In identity building, the student is constituted less as a curious learner than as a pragmatic navigator of requirements, whose educational subjectivity is defined by efficiency and compliance. At the level of world building, digital platforms emerge as the primary epistemic infrastructure, reshaping what counts as "real" knowledge by privileging immediacy and replication over critical reasoning. Connection building is likewise reorganized: rather than linking school knowledge to broader life-world concerns, students' practices align education with short-term instrumental goals, such as passing exams or satisfying parental oversight.

Within the hegemonic formation of contemporary schooling (Laclau, 2005), learning is invoked as a universally valid term but is increasingly reduced to procedural task completion and test preparation. The signifier thus stabilizes a field of meaning that privileges quantification, credentialism, and efficiency, while masking the ideological function of these priorities in sustaining neoliberal educational logics. Students' reliance on digital shortcuts can be read as both a symptom and a critique of this formation. While they comply with its demands, they also expose its hollowness by revealing that minimal effort is sufficient to reproduce its expected outcomes.

This pattern mirrors findings by Kopciewicz (2020), who documented how students' use of copy-paste techniques, online homework services, and other forms of digital expedience are tacitly tolerated by teachers and parents. The tolerance of such practices indicates not merely pedagogical negligence but a systemic accommodation to a model of learning centered on replication. Teachers' complicity—whether through silence or through reliance on repetitive, publisher-provided worksheets—contributes to a broader erosion of the formative and emancipatory potential of education. In this configuration, mobile technologies become instruments of procedural survival, narrowing their function to mechanistic cycles of information retrieval and reproduction.

An essential factor at play here is the production of what might be called "fictions" of learning. As long as a student's answer conforms to the expected register, tone, or style, its epistemic validity becomes difficult to verify. The ambiguity of whether the content originates from AI, from online repositories, or from the student's own synthesis is often ignored or tacitly accepted, thereby reinforcing superficial engagement with knowledge. A telling instance occurred during a history lesson at School 1, where students delivered a PowerPoint presentation that reproduced elementary facts in neutral language but lacked any references. The teacher, finding no errors, refrained from critique and did not raise the possibility that the work had been generated through digital shortcuts. The brief classroom dialogue captures the dynamics of this interaction:

> T:Okay, guys, so you looked up information on the Slavs?
> S:Of course.
> Teacher:In books of course?
> Students:Of course.
> Teacher:Oh really? (significant smile) Okay, take your seats.

Here, the teacher's ironic rejoinder foregrounds an implicit recognition of the digital mediation underpinning the students' work. By choosing irony rather than explicit confrontation, the teacher maintained authority while signaling awareness of the likely use of AI or Internet sources. This moment illustrates what Peters et al. (2018) and Abrams (2023) identify as a mode of "***knowing restraint***": an institutional tactic in which teachers preserve their status by neither endorsing nor openly challenging students' strategies. The result is a tacit pact between educators and learners. Both parties collude in maintaining the appearance of academic engagement while accepting its contrived nature. In this way, classroom practices drift toward a culture where surface compliance substitutes for genuine intellectual inquiry.

What appears, at first glance, as classroom pragmatics is more accurately understood as a mode of governance. Schools, operating under neoliberal imperatives, are compelled to demonstrate alignment with technological modernization while preserving core routines of procedural instruction. This dynamic resonates with Jessop's (2002) account of governance through spectacle. Institutions project reform and innovation without substantively transforming pedagogical relations. The teacher's stance thus exemplifies how authority is reconfigured in a postdigital environment—not by cultivating deeper epistemic reflexivity, but by sustaining the efficiency and legitimacy of existing routines through the performance of adequacy.

From the perspective of Fraser's (2009) dual framework of misrecognition and maldistribution, the exchange embodies a double bind. On the one hand, students' agency is reduced to procedural adequacy, recognized only insofar as it conforms to the expected form of a "presentation." On the other hand, structural inequalities in access to critical literacies and epistemic resources remain obscured, leaving students unequipped to interrogate the provenance and credibility of knowledge. The circulation of fictions—plausible but unexamined outputs—thus stabilizes the appearance of equality while reproducing epistemic hierarchies.

Seen through this lens, the postdigital school does not mobilize technology to expand learning possibilities. It instrumentalizes technology within an economy of appearances, where digital outputs serve as signs of engagement and innovation. The deeper potential of technological mediation—to open space for critical questioning, reflexive engagement, or alternative epistemologies—is subordinated to the institutional imperative of demonstrating control and efficiency. What is produced, then, is not transformative learning but a carefully managed simulation of it.

The construction of learner identity within contemporary learning discourse is increasingly shaped by mechanistic and standardized forms of knowledge production, where success is measured by the ability to replicate correct answers within predefined formats. In this model, learning is instrumentalized, bounded by worksheets, tests, and homework that demand efficiency. The learner is thus rendered into a functional subject, trained to interpret and fulfill institutional expectations through a process that often devalues individuality and deeper understanding. This subjectivity, once critiqued through Marxist frameworks as symptomatic of the knowledge worker's alienation, now takes on posthumanist dimensions when examined through the lenses of Haraway (2013), who explore how technologies contribute to the dehumanization and algorithmic optimization of identities. Here, identity is constructed around the empty signifiers of *survival* and *to pass*, encapsulating the affective and existential dimensions of schooling under high-stakes assessment regimes. These terms highlight the performative pressures students face in navigating systems that prioritize output and compliance over intellectual development.

This mechanized subjectivity is deeply intertwined with what Brown (1992) identifies as the Fordist logic of schooling, where educational processes mimic the industrial organization of labor. Students and teachers alike are embedded within systems that demand precision, replication, and conformity, reducing learning to a form of task execution. Brown's depiction of learning as the act of inserting correct information into assessment templates—later catalogued into centralized data systems—reveals how deeply this logic has infiltrated educational discourse (Brown, 1992, p. 397). Under the guise of lifelong learning, students are subject to an unceasing cycle of performance evaluation, where knowledge is commodified and credentials function as proof of productivity. The classroom thus mirrors the factory, not only in structure but in its demand for continuous output and standardization. In such environments, the learner becomes less a thinker and more a processor tasked with survival through compliance and assessed through metrics that reflect institutional priorities. This translation into education manifests in a structured and repetitive environment dominated by test preparation, memorization, and output-oriented practices. The industrial model reshapes schooling to replicate factory logic, privileging efficiency and standardization at the expense of holistic development. In such a paradigm, classrooms cease to function as spaces for exploration or critical inquiry and instead become sites of mechanical knowledge reproduction, where success is measured by conformity to predetermined answers. Both students and teachers are constrained by the demand for immediate, quantifiable outcomes, a pressure that suppresses creativity and diminishes intellectual autonomy. The educational subject, like the Fordist worker, is valued for their ability to conform to systemic expectations—thus transforming education from a transformative experience into a mechanized process of credential accumulation and institutional compliance.

This configuration is reinforced by the neoliberal rationality that permeates contemporary education, reframing learning as an economic investment, and rarely as a humanistic pursuit. Once transformative ideals such as "*creativity*" and "*problem-solving*" are reinterpreted through this lens, they risk becoming empty signifiers—concepts that legitimize a market-oriented system while losing much of their emancipatory potential. My argument here builds on Hanushek (2019) and Gromkowska-Melosik's (2015) critiques of the instrumentalisation and misunderstanding of such concepts, which show how their pedagogical value is narrowed to serve economic priorities. Within this framework, critical and creative capacities are cultivated not for intellectual enrichment but repurposed to serve economic productivity and adaptability. The elevation of credentialism—where the accumulation of standardized competencies is pursued primarily for labor market advantage—further commodifies education, reducing it to a transactional process aimed at producing economically viable subjects. The learner, in this reconfiguration, is positioned less as an autonomous thinker than as a strategic actor navigating institutional structures calibrated to optimize labor potential. The result is a narrowed, utilitarian model of education that erodes democratic participation and intellectual agency, subordinating meaningful engagement with knowledge to the demands of market value.

The rise of automated learning systems intensifies the Fordist logic already embedded in contemporary education, absorbing students into algorithmically governed environments that privilege efficiency, standardization, and predictability over intellectual risk and engagement. In both the industrial factory and the modern classroom, roles are predefined. Factory workers follow rigid production schedules, while students are confined to standardized curricula that reward compliance rather than curiosity. This alignment produces what might be called the "*Ford factory subject*"—a learner valued for producing quantifiable outcomes. The subject does not engage critically or creatively with knowledge. In such spaces, students become datasets, assessed through metrics that disregard the cognitive, emotional, and social dimensions of learning, reducing education to a mechanized process aimed at eliminating variability.

Against this deterministic order, Haraway's *Cyborg Manifesto* (2013) reframes the human–machine relation as a hybrid space in which the fusion of organic and technological can unsettle the very hierarchies such systems seek to entrench. This challenge to fixed boundaries converges with Rancière's vision in *The Ignorant Schoolmaster* (1991), which rejects the premise of pedagogical hierarchy and affirms the equal cognitive potential of all learners. Together, Haraway's cyborg and Rancière's emancipated learner disrupt the binary of technological domination versus human autonomy, suggesting that agency is not extinguished by mechanization but can emerge through the appropriation and reconfiguration of technological systems. Such a reimagining resists the reduction of education to a regimented pursuit of predetermined benchmarks, proposing instead an alternative grounded in equality and the willingness to embrace uncertainty as a condition for genuine intellectual growth.

The empty signifiers "*survival*" and "*to pass*," as voiced by students in informal conversations, show the reduction of education to a transactional pursuit in which institutional navigation takes precedence over intellectual enrichment. Their meaning is anchored in the performative demands of the educational apparatus, where success is defined by conformity to predefined outcomes and the ability to satisfy external benchmarks. Within this logic, learners are not animated by curiosity or critical engagement but by the imperative to overcome immediate hurdles—examinations—required to maintain institutional standing. Education thus becomes an exercise in symbolic compliance, where "*survival*" and "*passing*" mark not personal growth but the capacity to function within a system that privileges efficiency.

The increasing integration of artificial intelligence into this landscape adds a posthumanist inflection to what is, at its core, a Fordist paradigm. AI-driven tools—from adaptive learning platforms to automated assessment systems—reposition the learner within algorithmically governed assemblages where human and non-human agents co-produce the learning process. In this hybrid configuration, the student resembles a cyborg-like subject. Not an autonomous knower, but a node in a digitally mediated network that both enables and constrains agency. While this reframing complicates traditional understandings of the learner as a worker of knowledge shaped solely by human-centered production, it also exposes how algorithmic governance frequently intensifies the very logic it might be assumed to disrupt. Rather than dismantling standardization and output-driven evaluation, AI tends to reproduce them through data-driven processes that deepen the bureaucratic and performative dimensions of schooling—recasting "*survival*" and "*passing*" not as residual features of a pre-digital order, but as defining conditions of the postdigital educational experience.

In teachers' narratives, the learner is often cast as a fundamentally different kind of being—what one teacher described, half-ironically, as a "*different species*" permanently armed with a phone (T_4_school_2; T_1_school_1; T_6_school_2)). This image converges with Kopciewicz's (2019) figure of the cyborg child, a hybrid of human and machine that crystallizes anxieties over the dissolution of traditional childhood qualities under the pressures of digital technologie. The cyborg child is imagined as living in an always-connected state, immersed in screen-mediated interactions and algorithmically tailored content, rather than in relationships rooted in human presence. Teachers speak of this in elegiac tones, lamenting a perceived loss of the "soul" of childhood and implicitly invoking what Kopciewicz terms a "culture of death"—the gradual erasure of humanistic values in a society ordered by technological rationality. In this framing, hybridity is not celebrated as a site of creative potential. Instead it is treated as a symptom of depersonalization: a diminishment of the emotional and ethical dimensions of learning that once anchored pedagogy in mutual recognition.

This cultural imaginary is not sustained by sentiment alone. It is reinforced by the structural organization of schooling itself, where measurable output dominate the pedagogical landscape. Within this Fordist logic of production, learning is reduced to a sequence of discrete operations aimed at completing predefined tasks and achieving quantifiable benchmarks. The student becomes a task-executing subject, shaped by rigid curricula, digital platforms, and algorithmic assessments—produced as much by code and data flows as by classroom interaction. Haraway's cyborg metaphor is particularly incisive here, not only because it challenges the human–machine binary, but because it exposes the political stakes of technological integration in education: the risk that mechanization will subsume individuality and creativity under a regime of compliance and optimization. The educational system thus functions as an assembly line, manufacturing a form of subjectivity that is predictable and attuned to the demands of performance. In this configuration, the cyborg child is not simply a metaphor for technological hybridity, but the embodiment of an identity produced through algorithmic governance and institutional discipline—a subject whose formation is increasingly detached from relational engagement and oriented instead toward the imperatives of a tightly managed, postdigital order.

The cyborg child, as it appears in teachers' narratives, embodies the technologized dimension of contemporary subject formation. This is an identity shaped through constant connectivity, algorithmic mediation, and the erosion of relational pedagogy. Parallel to this, the learner as a Fordist subject reflects the industrial logic of the educational system, in which survival and passing become the central imperatives. While the cyborg child crystallizes anxieties over the hybridization of human and machine, the Fordist subject exposes the procedural, output-driven nature of schooling, where the execution of standardized tasks replaces inquiry and exploration. These two constructions, though analytically distinct, operate in tandem. Technological mediation strengthens the system's efficiency imperatives, while the Fordist logic lends structure and discipline to the cyborg condition. Together, they reveal an educational order in which subjectivity is produced through the convergence of mechanization and technological rationality, narrowing the scope for autonomy and reconfiguring the learner's place in the postdigital classroom. This dual construction sets the stage for the next discussion on the learner as the sovereign of knowledge, a counterpoint to the mechanized and technologized subjectivities that dominate the postdigital school.

4.2 Learner as the Sovereign of Knowledge

Digital technology is frequently celebrated as a democratizing force within education, embedded in the discourse of equal opportunity that underpins global consumer culture. This narrative, as Selwyn (2014) observes, promotes the notion that "everyone is basically the same" (p. 137), framing digital platforms as inherently egalitarian tools that offer universal access to knowledge and learning. Such optimism, however, conceals the structural inequalities and algorithmic constraints that spread through digital learning environments (Selwyn, 2014, p. 138). The assumption that digital tools automatically level the educational playing field disregards the socio-economic disparities that shape both access to and participation in digital learning. In the postdigital context, digital education emerges not as a neutral facilitator of empowerment, but as a complex and contested terrain in which learner autonomy is both enabled and systematically regulated.

As I have noted, students often claimed that the knowledge they considered "real" and genuinely useful in life was obtained through social media, positioning this form of learning in direct opposition to the learning offered at school. An example could be my informal exchange with students in the hallway of School No. 2.

R: Is what you learn at school useful to you?
S: Not really. I mean, it's necessary to pass the matura exam, but it won't be useful for anything else.
R: What would it need to be useful for?
S: I mean that today everything changes quickly, and the school doesn't know what we will need in our professional work. Artificial intelligence is changing

the job market very fast. Nobody knows this. I follow trends and can see for myself that even I can't keep up, so knowledge needs to change very quickly.
R: And what about general knowledge?
S: I don't know...

The student's positioning of school knowledge as simultaneously *necessary* for passing the matura but *useless* beyond that function can be read, via Gee and Green's framework, as a case of activity building. Learning is articulated as an instrumental task tied to assessment rather than a resource for life (Gee & Green, 1998). This aligns with research on performance-driven regimes that standardize curriculum and narrow purposes toward testability (Au, 2011; Sahlberg, 2016). Within this discourse, the learner is configured as a compliant subject whose engagement with knowledge is governed by the symbolic economy of exams.

By contrast, the same speaker frames social media as the locus of "*real*," useful knowledge because it keeps pace with rapid technological and labor market change. This constructs a different world for learning, which is—dynamic and, adaptive, constantly updating—set against the school's "static" curriculum (Gee & Green, 1998). It also performs identity building. The learner casts themselves as an active agent who "follows trends" and manages uncertainty, embodying the neoliberal ideal of the self-responsible, continuously upskilling subject (Brown et al., 2011). The hesitation around "general knowledge" ("*I don't know...*") is a discursive gap between inherited humanistic aims—broad cultural literacy and civic formation (Biesta, 2017; Nussbaum, 2010)—and the contemporary privileging of agile, market-oriented competencies.

Read through Laclau, key terms in the exchange—"*usefulness*," "*needs*," "*general knowledge*"—operate as empty signifiers. They appear self-evident but are filled with competing meanings (Laclau, 1996, 2005). "*Usefulness*," for students, condenses employability and speed in an AI-mediated economy. "*General knowledge*" becomes vague, even dispensable. The opposition "*school knowledge*" vs. "*real knowledge*" organizes the discourse It is based on institutionally validated content on one side, and fast, interest-driven, renewable knowledge on the other. The opposition emphasizes the ideological work being done. It naturalizes responsibilized autonomy while downplaying the data economies and inequalities that condition access to "*real*" knowledge.

Placing the student's account within youth learning cultures online clarifies the appeal. Social media foregrounds interest-driven and rapidly updated forms of participation (Ito et al., 2013, p. 14). In Gee & Green's terms, the platforms support specific activities (liking, sharing, trend-tracking, exchanging), stabilize identities (self-updating learner), and build connections that privilege immediacy and affect. The student's closing "*I don't know...*" is thus not merely personal uncertainty. It indexes a structural tension between educational ideals of general formation and the epistemic logics of a postdigital, AI-intensified knowledge economy (Brown et al., 2011; Sahlberg, 2016).

Social media analysis indicates that technocratic knowledge about the contemporary world is produced very fast. The analyses of artificial intelligence to which the student referred were appearing literally days after new AI versions were released, creating a sense that the knowledge was highly up to date. It must be acknowledged that many of these analyses were in-depth, drew on reputable sources, and introduced Polish audiences to content from the agenda-setting international press. On the other hand, as a researcher, the speed at which these materials are produced leads me to doubt their full reliability.

Social media users often articulate a strong sense of autonomy in determining what knowledge they acquire. This perception resonates clearly in students' narratives, which emphasize self-direction and personal relevance in their learning choices. As my conversation with a student illustrates:

> *S_6: "- On the internet we decide for ourselves what we want to watch—things that are more useful and interesting."*
> *R: "- And what does 'useful and interesting' mean for you?"*
> *S_6: "- For example, history—things that concern us, information about our ancestors that you don't find in school, or even if it's there, in school it's presented in such a boring way. A teacher can make everything off-putting [laughter]."*
> *R: "- And you want to learn this kind of information?"*
> *S_6: "- Yes, I decide for myself what is useful for me, or what will be useful for my future work. I won't learn that at school." (S_IC_School_1)*

In Gee and Green's (1998) terms, this account constructs a particular world of learning, one defined by interest and personal utility, and never by institutional authority or fixed curricula. The activity of learning is positioned as voluntary selection and consumption of digital content, a practice framed as intrinsically engaging in contrast to the compulsory routines of school. Through identity building, the student positions themselves as an agentive learner—someone who decides what knowledge is valuable. The learner rejects the monotony of formal instruction and aligns learning with future professional goals. Connection building further situates this practice within temporal and cultural horizons History is valued not as abstract knowledge but as affectively meaningful, linked to ancestors and future work, thereby legitimizing its relevance.

From a Laclauian perspective, the student's invocation of "*useful and interesting*" operates as an empty signifier. It condenses heterogeneous desires—pragmatic employability, affective connection to ancestry, and resistance to boredom—into a single marker of value. This signifier organizes a discursive antagonistic opposition. On one side stands school knowledge, dismissed as irrelevant, monotonous, and imposed. On the other side stands digital knowledge, figured as dynamic, engaging, and freely chosen. The very articulation of autonomy here conceals the infrastructural logics shaping what appears as choice. As Fraser and Honneth (2003) argue, neoliberal discourses of self-responsibility position individuals as entrepreneurial subjects responsible for maximizing their own capacities. The "*sovereign of knowledge*" thus emerges as an ideological figure A learner imagined as free and self-directed, but whose agency is profoundly mediated by algorithmic systems that delimit what can be known and valued.

In this sense, the student's laughter at the "boring teacher" is not simply anecdotal but a discursive act of differentiation, separating the sphere of authentic, engaging learning from the discredited practices of schooling. The apparent freedom of digital autonomy is embedded within circuits of digital capitalism. The more personalized the algorithmic curation, the narrower the epistemic horizon becomes, as learners' "choices" are invisibly structured by optimization logics and commercial imperatives. The sovereign learner is therefore less a description of lived autonomy than an ideological artifact, sustaining the illusion of agency while embedding learning within infrastructures that reproduce existing hierarchies of recognition and distribution (Laclau, 2005; Couldry & Mejias, 2019).

The illusion of autonomy in digital education is central to the contemporary construction of learner identity. Within the knowledge-based economy, the figure of the learner is increasingly imagined as a self-directing "*sovereign of knowledge*," free to navigate the vast expanse of digital content. This sovereignty is more rhetorical than real. Lifelong learning platforms and digital infrastructures embed learners in systems of algorithmic curation and personalized recommendation engines that do not merely mediate access to knowledge but actively govern it. These architectures channel attention toward content aligned with marketable skills and economic imperatives, sidelining critical or emancipatory forms of knowing. What appears as choice is, in practice, a managed trajectory, where agency is exercised within boundaries designed to produce economically and optimizable subjects.

However, as the analysis in the next part on *dangerous epistemologies* has demonstrated, the construction of knowledge is simultaneously a process of inclusion and exclusion—not only of information, but also of particular ways of thinking about the world. Social media content identified by students as valuable is deeply embedded in this dynamic, often saturated with denialist and nationalist discourses. This was evident in my own observations when analyzing the TikTok accounts they followed, as well as in the material I encountered while exploring hashtags such as *#polska (poland)*, *#dumanarodowa (nationalpride)*, and *#polacy (poles)*. These digital spaces function as both repositories and amplifiers of ideologically charged narratives, where the boundaries of belonging and exclusion are drawn through symbolic markers of identity. In this way, they do not merely reflect existing social divisions but actively participate in shaping epistemic landscapes, reinforcing particular visions of the nation and history while marginalizing alternative perspectives. Social media platforms—key spaces in which learners encounter knowledge outside formal education—serve as powerful sites of national identity formation. The narratives encountered here often diverge from those sanctioned in school curricula, but the choice to engage with them is shaped by the same algorithmic architectures that govern educational content. As in the economic sphere, the freedom to choose one's national narrative is an illusion. Exposure is curated, and engagement is guided toward particular ideological framings, often reinforcing ethnonationalist or exclusionary discourses while suppressing alternative perspectives.

Foucault's (2007) concept of pastoral power helps to make sense of the contemporary portrayal of the learner as a "*sovereign of knowledge*." Pastoral power, unlike direct coercion, works through quiet forms of guidance, leading individuals to adopt goals that reflect wider societal priorities. In digital learning, this operates through the architectures of search algorithms and platform design—mechanisms that act as unseen guides, shaping what information comes into view and reinforcing particular ways of knowing. Within this environment, the image of the learner as an autonomous and discerning subject—able to move through endless digital resources and define their own learning path—has become a central ideal in education. This autonomy is often more rhetorical than real. The same infrastructures that promise freedom also determine what is framed as relevant and what slips from sight. In doing so, they steer learning toward the priorities of economic productivity and market value, leaving less room for critical questioning or alternative visions of knowledge.

In this configuration, the learner's identity is tied closely to the neoliberal ideal of constant self-improvement. Education is framed not only as a route to personal growth but as a moral and economic obligation. The "good" learner is imagined as an entrepreneurial figure, always updating skills to stay relevant in an unstable labor market. This framing shifts attention away from the structural causes of insecurity—the extractive practices of platform capitalism—and places the burden on individuals to adapt endlessly. What emerges is a form of disciplined autonomy The learner experiences a sense of independence, but their choices are already shaped by the economic and algorithmic systems that set the terms of participation.

The disciplinary side of this ideal becomes clear in the use of AI-driven analytics and assessment. Predictive algorithms and ranking systems turn education into a cycle of constant monitoring and adjustment. These tools do more than record progress. They influence what counts as progress, steering learners toward outcomes that match institutional targets and labor market needs. In this way, analytics foster a compliant orientation, where meeting quantifiable benchmarks takes precedence over critical inquiry. The learner who appears sovereign becomes a self-monitoring performer, aligning behavior with the metrics built into the system.

The promise of digital freedom is central to sustaining this model. Learners are encouraged to personalize and explore their own studies, however these freedoms operate within boundaries set by algorithms and economic priorities. Social media, often perceived as an open arena for alternative learning, plays a double role here. While it provides spaces for interest-driven knowledge exchange, it also amplifies content aligned with dominant political currents, including nationalistic narratives and values. Such content often blends emotional appeal with simplified historical or cultural frames, reinforcing identity-based allegiances and narrowing the scope of acceptable perspectives. In this configuration, knowledge that supports productivity and measurable competence is prioritized, while both critical perspectives on the economy and challenges to prevailing national narratives are marginalized or rendered invisible. Learning becomes less an open-ended search for understanding and more a managed pathway to both economic utility and ideological conformity. It helps producing human capital attuned to the demands of the market and the symbolic boundaries of the nation.

Understanding the learner as a "*sovereign of knowledge*" requires situating this figure within the socio-technical, political, and economic arrangements that both enable and constrain it. What is presented as independence often emerges from forms of governance that operate without overt coercion, shaping dispositions toward knowledge that appear natural and self-chosen (Foucault, 2007). In the postdigital condition, digital sovereignty is not an intrinsic quality of the individual but the product of the economic imperatives of the knowledge economy, and the hierarchical structures that regulate value in knowledge production.

This dynamic extends beyond economic productivity to encompass the ideological dimensions of learner formation. The circulation of nationalistic narratives through social media, for example, places epistemic authority within particular cultural and historical frames, reinforcing identity-based allegiances while narrowing the range of legitimate perspectives. Algorithmic filtering and the selective amplification of content further delimit the field of possible knowledges, even as the appearance of choice is maintained.

Within this configuration, learner autonomy functions as a regulated construct. The figure of the "*sovereign*" is sustained through systems that align educational orientations with market imperatives and prevailing political narratives, producing a subject whose agency is exercised within pre-structured boundaries. The analysis of this process requires attention to how governance logics and identity politics intersect to shape what counts as and valuable knowledge in the contemporary educational landscape.

4.3 The Discourse of Ignorance

At the onset of fieldwork, the students' reactions to my interest in how they learn revealed a profound and internalized disconnection from the concept of themselves as learners. Remarks, such as "*But we don't know anything*," delivered with laughter, signaled not defiance but a deep alienation from the act of learning itself. Students did not view education as a participatory or generative process. They experienced it as something external, enacted upon them rather than with them. This perspective was consistently reinforced through classroom interactions, where even minor linguistic ambiguities—such as the unfamiliarity with the phrase "flip through"—led to complete inaction. The students' silence in response to emphasizes their conditioned passivity and the erosion of their epistemic agency. Rather than responding with curiosity or collective experimentation, the students froze, awaiting explicit instructions. This moment, seemingly trivial, encapsulates a pedagogical culture wherein the teacher is the singular source of meaning, and the student's role is reduced to passive reception and mechanical compliance.

The discourse of ignorance in educational settings functions not merely as a recognition of knowledge gaps between teachers and students but as a deeply entrenched mechanism of power that structures classroom relationships, institutional hierarchies, and learner identities. Observations revealed that students were repeatedly positioned as epistemically deficient through subtle and overt rhetorical practices—from teachers' impatient remarks to frustrated exhortations like "*Wake up!*," "*pull yourselves together*," "*you really know very little*," and "*what times we live in*," "*children of the internet*"—which collectively framed student ignorance as a defining and naturalized characteristic.

Although teachers are increasingly expected to integrate digital tools into their practice, many struggle with limited competences, particularly in relation to advanced or AI-powered applications (Pyżalski, 2025). In the studied schools, teachers prohibited AI use in lessons and treated AI-assisted work with suspicion, often designing assignments to make such tools unusable. They frequently assumed that students' skills were limited to "*inputting tasks into Chat*," overlooking more complex forms of engagement. At the same time, teachers expressed frustration at competing for students' attention with smartphones and platforms like TikTok, often describing them as an "*entertain me generation*" (T_3_school_2) that demands constant stimulation, like quizzes, videos, or games, to remain engaged. Such descriptions, framing students as lazy or screen-dependent, neglect the wider social and institutional factors shaping these behaviors.

This positioning reinforces a pedagogical hierarchy in which the teacher is constructed as the sole legitimate knower, and students are relegated to the role of passive recipients in need of intellectual correction. Such practices are rooted in broader epistemological traditions that sustain structural ignorance, as theorized by Medina (2013), who describes meta-ignorance as a condition where epistemic limits are normalized and reproduced through social and institutional exclusion. Within schools, ignorance is not a neutral absence but a produced and maintained state that legitimizes teacher authority and marginalizes student agency. As students are expected to accept their constructed deficiencies, educational practices shift away from dialogic co-construction of knowledge and toward a unidirectional model of transmission, reinforcing unequal power dynamics and silencing alternative epistemic contributions.

The public understanding of science illustrates a broader, structural dimension of ignorance, emphasizing that epistemic gaps are not simply individual deficits but outcomes of systemic inequalities and institutional design. Schools, situated within larger socio-political frameworks, function as arenas where dominant knowledge systems are reproduced and legitimized. In this context, ignorance within educational settings often operates to preserve existing hierarchies, maintaining the authority of particular knowledge forms while sidelining others. As Sullivan and Tuana (2007) and Vianna (2013) highlight, cultural ignorance in schools can result in the misrecognition and exclusion of students from historically excluded backgrounds, reinforcing their status as "others" and constraining their ability to form empowered identities within the educational space. In this case, however, exclusion concerns not only students from specific backgrounds but an entire generation.

A postcolonial perspective sharpens the analysis of ignorance in education by framing it not as a passive absence of knowledge but as an active practice of epistemic control. Perera (2015) and Spivak (1999) have shown how Western-centered educational paradigms sustain ignorance by erasing or silencing non-Western epistemologies. This form of epistemic violence consolidates the authority of Western knowledge by excluding other intellectual traditions from the curriculum, presenting Eurocentric frameworks as both universal and self-evident. Ashcroft et al. (1995) trace this logic to the colonial civilising mission, in which education was used to discipline and assimilate colonized populations into a dominant epistemic and moral order. In this model, the learner is not regarded as a co-producer of knowledge but as a subject to be reshaped and corrected, reproducing the colonial trope of education as a transformative tool for the "uncivilised." Such legacies remain visible in contemporary schooling, where the suppression of epistemic plurality continues to regulate legitimacy.

Within the contemporary educational framework, ignorance operates not merely as an absence of knowledge but as a constitutive element of pedagogical relations. It functions simultaneously as a mechanism of control and, potentially, as a space from which to reimagine educational practice. Rancière's (1991) critique of negative ignorance is particularly instructive here. In the dominant model of schooling, ignorance is actively produced and maintained in order to legitimize hierarchical asymmetries between teachers and students. The teacher is positioned as the exclusive bearer of valid knowledge, while students are cast as epistemically deficient subjects, whose value lies in their capacity to receive and reproduce sanctioned content. This dynamic is reinforced through pedagogical practices centered on memorization, standardization, and exam preparation, all of which restrict the possibilities of inquiry and reduce learning to procedural compliance. The logic was articulated with striking clarity by one teacher: "*They don't need to understand everything. They need to know what the exam expects from them. That's my job—to prepare them for that, not to discuss unnecessary details*" (T_4_School_2). Here, the teacher's self-description illustrates how institutionalized assessment regimes subordinate intellectual exploration to the instrumental demands of test performance, narrowing education to the production of examinable outputs.

The category of "*ignorance*" itself can be read as an empty signifier that brings together disparate anxieties—about student apathy, lack of preparation, or inability to cope with curricular demands—into a unified deficit construct. Its apparent universality ("*students do not know*") masks its ideological function. It is aimed at naturalizing hierarchical educational arrangements and render them commonsensical. As Laclau (2005) argues, such signifiers secure hegemony not through their precision but through their very indeterminacy, enabling multiple meanings to be condensed into a single, seemingly self-evident notion. Thus, ignorance does not merely describe a lack. It performs a political function in sustaining the authority of the teacher and the legitimacy of the system.

At the same time, Rancière's (1991) proposition that ignorance can be reframed as a shared point of departure in inquiry offers a counter-hegemonic articulation. Here, ignorance is detached from its deficit connotation and re-signified as a condition of possibility for collaborative discovery. In this rearticulation, the authority of the teacher is no longer anchored in superior knowledge but in the facilitation of questioning and exploration. Such a move destabilizes the binary of "knower" and "learner," enabling pedagogical relations grounded in co-investigation rather than subordination.

Within prevailing institutional logics, the discourse of negative ignorance—articulated as deficiency and lack—remains hegemonic. It is reinforced not only by performance-driven regimes but also by deeper epistemic hierarchies, often rooted in colonial traditions, that construct certain subjects as perpetually "behind" or "in need of catching up." Ignorance thus functions as a disciplinary technology. It organizes classroom interactions around compliance and suppresses opportunities for students to exercise agency in shaping knowledge. Seen through both Rancière and Laclau, ignorance is never a neutral category; it is a site of struggle, whose meaning can either stabilize domination or open possibilities for reconfiguring education as a democratic space of inquiry.

The implications of this mechanized approach to knowledge are evident in how student identity is constructed within the discourse of ignorance. Students who deviate from expected responses, who challenge the dominant narrative, or who seek alternative ways of understanding are often disciplined, marginalized, or dismissed. The following classroom exchange illustrates this mechanism:

> *"The previous day, the class watched The Zone of Interest. Today, the teacher starts the lesson by asking how they liked it. A few students complain about the cinema educator, while others nod in approval. The teacher then begins asking structured questions:*
> *'How did the commandant's family live? What is the evidence that they were indifferent to the fate of the prisoners?' Several students volunteer answers, and the discussion proceeds smoothly. But then M. and A. interject:*
> *M: I don't think Hoess was a bad person. In my opinion, you can't judge someone by just one deed.*
> *Teacher: Oh, M., you again. You always have to say something. Please, who will answer the question?*
> *The other students, still waiting to answer, ignore M. and A., while the teacher redirects the discussion.*
> *M: After all, we don't know him from other situations, we don't know what kind of person he really was.*
> *A.: Exactly. We don't know.*

Teacher: This is really not the time for this kind of discussion. Please, K., you want to answer?
K.: Hoess didn't pay attention to the situation of the prisoners, he was cruel, and we know by that that he was a bad man. M., stop provoking us.

The classroom exchange highlights how student identity is discursively produced at the intersection of ignorance and conformity. From the perspective of Gee and Green (1998), discourse is always "world-building," structuring not only the content of knowledge but also the identities and forms of participation that are made possible within interaction. The teacher's structured questions—"*What is the evidence...?*"—set the frame of activity building: knowledge is not collectively constructed but retrieved according to pre-established evaluative criteria. Within this logic, students are positioned as compliant respondents whose task is to echo the sanctioned interpretation. When M. and A. attempt to shift the frame by proposing a morally ambiguous reading of Höss, their contributions disrupt the expected identity building. They implicitly claim the role of critical inquirers rather than compliant test-takers. This move is immediately delegitimized The teacher frames their intervention as provocation, while peers reinforce the dominant narrative, effectively closing down the possibility of alternative epistemic positions. In Gee and Green's terms, the discursive building tasks of the classroom consolidate authority, normalize compliance, and marginalize dissent.

From a Laclaudian perspective, the episode illustrates how the category of ignorance functions as a floating signifier within the classroom's hegemonic order. M. and A.'s contributions are not engaged as legitimate attempts at inquiry but are rearticulated as provocations, aligning them with ignorance-as-deviation rather than with knowledge-seeking. This discursive re-signification secures the dominance of the "correct" moral interpretation, which operates as a nodal point around which classroom consensus is organized. The figure of Höss as unequivocally "a bad man" stabilizes the moral framework by bringing together disparate elements—curricular expectations, collective memory, affective investment in Holocaust education—into a coherent chain of equivalence. The indeterminacy of ignorance enables this process It is deployed flexibly, both as a marker of students' supposed deficiency and as a means to delegitimize perspectives that threaten the stability of the hegemonic articulation. As Laclau (2005) reminds us, hegemony works precisely through this play of inclusion and exclusion, where certain interpretations are made to appear natural and unchallengeable, while others are rendered unthinkable or disruptive.

Seen through the integration of Gee and Green with Laclau, the classroom emerges not as a neutral space of historical reflection but as a site where discourse actively constructs boundaries of legitimate knowledge and identity. The refusal to engage with M. and A.'s interventions is not a simple pedagogical choice. It is a hegemonic operation that transforms critical reflection into deviance. What appears as "teaching history" is simultaneously a process of disciplining subjectivities, where the roles of "good student" and "ignorant provocateur" are continuously re-inscribed.

This interpretation complicates conventional understandings of Holocaust education as a moral safeguard against forgetting. In practice, the insistence on consensus suppresses precisely the kind of dialogical, open-ended inquiry that would allow students to grapple with ethical ambiguity. By reducing the lesson to the reproduction of an already-authorized script, the classroom turns moral learning into procedural compliance. Students like M. and A., who resist this script, embody the possibility of alternative epistemic trajectories, however their positioning at the margins illustrates how the hegemonic order of schooling neutralizes such potential. Thus, ignorance in this context is not a neutral deficit but a politically charged construct. It is deployed to exclude disruptive perspectives while stabilizing authority and the institutional demand for controllable knowledge.

This pedagogy of passivity is not incidental but structurally embedded in schooling, shaped by high-stakes assessments and standardized curricula where ambiguity is framed as a liability rather than an invitation to inquiry. Within such a regime, learning becomes synonymous with error-avoidance, and achievement is measured by correctness rather than creativity. Students are positioned as self-monitoring agents of compliance, habituated to interpret failure as personal deficiency instead of as an integral part of intellectual development. This logic explains why dissenting or unorthodox contributions, such as those voiced by M. and A., are dismissed not only by teachers but also by peers. Such interventions disturb the fragile performative order of the classroom, which depends on predictable exchanges and rehearsed answers. In this way, the form and function of knowledge are diminished. Classrooms operate as stages for enacting pre-scripted forms of knowing, while curiosity and critique are reclassified as deviation. Over time, these patterns sediment into what Gee and Green (1998) would call the building tasks of discourse—forming a linguistic and cultural residue in which conformity is equated with intelligence, and silence with learning.

What emerges is not merely a transmission of knowledge but an active construction of subjectivities, where students internalize what they are permitted to know and who they are allowed to become as learners. This architecture of constraint rests on the erosion of learner agency and the cultural normalization of compliance. The resulting pedagogical subject is present but disempowered, responsive but untransformed. Within this framework, the learner is mechanized—trained less for intellectual engagement than for procedural task completion. Despite the rhetoric of personalization and competencies, the model is rigidly normative, anchored to evaluative mechanisms that privilege performance over understanding.

Szkudlarek and Zamojski (2020, p. 581) emphasize the deeper logics underpinning this configuration, observing that "*the construction of the knowledge society depends not only on the lines of knowledge production, innovation, and learning, but also on the lines of knowledge exclusions.*" Their insight resonates with Laclau's (2005) notion of the constitutive outside. Knowledge acquires its authority through contrast with what is marked as ignorance, delineating boundaries, legitimizing hierarchies, and stabilizing hegemonic orders. In this sense, the "knowledge society" is not an open arena of inquiry but a regulated regime in which access is contingent on exclusion. Postdigital schooling, governed by procedural learning, produces learners who navigate systems premised on behavioral predictability. The empty signifier of "*survival*" encapsulates this condition. The imperative to pass exams or complete schooling becomes the organizing principle of education, displacing curiosity and discomfort in favor of routinized outcomes. Ignorance here is not a cognitive failure but a structurally produced condition that secures institutional authority by marginalizing precisely those forms of thought that could resist or reconfigure dominant frameworks.

From this perspective, ignorance must be understood not as absence but as an outcome of discursive and institutional design. It is actively generated through pedagogical practices that demarcate what counts as legitimate knowledge and who may claim it. This relational ignorance sustains not only the micro-politics of the classroom but also the macro-politics of the educational system, which mirrors broader market logics, reproduces social stratifications, and neutralizes dissent. In this way, the management of ignorance becomes central to the maintenance of institutional order. It defines insiders and outsiders, regulating epistemic legitimacy. Moreover it suppresses alternative knowledges that might destabilize dominant discourses. Schooling, thus conceived, operates less as a space of exploration than as a technology of epistemic containment.

It is within this disciplinary regime that the concept of dangerous epistemologies gains critical traction. If school knowledge is maintained through the exclusion of its "constitutive outside," then what happens to knowledges that challenge curricular orthodoxy or contest the authority of the national canon? Students who bring alternative political, historical, or affective frameworks into the classroom—often shaped by digital environments and social media networks—are not merely deviating from educational norms. They are performing epistemic resistance. These "dangerous epistemologies" unsettle the tightly regulated logic of schooling, revealing students as participants in multiple, intersecting knowledge systems that frequently diverge from institutional expectations. The move from mechanized, performative learning to dialogical knowledge practices exposes the fault lines between formal education and peer-validated discourse, between compliance and criticality. As the following chapter will explore, these epistemologies do not simply disrupt classroom routines. They reimagine the conditions of learning itself, offering a potent counter-narrative to the hegemonic epistemic order and foregrounding youth as active agents of knowledge production in the postdigital age.

4.4 New Sources of Knowledge and Dangerous Epistemologies

The contemporary educational landscape is marked by profound epistemic tensions in which students increasingly contest the authority and relevance of school-sanctioned knowledge, drawing instead on extra-institutional sources such as digital media, online communities, and peer-based epistemic networks. This contestation reflects not simply disengagement but a renegotiation of epistemic authority. Learners are no longer passive recipients of curricular content but active participants in competing truth regimes. Classroom engagement, under such conditions, often narrows to the strategic acquisition of exam-oriented knowledge, while, in parallel, students cultivate alternative epistemologies shaped by Internet culture, meme logic, conspiracy-laden discourses, and anti-establishment critiques.

An illustrative case from participant observation occurred in a philosophy class in School No. 1, where students lodged a formal complaint against their teacher for "spreading fake news" during a lesson on George Berkeley's immaterialism. The claim that "*materiality does not exist*," a foundational philosophical proposition, was reframed by the students as an empirically falsifiable statement—and thus fake. By invoking the verificationist logic characteristic of digital platforms, where truth is equated with demonstrability and fact-checking protocols, the students displaced the legitimating authority of philosophical tradition with criteria derived from the digital public sphere. In Gee and Green's (1998) terms, this was an act of world building. They redefined the epistemic parameters of the classroom by aligning them with the epistemic norms of digital culture, where validity is contingent upon proof and visibility. What was once a philosophical inquiry into the nature of reality was recoded as a contest over factual correctness, thereby collapsing ontological questions into empiricist verification. In Laclau's framework, this reveals how the signifier "*truth*" itself is emptied and refilled—its meaning shifting from philosophical lineage to digital empiricism. Such moments exemplify a broader epistemological rearticulation, in which students position themselves as arbiters of validity and, in doing so, destabilize the authority of teachers and the institutional order of schooling.

A second case further illustrates how students integrate external digital discourses into their school interactions, but with different consequences. During a history lesson in School No. 2, the teacher assigned work on the topic of the Vikings. At the back of the classroom, a group of boys who typically did not participate began browsing YouTube, searching for their own information. When the teacher later reviewed the task, these students contributed answers about runes and Germanic mythology—responses that exceeded the assignment's requirements. Although the teacher acknowledged them with a nod, he did not integrate their contributions into the structured discussion. The boys, however, remained unperturbed. In an informal conversation afterward, they explained that the topic genuinely interested them, that they had deep knowledge from online sources, and that they sought to assert this knowledge despite the teacher's lack of recognition. Their insistence that runes were important because Germanic and Slavic mythologies were part of "cultural heritage" further emphasizes how extra-institutional epistemologies circulate within the classroom. Here, Gee and Green's identity building is at work. The boys positioned themselves as knowledgeable outsiders, drawing cultural legitimacy not from curricular validation but from online epistemic communities that valorize mythological knowledge as heritage.

Taken together, these cases illuminate the shifting epistemic terrain of postdigital schooling. Authority is no longer monopolized by institutional scripts but is constantly contested by alternative articulations that students import from digital networks. In Laclau's terms, this produces antagonisms around empty signifiers such as "*truth*," "*heritage*," and "*knowledge*," which are redefined through competing logics of digital and cultural. The school's pedagogical routines attempt to stabilize meaning by privileging correct answers and minimizing deviation, but the proliferation of external epistemologies undermines this stability, exposing the fragility of institutional authority. From Fraser's (2009) perspective, these dynamics reflect a dual axis of maldistribution and misrecognition. Students' contributions are excluded from curricular legitimacy (maldistribution of epistemic resources) while their identities as knowers are devalued (misrecognition).

What emerges is a paradoxical configuration. On the one hand, the classroom remains anchored in standardized procedures that reward compliance and constrain inquiry. On the other, students increasingly mobilize external epistemologies that challenge the legitimacy of curricular knowledge, whether through the empiricist verification logics of digital culture or through cultural claims rooted in alternative discourses. These practices signal not a simple decline of school authority but a transformation of the epistemic field itself, where schooling functions less as the sole arbiter of knowledge and more as one arena within a broader, contested ecology of truth production.

A closer analysis reveals that the students' discursive construction of their experience aligns with broader rhetorical patterns prevalent in right-wing digital discourse, particularly the valorization of cultural heritage through selective historical motifs. Their emphasis on runes and Germanic mythology, positioned alongside Slavic mythology as central to "authentic" culture, reflects a mode of knowledge validation that bypasses institutional criteria and draws authority from ideologically saturated online communities. This moment illustrates the increasingly complex epistemic landscape of the classroom, in which school knowledge must compete with culturally and politically charged narratives circulating in digital spaces. In such contexts, students' meaning-making is shaped by hybrid frameworks in which Internet culture plays a central role in establishing truth claims. For educators, this creates a dual challenge. Confronting resistance to institutional authority while addressing the growing influence of extra-institutional, ideologically embedded discourses that destabilize traditional hierarchies of knowledge. Ultimately, this dynamic signals a broader crisis in educational authority, as the locus of epistemic legitimacy shifts from the school to the digitally mediated public sphere.

Participant observation in both schools and digital spaces reveals a significant shift in how students construct knowledge, blending academic and Internet-based discourses in ways that undermine traditional epistemic hierarchies. Students increasingly treat school-based and digital knowledge as interchangeable, drawing from a wide array of ideological and rhetorical sources without necessarily recognizing disciplinary boundaries. This fluid engagement disrupts the authority of institutional education, replacing it with a decentralized and algorithmically curated knowledge decorum.

Students admitted that they prefer learning from YouTube or TikTok videos and animations. They shared historical animations and animated lectures, which they described as more engaging and aesthetically appealing than traditional classroom materials. One example frequently mentioned were animations depicting the Battle of Vienna, where dramatic visuals and concise narration transformed historical content into a compelling spectacle. Such preferences point to a broader shift in how learning is experienced. Digital media are not simply supplementary resources but primary sites where students negotiate, and evaluate knowledge.

The three TikTok videos analyzed here illustrate this process clearly. They do not merely transmit information about the past. They construct and perform what it means to learn history. In this sense, learning is less a neutral act of receiving facts than a discursive practice embedded in cultural and political struggles. Following Gee and Green's (1998) matrix it becomes possible to trace how learning is enacted differently across these short films and their comment threads. What is at stake in these exchanges is not only the interpretation of seventeenth-century events but also the very definition of learning itself.

The first video is particularly revealing because most of the epistemic work takes place not in the images or captions, but in the comment section. Here users reimagine Poland's geopolitical position. Should

Sobieski have turned against Prussia? Was an alliance with the Ottoman Empire possible? Was the real threat Austria rather than Turkey? In these exchanges, learning is constructed as a form of debate, a collective act of reopening questions that in the classroom are usually closed. The world that is built is one of contingency and possibility, and not chronology. The activity is speculation and argument, not memorization. Participants position themselves as independent and sometimes oppositional subjects—"*I said this at school and was shut down*"—which is to say, learning is also an act of identity building against the authority of teachers. Connections to the present are explicit. Seventeenth-century alliances are weighed in light of today's international politics. In this mode, learning appears not as the passive reception of facts but as the discursive testing of alternative narratives.

The second video offers a stark contrast. It constructs learning as immersion in a patriotic myth. AI-generated images of Sobieski and the hussars, combined with martial music and declarative captions, leave little space for debate. The world here is one of civilization defended and Europe saved. The activity is receptive: to learn is to watch, feel, admire. The learner's identity is fashioned through interpellation. One is invited to see oneself as the descendant of heroes, charged with carrying forward their virtues. Connections between past and present are direct and moralizing. The victory at Vienna becomes a template for contemporary patriotism. In this configuration, learning means recognizing and internalizing a national lesson. It is a construction that echoes the formative role long attributed to schooling in Poland, where history functions not only as information but as moral pedagogy (Dudzikowa, 2001).

The third set of materials shows how these two constructions collide. The video itself adopts the same heroic tone as the second, but the comments refuse closure. Users raise questions about whether the battle truly served Poland's interests, whether Austria was ever a trustworthy ally, or whether the outcome should be regarded as a betrayal. The result is a hybrid discursive space. On the one hand, the video advances a mythic and affective pedagogy. On the other, the comment section re-opens the field for negotiation. Learning here is doubled. It is at once absorption of patriotic narrative and its contestation through dialogue. This hybridity illustrates the postdigital condition, in which the same platform circulates authoritative myths and their subversions in a single communicative environment.

Taken together, these cases demonstrate that learning itself is unstable and contested. In the videos, it is equated with identification, however in the comments, it is reframed as speculation and critique. Neither version is definitive, Both circulate simultaneously. To borrow Laclau's (1996) vocabulary, *learning* functions as an empty signifier that is constantly filled with different meanings: moral pedagogy, critical debate, patriotic inheritance, ironic counter-narration. No single articulation closes the field. This instability reflects a broader erosion of pedagogical authority. Schools no longer monopolize the power to define what it means to learn; learners encounter rival constructions daily, embedded in the cultural logics of digital platforms.

This raises significant implications for educational research. To treat learning as neutral acquisition is to miss how it is discursively produced and contested. In the analyzed material, young people position themselves in multiple ways. Sometimes they see themselves as heirs of Sobieski, sometimes as revisionists who claim to know better than their teachers. They may be also ironic participants in meme-like debates. The same discursive strategies that open space for critique can also reinforce exclusionary or nationalist worldviews. What is needed is an account of learning that recognizes its ambivalence. It is simultaneously reproduction and resistance, absorption and appropriation.

The TikTok examples make visible what is often obscured in classroom settings. Learning as an ongoing discursive struggle. Through the discursive space, learners engage with history not as a settled record but as a terrain on which meanings are continually fought over. In the postdigital environment, learning does not simply involve the acquisition of knowledge. It entails inhabiting and negotiating the discourses through which knowledge and identity are produced.

At the same time, these practices intersect with a broader ideological formation that has come to dominate educational discourse: the valorization of autonomous learning. This notion is organized around the mentioned before empty signifier "*needs*," which, as Laclau (2005) suggests, gains persuasive force by appearing universally valid while concealing its ideological function. In contemporary education policy and practice, "*needs*" are invoked to legitimate a shift from collective, curriculum-based instruction toward individualized, interest-driven pathways. What is naturalized in this move is not simply learner agency but a neoliberal logic of responsibilization. The learner is expected to identify their own educational needs, becoming an entrepreneur of the self. Within this framework emerges what may be described as the discourse of the sovereign of knowledge, in which learners are imagined as self-sufficient agents fully accountable for their educational trajectories.

The changing epistemic landscape of digital learning has attracted significant scholarly attention, particularly with regard to how students engage with knowledge in the postdigital era. As participant research demonstrates, many students construct meaning less through sustained analysis of curricular content than through affective identification with binary oppositions. The recurring "rich versus poor" dichotomy exemplifies this dynamic, functioning as a simplified lens through which students interpret social complexity. This mode of sense-making mirrors what Laclau (2005) identifies as the populist logic of equivalence. Heterogeneous grievances and positions are condensed into antagonistic camps, producing clarity through opposition. The appeal of this framing lies in its affective immediacy. It provides students with narratives that feel both morally charged and self-evident, while circumventing the slower, more ambiguous processes of critical engagement fostered by school knowledge.

Within classrooms, challenges to moral and epistemic authority often emerge not as reasoned debates but as affectively charged assertions that draw upon the oppositional logics circulating in online populism. Here, digital culture does not simply provide content but reconfigures the epistemic modes through which students participate in knowledge construction. A telling instance occurred during a discussion about Agnieszka Holland's film *Green Border* in School No. 2. None of the students had seen the film, but nearly all voiced strong condemnation, framing it as "*an attack on Poland*," "*an insult to Poles*," and "*an effort to damage the nation's international reputation*." When prompted to reflect on the narrative itself, their responses bypassed the humanitarian dimensions of migration and instead mobilized national-security frames: "*You can't let everyone in; this is a hybrid war. These people aren't coming here to work*" (IC_S_School_2).

Such responses articulate an epistemic closure in which engagement with certain issues is foreclosed before it can begin. The refusal to watch the film, justified on the grounds that there was "*nothing to learn*" from it, exemplifies what Nguyen (2020) conceptualizes as an echo chamber. This is an epistemic environment that not only filters information but actively discredits dissenting perspectives, reinforcing loyalty to the dominant narrative. The effect in the classroom is that inquiry is short-circuited, as students position themselves as guardians of a nationalized moral order. They cannot see themselves as learners exploring contested realities.

In Gee and Green's (1998) terms, what is at stake here is identity building. Students construct themselves as defenders of the nation, policing the boundaries of what can be said and known in school. This self-positioning is affectively sustained by discourses encountered on TikTok and other social media platforms, where irony frames critiques of national heroism or Poland's geopolitical role as insults to collective identity. The affective pull of such discourse intensifies students' sensitivity to perceived slights against Polishness, producing a defensive epistemic stance that privileges loyalty over learning.

What appears as classroom pragmatics is thus better understood as the circulation of populist logics within the micro-politics of schooling. Through Laclau's lens, "*the nation*" operates as an empty signifier, capable of condensing diverse anxieties—about borders, migration, sovereignty, or recognition—into a singular antagonism: the defense of Poland against external and internal enemies. The pedagogical consequence is a narrowing of epistemic horizons, where engagement with curricular material is subordinated to the affective reproduction of national identity. In this sense, digital populism does not merely supplement school learning. It reshapes the very conditions under which knowledge is recognized as legitimate or excluded as threatening.

Students do not merely passively consume social media content curated by algorithmic processes. They also actively shape their own digital environments, filtering out perspectives they find disagreeable. Unlike older generations, who still engage in open comment sections or platforms like Reddit, younger students retreat into closed spaces such as Discord or Messenger groups. Within these networks ideological content circulates without exposure to external critique. In these contexts, students follow TikTokers or YouTubers not only as entertainers but as epistemic authorities, figures who provide guidance on how to interpret contemporary reality. Trust is transferred from institutional knowledge to influencer-based knowledge, however it is always mediated by algorithmic selection and group curation, producing what Nguyen (2020) calls echo chambers: epistemic communities that both amplify and immunize beliefs.

The empirical material resonates with studies on right-wing digital discourse (Staykova et al., 2016), where themes such as anti-immigration, ethnic identity, and rejection of progressive gender policies dominate.

These discourses operate not merely as informational resources but as mechanisms of political identification. Laclau's (2005) analysis of populism clarifies how such identity formations are created. Diverse social anxieties are aggregated around antagonisms with a common adversary—"*the elites*," "*the West*," or "liberals." Empty signifiers such as "*the nation*," "*freedom*," or "*truth*" serve to unite otherwise disparate grievances under a shared symbolic horizon. When students in classrooms discuss migration, abortion, or Poland's role in Europe, their arguments—often citing TikTok—exemplify this logic. Social media does not simply supplement school knowledge. It offers students a parallel epistemic order, one they position as more authentic than curricular content.

The construction of this "authenticity" is particularly significant. Several TikTokers, indicated by students, present their content as knowledge suppressed by the school system, positioning themselves as guardians of truths deliberately excluded from curricula. For students, engaging with this material becomes an anti-establishment act, a performative rejection of institutional authority. Within Gee and Green's (1998) framework, this represents a distinct form of identity building. Students construct themselves as bearers of hidden truths, staging their classroom interventions as epistemic challenges to teachers. These interventions are not necessarily grounded in critical inquiry. They reproduce the populist logics of exclusion and boundary-making. What is learned is less a set of facts than a mode of positioning oneself against institutionalized knowledge.

This becomes evident in discussions on migration. Students readily cite TikTok-originated claims about welfare fraud, and economic migrants. Even when acknowledging that such information comes from the Internet, they grant it unqualified credibility. The appeal lies not in evidentiary rigor but in the aura of subversiveness. The claim to possess knowledge "*they don't want you to know*" (S_IC_School_2). In this sense, social media knowledge functions as an epistemic commodity—marketed as exclusive and oppositional to official school knowledge. But rather than opening deliberative space, this form of knowledge solidifies ideological boundaries. The performance of learning is entangled with the performance of resistance, where adopting certain discourses signals belonging to a community defined not by inquiry but by antagonism.

The blending of digital epistemologies with school learning is reshaping how young people understand knowledge. In a postdigital world, where Internet discourses compete with formal education, students no longer see academic knowledge as inherently authoritative. Instead, they construct their own epistemic hierarchies, often privileging social media over institutional learning. This challenges traditional models of education, demanding new approaches to critical pedagogy that acknowledge the realities of digital epistemology while resisting the commodification of knowledge within populist frameworks. Young people are subjected to the same mechanisms of populist and anti-establishment mobilization as adults in online spaces. What distinguishes them, however, is that Internet-driven populism does not only position itself against political elites but also fosters resistance to school-based knowledge, turning that resistance into an anti-elitist act. For many students, school knowledge is not perceived as "real" knowledge but rather as an imposed system designed to serve the interests of the ruling elite (S_IC_School_1). The instrumentalized, test-oriented nature of school learning reinforces this perception—education becomes a game of survival rather than an authentic intellectual pursuit. Teachers, often seen as messengers of the state and enforcers of a bureaucratic curriculum, are equated with politicians and governmental figures who dictate what students must learn (S_IC_School_1; S_IC_School_1).

This distrust of school knowledge becomes particularly visible in the ways students construct and affirm their national identity within digital environments. Epistemologies perceived as undermining national unity are systematically excluded from their interpretive frameworks, while identity formation takes place within tightly controlled echo chambers. Most of the social media accounts students recommended to me as "teaching history" presented a singular, unchallenged perspective. Successive videos carried identical hashtags—*#chrzescijanstwo* (*#Christianity*), *#polska* (*#Poland*), *#polacy* (*#Poles*), *#dumanarodowa* (*#nationalpride*), *#polscyzolnierze* (*#Polishsoldiers*), *#ulani* (*#uhlans*)—signaling a coherent ideological alignment, Critical discourse analysis revealed that the content of these accounts predominantly reflected a right-wing worldview, and employing historical narratives that reinforced nationalist pride while omitting alternative or contested interpretations.

Particularly striking was the aesthetic dimension, often enhanced through AI-generated imagery. Pivotal battles in Polish history, national heroes, and known figures were depicted in visual hyperbole, rendered with the grandeur of cinematic epics. Such representations amplified emotional and political engagement. Historical actors appeared not merely as figures of the past but as mythic heroes embodying timeless virtues. In informal conversations, students repeatedly told me that watching these videos made them "*feel proud to be Polish*" (S_IC_School_2)—a sentiment they explicitly contrasted with their experience of history lessons in school, where they reported never feeling the same sense of pride or connection. The contrast here reveals an important epistemological boundary. The classroom's commitment to factual accuracy and critical distance is experienced as emotionally flat, while digital media's dramatized historicism generates affective attachment and belonging.

From a discursive perspective, these practices illustrate what Laclau (2005) theorizes as the work of empty signifiers. Categories such as "*Poland*" or "*Poles*" operate as unifying symbols, aggregating disparate narratives of Christianity, military glory, and cultural heritage into a coherent, emotionally resonant identity. Within the students' digital environments, such signifiers acquire their authority not through rational debate or critical testing but through their affective charge, their capacity to mobilize pride and solidarity. In this sense, national identity becomes not a historical inquiry but an affectively sustained discursive project in which the exclusion of contesting perspectives is constitutive.

Gee' and Greens (1998) notion of world building is helpful here. Students construct an interpretive universe in which Poland is imagined as timeless and heroic, while activity building takes place through the ritualized acts of liking, sharing, and commenting on ideologically aligned content. These digital practices simultaneously reconfigure identity building, as students align themselves with a community of proud defenders of the nation against perceived external or internal threats. Importantly, this epistemic community is not pluralist but tightly bounded, operating according to logics of inclusion and exclusion that mirror both algorithmic filtering and nationalist discourse itself.

The privileging of visually mediated, affectively saturated narratives over the fragmented, critical, and multiperspectival forms of school knowledge reflects a deeper reconfiguration of epistemic legitimacy. As Rancière (1991) observed, schools often sustain their authority through the presumption of student ignorance. Here, students invert this hierarchy, positioning themselves as already knowing and the school as the site of ignorance or ideological concealment. This inversion, however, does not lead to emancipatory inquiry but to a different form of closure, reflected in a refusal of critique. In doing so, students redraw the boundaries of historical truth and national belonging within the parameters of digitally mediated, ideologically saturated discourse.

Postdigital reality no longer functions as a supplement to students' schooling. It has become an equivalent, and in many cases a significant, arena in which Polish youth engage with knowledge. This is particularly visible in the realm of national identity, where digital platforms circulate narratives that diverge sharply from those advanced in formal curricula. The tension was especially evident during my fieldwork, coinciding with the introduction of the History and the Present (HiT) curriculum by Minister Przemysław Czarnek. Designed to impose a standardized interpretation of Polish history from 1945 to 2015, HiT was widely criticized for its nationalist orientation and exclusionary ideological framing. While its aim was to consolidate a cohesive national narrative, students instead gravitated toward social media, where alternative historical accounts—often framed as "forbidden knowledge"—offered them both a sense of epistemic dissent and an avenue for anti-establishment identification.

The political shift following the October 15 elections, and the subsequent abolition of HiT as a mandatory subject, only intensified the contested nature of history education in Poland. In the classroom discussion students increasingly came to see school-based knowledge as even more politically motivated and detached from their own lived realities. Observations from this period indicate that digital platforms now serve as the principal spaces in which national identity is negotiated, shaped by personalized content feeds and ideologically selective curation. Within this environment, the authority of formal education is not simply questioned—it is actively reversed. School knowledge is recast by students as elitist propaganda, while digitally mediated epistemologies grounded in nationalism and populism gain legitimacy. This inversion marks not only a profound crisis of epistemic authority but also highlights the need for educational approaches capable of addressing misinformation while engaging with the modes of meaning-making that dominate students' digital worlds.

Analysis of the textbook content shows that the discourse of learning focuses primarily on the acquisition of national knowledge, with tools and teaching techniques designed less for inquiry than for the reinforcement of sanctioned narratives. Exercises require students to justify statements, argue in discussions, explain, and provide answers to questions, but the space for independent reasoning is curtailed by the fact that arguments are often already supplied within the materials. For instance, on page 20 of the *History and the Present* textbook, a photograph of the Ordynacja Krasińskich Library in Warsaw is accompanied by the inscription Amor Patria nostra lex. The instruction beneath it asks students to explain the attitude expressed by this motto and to consider why collections were gathered there, "*bearing in mind that at the time the library was established, Poles lived under partitions.*" On the following page, a propaganda poster from the Polish-Bolshevik War of 1920 is reproduced, accompanied by an exercise directing students to present its message within the interpretive frame that "*the communist internationalism of Bolshevik Russia clashed with the Poles' desire to build an independent national state*" (*History and the Present 1*, p. 21).

Such tasks position knowledge within a narrow discursive horizon. They do not invite students to interpret sources through open inquiry. They embed expected answers into the exercise itself, leaving students to reproduce what is already coded as legitimate. Even identity-oriented exercises, such as "*Explain what the statement 'I am local' means. Can you indicate a place where you feel like a local?*", function less as explorations of self and place than as ritual affirmations of belonging. In both HiT lessons—where the textbook was often avoided due to its perceived ideological bias—and traditional history lessons, students interpreted such exercises as tests of compliance. Their responses were pragmatic and unenthusiastic, delivered with the singular aim of meeting the formal requirement.

From a discourse-theoretical perspective, these tasks illustrate what Laclau (2005) terms the work of empty signifiers. Phrases such as "*Poles' desire for independence*" or "*I am local*" acquire their force not from critical interrogation but from their function as nodal points in a nationalist narrative. The exercises structure what Gee and Green (1998) would call world building. They create a discursive universe where the meaning of the past is pre-structured by national struggle, patriotism, and territorial belonging. In this setting, students are positioned not as interpreters but as confirmers of identity, required to articulate themselves within pre-authorized categories. The effect is what with reference to Rancière (1991) could be described as a pedagogy of explication, where the teacher (and, by extension, the textbook) presumes the ignorance of students and sets the boundaries of legitimate knowledge in advance. The student's task is not to question or produce knowledge but to demonstrate alignment with the sanctioned narrative. This explains the observed lack of enthusiasm. The exercises are less opportunities for intellectual discovery than performative rituals of national affirmation.

Students frequently distance themselves from this patriotic discourse, often mocking or parodying it. A telling example involved the use of a photograph of John Paul II in a student PowerPoint presentation, where the figure of the pope—promoted in school education as the emblematic "great Pole"—was as a meme that triggered laughter. Similar reaction was directed toward concepts heavily embedded in school discourse, such as Solidarity, democracy, communism, Lech Wałęsa or the parliament. Digital technologies provided students with a repertoire of remixing and irony that allowed them to destabilize national knowledge and reframe it as material for ridicule. On Messenger groups, students showed me circulated memes and jokes targeting official symbols and political figures, constructing alternative registers of meaning outside the classroom.

In this context, the construction of the learner's identity reveals a tension between the forms of national and civic knowledge promoted at school and the ways students actively re-appropriate or reject these same symbols in digital environments. The very semiotic resources employed in textbooks are displaced, re-entering student culture in parody, meme, and affective play. School spaces enforce solemnity and consensus, while social media afford arenas of selective re-signification, where knowledge is not simply consumed but remixed and contested.

From a discourse-theoretical perspective, the empty signifiers organizing the textbook discourse of Polishness—"*patriot*" and "*nation*"—fail to anchor student identification. Instead, they operate as what Laclau (2005) would describe as signifiers emptied of affective investment, assimilated within the Fordist logic of the knowledge factory. National knowledge is memorized as curricular output but stripped of symbolic force. The textbook's discourse situates Poland as something to be learned, while students situate it differently. They perceived it as something to be lived and felt in spaces not accessible to the school.

This distinction was evident in informal conversations with students, who expressed genuine interest in Poland but resisted associating the knowledge they valued with school learning. The term itself was reserved for the procedural, test-oriented work of schooling. By contrast, their engagement with Polishness—whether through digital reconstructions of history, mythologies shared in online communities, or affective attachments forged through memes and cultural narratives—was articulated as self-discovery and never as education. In this divergence, I see the formation of parallel epistemic processes. There is the institutional economy of national knowledge that scripts identity through repetition, and the student-led economy of digital circulation, where symbols are re-appropriated and mocked with alternative meanings.

Affective identification is the most visible mechanism in the discourse of digital media. Much of the content indicated by students themselves—and observed on their phones during participant research—centered on Polish history. One illustrative example was a multi-part TikTok post devoted to Tadeusz Kościuszko. Although much of the footage came from the public broadcaster TVP Historia, the clips were reframed with memes, infographics, and commentary to heighten their affective appeal. Kościuszko was portrayed not primarily as a historical figure embedded in the complexities of eighteenth-century geopolitics, but as an exceptional Pole whose personal traits and achievements symbolized the virtues of the nation. Users' comments repeatedly complained that such stories were absent from schools, questioning whether teachers deliberately suppressed this "real" knowledge.

Through the lens of Gee and Green's (1998) framework, these practices constitute more than entertainment. They are discursive acts of identity, world, activity, and connection building. The Kościuszko videos positioned him as a mirror of the Polish character (identity building). The videos framed history as a moral struggle between nations (world building). They embedded the act of sharing and remixing into youth cultural practices (activity building), and linked individuals into imagined digital communities via hashtags (connection building). Such multimodal practices illustrate how young people actively participate in the rearticulation of history as a lived identity project rather than as curricular content.

The affective and symbolic coherence of these practices resonates with Laclau's (2005) theorization of populist logic. Figures such as Kościuszko, or in other contexts the Cursed Soldiers, function as empty signifiers. Their symbolic force derives not from historical complexity but from their capacity to unify affective investments and organize identity around national pride. The result is a populist condensation in which historical figures become containers of affect.

This dynamic stands in sharp contrast to the textbook-based pedagogy observed in schools. Textbooks also deploy empty signifiers—*patriot, nation, freedom*—but within a Fordist framework that reduces them to memorized units for assessment. History is fragmented into disconnected tasks and evaluation points, producing what Hobsbawm and Ranger (1983) called "invented traditions". The context-free rituals of repetition that sustain authority through form rather than meaning. In the digital domain, by contrast, history is also fragmented into TikTok videos, but the effect is affective amplification and commodification. Historical content is repackaged as consumable spectacle, its narrative coherence secured less by historical accuracy than by emotional intensity. Both the textbook and the digital remix operate through simplification and ritualization, however they diverge in their affective force: where the textbook evokes compliance, the TikTok post cultivates pride and belonging.

Taken together, the discoursive perspective allow us to see how these two epistemic infrastructures—schooling and social media—mirror each other. Both fragment and ritualize history, both are organized around similar empty signifiers. While the schoolbook organizes knowledge through the procedural logic of conformity, the digital post organizes it through the populist logic of affective identification. TikTok creators styling themselves as "truth-tellers," claiming to reveal "what schools won't teach you," explicitly position themselves against institutional authority, drawing legitimacy from their proximity to "the people." In this sense, the digital circulation of historical figures is not simply an alternative pedagogy but an alternative politics of knowledge. Consequently, students' learning becomes inseparable from the populist construction of identity. In this sense, the online environments students inhabit resemble what Nancy Fraser (1990) describes as counterpublics—parallel discursive arenas where subordinated groups produce and circulate counternarratives that contest dominant public spheres. Excluded from the authoritative version of history and identity advanced in school, young people increasingly locate their epistemic and political affiliations in these digital counterpublics, where belonging is forged through algorithmic curation and a shared rejection of institutional authority.

Mouffe's (2005) account of politics as an agonistic field of competing hegemonic projects further clarifies the stakes. In Poland's postdigital knowledge society, schooling represents one hegemonic project. It is characterized by an attempt to reproduce a rational-civic model of national identity grounded in institutional legitimacy. Digital populist discourse constitutes another, premised on affective mobilization and aestheticized narratives of belonging. To students caught between these poles, formal education often appears irrelevant—not because its content fails to meet curricular standards, but because its authority no longer commands recognition.

This is, at its core, a crisis of epistemic legitimacy. As Noack and Eckstein (2023) demonstrate in *Populism in Youth: Do Experiences in School Matter?*, students' sense of being heard and respected within school strongly correlates with their receptivity to populist narratives. Where institutional authority is experienced as unresponsive or alien to lived realities, populist counterpublics provide a readily available framework for knowledge. Returning to Fraser (2007), the school's failure to operate as an inclusive public sphere creates precisely the vacuum in which these counterpublics thrive.

In this light, populism functions not merely as a political style but as an epistemic order—an alternative architecture of meaning-making in which authority and legitimacy are negotiated through the aesthetics and affect of digital culture. The struggle over national identity and historical memory is thus not confined to textbooks or classrooms. It is enacted in algorithmic feeds, viral imagery, namely and the performative gestures of digital partisanship. For schools to remain relevant, they must confront this reality directly, engaging not only with the content of misinformation but with the communicative forms and affective economies through which students are already reimagining what counts as knowledge.

In the sphere of knowledge-building and the construction of learning discourses, class-based differences are evident across the student groups, though not in a strictly dichotomous manner between schools. Students in both institutions draw on heterogeneous repertoires of knowledge, but their capacity to contextualize what they encounter online is shaped by the resources available to them throughcultural background and social networks.

When I asked whether they questioned the accuracy of digital content, some students—often those with access to broader cultural capital—described triangulating between sources. One explained: "*Generally I agree, but I often talk with my dad about history; he has a lot of knowledge, he's really interested in it, and I learn a lot from him. He doesn't really agree with TikTok, says it's a Chinese app and that they're definitely spying on us. But yes, we talk about it*" (S_IC_2_School_2). Another highlighted the role of international podcasts in supplementing digital media: "*No, I don't just listen to one source, I compare different ones because I want to have my own opinion. I listen to different podcasts, not only Polish ones. Do you know Hardcore History? I listen to that too*" (S_IC_

2_School_2). Such examples show how some students, while consuming the same TikTok streams as their peers, integrate additional references that expand their interpretive repertoires. In Gee's terms (2014), they mobilize several building tasks at once: world building (framing history as contested), identity building (claiming a position of autonomy), and connection building (linking local and transnational perspectives). These practices echo Bourdieu's notion of habitus, where class resources extend what counts as credible knowledge and how it is contextualized.

At the same time, many students framed their responses in more affective and reactive ways. Asked about alternative references, one student remarked:

> S: *"Of course not everything we like, we want to have our own opinion. For example, I don't like how non-binary people are presented, and I always say it out loud."*
> R: *"And what do you refer to in order to express your opinion?"*
> S: *"I don't know, are you asking about books? ... I don't think so." (S_IC_1_School_1)*

Here, the building task of identity construction ("*having my own opinion*") is emphasized, but without a strong world or connection building. The absence of alternative repertoires means critique remains at the level of impression. It is not a structured comparison. This does not mean such students are passive. However their practices are constrained by the limited epistemic repertoires embedded in their social environments.

Through Laclau's (2005) lens, both groups negotiate the same populist signifiers—"*Poland*," "*nation*," "*tradition*"—but articulate them differently. For some, these signifiers can be relativized and set against transnational discourses. For others, they operate as immediate markers of belonging, closed to contestation. In both cases, the signifiers function as empty containers filled with affective charge, anchoring students' sense of identity in ways that echo the populist logic of equivalence.

Importantly, neither group named the school as a significant source of epistemic authority. For those with high cultural capital, school knowledge seemed redundant beside family expertise or global podcasts. For those with fewer resources, school provided little support to transform affective stances into comparative critique. Thus, the institution does not disrupt the closure of populist signifiers nor support the full range of Gee's building tasks.

In this way, digital infrastructures do not equalize learning but intensify class-based inequalities. Access to the same TikTok feeds or YouTube channels does not produce the same epistemic practices, because what students can do with this content depends on broader social conditions.

It is important to note, however, that alongside class-based differences in learning practices, there were also areas where students—regardless of background—reacted in remarkably similar ways, suspending verification or critical scrutiny. A striking example during fieldwork was the case of Andrew Tate, whose figure provoked particularly intense discussion among boys. Their positions were uncompromising. They defended him with passion, expressed a strong sense of injustice regarding his portrayal in mainstream media, and articulated their views with emotional intensity and unwavering loyalty. In conversations, they repeatedly stressed that this was the issue from which they had "l*earned the most*."

A particularly telling situation took place during an off-site event involving School No. 2. "During Democracy Day, students participated in an event at a cultural institution. At the end of the event, everyone was invited on stage to take a group photo. When the young people came on stage, we saw that the boys had arranged their hands in the so-called Tate hands, that is, resting their hands in front of their abdomen or chest with the fingertips touching the index fingers to form a triangular shape. Most of the adults, including me, didn't know at first what was going on or how to react. One of the teachers confirmed that it was Andrew Tate's symbol. None of the adults reacted or commented on the situation. The photo was taken. The next day at school, I tried to ask the students why they did it, but I only found out that it was important to them. No one wanted to talk to me about Andrew Tate" [field note_School No. 2_18.09.2023]. This suggests that in the postdigital environment, learning can no longer be fully understood as the acquisition of information but must be analyzed as the affective and discursive constitution of subjectivity.

The case of Andrew Tate illustrates how learning in the postdigital environment is driven less by rational verification than by affective attachment and the construction of identity within discourse. The boys' uncompromising defense of Tate, their strong sense of injustice, and their insistence that they had "*learned the most*" from this controversy reveal how affect functions as a central mechanism of meaning-making.

In Laclau's (2005) terms, Tate operates as a nodal point around which heterogeneous frustrations are condensed, providing a unifying discourse of resistance to perceived elites and hostile media. The students' affective investment transforms learning into a process of identification, where knowledge is less about facts or evidence and more about belonging, loyalty, and solidarity. What emerges, then, is a form of learning that is deeply populist its logic: the subject is constituted not through critical engagement with multiple perspectives, but through affective alignment with a discourse that positions itself against an antagonistic "other."

The mechanized subject, shaped by the proceduralism of standardized assessment, the disciplining gaze of surveillance of digital platforms, embodies the fusion of human learning with machinic control. Within this apparatus, reversive knowledge emerges. It is expressed in inversions and parodies of school-sanctioned content that redirect its meaning toward alternative epistemic projects. These reversals expose the instability of pedagogical authority, revealing that control is never absolute and that meaning-making remains contested. Their ambivalence, however, is critical. The same strategies that unsettle exclusion can equally sustain reactionary worldviews, as seen in the impassioned defense of Andrew Tate by male students, whose affective investments transformed his figure into a nodal point of identity and belonging. Here, learning unfolds less through verification than through emotional alignment, echoing Laclau's account of collective identities articulated around empty signifiers. What emerges is the postdigital collapse of boundaries between institutional and extra-institutional knowledge, where legitimacy is no longer secured by schools but negotiated across classrooms, peer networks, and algorithmic publics. For critical pedagogy, the challenge is not only to resist this collapse but to inhabit it. It requires engaging the contradictory ways students reconfigure learning through solidarity and antagonism and recognizing that subjectivity is produced as much through these contested architectures of knowledge as through their disruption.

References

Abrams, A. (2023). *Shortchanged: How advanced placement cheats students*. John Hopkins University Press.

Au, W. (2011). Teaching under the new Taylorism: High-stakes testing and the standardization of the 21st century curriculum. *Journal of Curriculum Studies, 43*(1), 25–45. https://doi.org/10.1080/00220272.2010.521261

Ashcroft, B., Griffiths, G., & Tiffin, H. (1995). *The post-colonial studies reader*. Routledge.

Biesta, G. (2017). *The rediscovery of teaching*. Routledge.

Britzman, D. P. (1998). *Lost subjects, contested objects: Toward a psychoanalytic inquiry of learning*. State University of New York Press.

Brown, M. (1992). Ford factory learning. In M. Brown, F. Oatrick, D. Tate, & S. Wright (Comps.), *A collection of readings related to competency-based training* (pp. 393–397).

Brown, P., Lauder, H., & Ashton, D. (2011). *The global auction: The broken promises of education, jobs, and incomes*. Oxford University Press.

Couldry, N., & Mejias, U. A. (2019). *The costs of connection: How data is colonizing human life and appropriating it for capitalism*. Stanford, CA: Stanford University Press.

Dolata, R., & Sitek, M. (Eds.). (2015). *Raport o stanie edukacji 2014: Egzaminy zewnętrzne w polityce i praktyce edukacyjnej*. Instytut Badań Edukacyjnych.

Dole, S., Bloom, L., & Kowalske, K. (2016). Transforming pedagogy: Changing perspectives from teacher-centered to learner-centered. *Interdisciplinary Journal of Problem-Based Learning, 10*(1). https://doi.org/10.7771/1541-5015.1538

Dudzikowa, M. (2001). *Mit o szkole jako miejscu wszechstronnego rozwoju*. Eseje etnopedagogiczne. Impuls.

Foucault, M. (2007). *Security, territory, population: Lectures at the Collège de France, 1977–1978* (G. Burchell, Trans.; M. Senellart, Ed.). Palgrave Macmillan.

Fraser, N. (1990). Rethinking the public sphere: A contribution to the critique of actually existing democracy. *Social Text, 25/26*, 56–80

Fraser, N., & Honneth, A. (2003). *Redistribution or recognition?: A political-philosophical exchange*. Verso.

Fraser, N. (2007). Transnational public sphere: Transnationalizing the public sphere: On the legitimacy and efficacy of public opinion in a post-Westphalian world. *Theory, Culture & Society, 24*(4), 7–30.

Fraser, N. (2009). *Scales of justice: Reimagining political space in a globalizing world* (Vol. 31). Columbia University Press.

Gee, J. P., & Green, J. L. (1998). Chapter 4: Discourse analysis, learning, and social practice: A methodological study. *Review of research in education, 23*(1), 119–169.

Gobby, B., Keddie, A., & Blackmore, J. (2018). Professionalism and competing responsibilities: Moderating competitive performativity in school autonomy reform. *Journal of Educational Administration and History, 50*(2), 141–154. https://doi.org/10.1080/00220620.2017.1399864

Gromkowska-Melosik, A. (2015). Orientacja na testy w szkolnictwie współczesnym–Kontrowersje ideologiczne i pedagogiczne. *Studia Edukacyjne, 36*, 19–32.
Hanushek, E. A. (2019). Testing, accountability, and the American economy. *The ANNALS of the American Academy of Political and Social Science, 683*(1), 110–128. https://doi.org/10.1177/0002716219841299
Haraway, D. (2013). A cyborg manifesto: Science, technology, and socialist-feminism in the late twentieth century. In *The transgender studies reader* (pp. 103–118). Routledge.
Hobsbawm, E. J., & Ranger, T. (Eds.). (1983). *The invention of tradition*. Cambridge University Press.
Ito, M., Gutiérrez, K., Livingstone, S., Penuel, W., Rhodes, J, Salen, K., Schor, J., Sefton-Green, J. & Watkins, C. (2013). *Connected Learning: An Agenda for Research and Design*. Irvine, CA: The Digital Media and Learning Research Hub Reports on Connected Learning.
Jerrim, J., Morgan, A., & Sims, S. (2023). Teacher autonomy: Good for pupils? Good for teachers? *British Educational Research Journal, 49*(1), 15–35. https://doi.org/10.1002/berj.3892
Jessop, B. (2002). *The future of the capitalist state*. Polity Press.
Klus-Stańska, D. (2012). Wiedza, która zniewala–transmisyjne tradycje w szkolnej edukacji. In *Forum oświatowe* (Vol. 24, No. 1 (46), pp. 21–40).
Klus-Stańska, D. (2020). Konstruktywizm edukacyjny–niejednoznaczność, kontrowersje, dylematy. *Problemy Wczesnej Edukacji, 16*(4 (51)), 7–20.
Kopciewicz, L. (2019). Szkolne technolęki. Jak nauczyciele rozumieją rolę i skutki obecności technologii mobilnych w szkolnej przestrzeni. *Teraźniejszość–Człowiek–Edukacja, 22*(1 (85)), 51–64.
Kopciewicz, L. (2020). Oblicza reformy szkolnej–technologiczne praktyki równościowego uczenia się. *Czas Kultury, 36*(01), 39–48.
Laclau, E. (1996). The death and resurrection of the theory of ideology. *Journal of political ideologies, 1*(3), 201–220.
Laclau, E. (2005). *On populist reason*. Verso.
Medina, J. (2013). *The epistemology of resistance: Gender and racial oppression, epistemic injustice, and resistant imaginations*. Oxford University Press.
Mouffe, C. (2005). Politics and the political. *On the Political*, 8–34.
Nguyen, C. T. (2020). Echo chambers and epistemic bubbles. *Episteme, 17*(2), 141–161. https://doi.org/10.1017/epi.2018.32
Noack, P., & Eckstein, K. (2023). Populism in youth: Do experiences in school matter? *Child Development Perspectives, 17*(2), 90–96. https://doi.org/10.1111/cdep.12481
Nussbaum, M. C. (2010). *Not for profit: Why democracy needs the humanities*. Princeton University Press.

Özhan, Ş. Ç., Tekeli, P., & Altun, A. (2024). Investigating the role of cognitive flexibility in shaping teacher engagement in a simulated virtual classroom. In *INTED2024 Proceedings* (pp. 6475–6480). IATED. https://doi.org/10.21125/inted.2024.1697

Perera, S. (2015). Visibility, atrocity and the subject of postcolonial justice. *Borderlands e-Journal, 14*(1), 1–27.

Peters, M. A., Besley, T., & Jandrić, P. (2018). Postdigital knowledge cultures and their politics. *ECNU Review of Education, 1*(2), 23–43. https://doi.org/10.30926/ecnuroe2018010202

Pyżalski, J. (Ed.). (2025). *Generatywna sztuczna inteligencja w polskiej szkole: Przecieranie szlaków. Badania ilościowe i jakościowe nauczycieli klas 4–8 szkół podstawowych.* NASK – Państwowy Instytut Badawczy.

Rancière, J. (1991). *The ignorant schoolmaster: Five lessons in intellectual emancipation* (K. Ross, Trans.). Stanford University Press.

Sahlberg, P. (2016). The global educational reform movement and its impact on schooling. In K. Mundy, A. Green, B. Lingard, & A. Verger (Eds.), *The handbook of global education policy* (pp. 128–144). Wiley-Blackwell.

Selwyn, N. (2014). *Distrusting educational technology: Critical questions for changing times.* Routledge

Sullivan, S., & Tuana, N. (Eds.). (2007). *Race and epistemologies of ignorance.* State University of New York Press.

Spivak, G. C. (1999). *A critique of postcolonial reason: Toward a history of the vanishing present.* Harvard University Press.

Staykova, E., Otova, I., & Ivanova, V. (2016). Anti-elitism as a populist strategy of defending 'the people'. In *Populism, media and education* (pp. 105–123). Routledge.

Szkudlarek, T., & Zamojski, P. (2020). Education and ignorance: Between the noun of knowledge and the verb of thinking. *Studies in Philosophy and Education, 39*, 577–590. https://doi.org/10.1007/s11217-020-09718-9

Vianna, E. (2013). *Absences and epistemologies of ignorance: A critical multi-sited study on the teaching of the Danish colonial and slave trading past.* The City University of New York.

Zalewska, E. (2015). Porównywanie wyników testów egzaminacyjnych. *Wiadomości Statystyczne. the Polish Statistician, 60*(12), 70–81.

CHAPTER 5

CEE Postdigital Knowledge Societies and Education

The postdigital knowledge society is characterized by the collapse of boundaries between digital and social life, reshaping how knowledge is produced and legitimized. What was once framed as "using technology" now constitutes the very fabric of students' everyday learning practices. The platforms they inhabit, the algorithms that recommend content, and the devices through which they communicate all blur the line between formal schooling and informal knowledge-making. For learners, this collapse does not appear as an abstract societal shift but as a daily negotiation of authority and meaning. They move between textbooks and YouTube tutorials, teachers' instructions and algorithmic suggestions, exam preparation and social media debates. To speak of a postdigital knowledge society, then, is not only to describe macro-level infrastructures but also to recognize how these infrastructures permeate the micro-practices of learning, shaping what students count as knowledge and which identities they construct in the process.

Chapter 2 showed how institutional discourse narrows learning to task performance—learning-as-labor, survival, necessity, and a thin autonomy—while surveillance platforms and competency talk secure this order under the sign of modernization. The effect is not transformation but selective adaptation. Digital tools brighten the surface while leaving pedagogical hierarchies intact.

M. Popow, *Learning in the Postdigital Knowledge Society*, Palgrave Studies in Educational Media,
https://doi.org/10.1007/978-3-032-21956-5_5

Chapter 3 traced the subjectivities produced inside that field. The mechanized learner is calibrated to standardized outputs. The responsibilized "autonomous" learner and reversive practices redirect institutional demands without guaranteeing emancipation. AI and platform governance do not displace the regime. They intensify its predictability and pace.

This chapter takes those findings as its starting point. Its concern is not whether schools "use technology," but how postdigital infrastructures organize knowledge. What is recognized as valid, how authority is allocated, and which epistemologies are excluded? It treats digital systems as dispositifs that regulate participation and legitimacy, while asking where counter-hegemonic work might be done under conditions of parity of participation that require both recognition and redistribution.

The postdigital knowledge society should not be understood solely as a macro-discursive formation imposed on schools from above. It is also a dynamic condition co-constituted through everyday pedagogical practices, including institutional routines and student engagements. As Jandrić et al. (2018) emphasize, the postdigital is not reducible to a toolkit of devices or applications. It denotes a socio-material condition in which the digital and the social are inseparably entangled. This duality means that the knowledge society is simultaneously structured by global infrastructures of platform capitalism, governance, and datafication (Knox, 2019; Williamson, 2017), while also being reshaped through the micro-practices of learners who negotiate algorithmic publics, school policies, formal learning requirements and peer digital interactions in their everyday lives. As Selwyn (2022) reminds us, education is not a passive recipient of technological change but an active site in which digital society is reproduced.

The postdigital condition does not simply add technology to schooling. It rewrites the very coordinates within which schooling is thinkable. Digital infrastructures seep into pedagogy and administration alike, shaping rhythms of work, attention, and temporality. What is advertised as "enhancement" or "efficiency" often installs a market rationality that configures students as entrepreneurial subjects, responsibilized to manage their own performance, while positioning teachers as operatives within systems of control and reporting. The architecture of datafication—inclusing learning analytics and algorithmic tracking—folds teaching into routines of surveillance and accountability, naturalizing the assumption that educational value can be captured through metrics (Knox, 2019; Williamson, 2017). Material conditions amplify these dynamics. Access remains uneven, infrastructures are fragile, and the data that circulate through them are never neutral. As Noble (2018) and Eubanks (2018) demonstrate algorithms may encode long-standing social biases, embedding patterns of exclusion into the very architectures of participation. To describe education as postdigital, then, is to recognize that the online/offline distinction no longer maps practice. Instead, data are interwoven with pedagogy across contexts (Fawns, 2022).

Technology has been central to the political and economic imaginary of the knowledge-based society from its very inception. Theorists such as Bell, Gouldner, Lyotard, Fukuyama, and Castells cast the rise of knowledge economies as a civilizational rupture. It was an epochal transition in which technological fluency would displace material labor as the primary sources of value and social organization (Fuller, 2006, p. 67). This narrative was not merely descriptive but prescriptive. It promised an order governed by intelligence rather than force, creativity rather than exploitation, and the circulation of ideas rather than the extraction of resources. As Fuller (2006, p. 29) reminds us, this celebratory framing consistently masked the commodification of knowledge and the massification of higher education—developments euphemistically recoded in managerial discourse as "knowledge management." For Fuller, such terminology functions as a kind of Orwellian narrative, depoliticizing the economic capture of knowledge while presenting it as neutral modernization. What had once been theorized as a shared resource essential to collective progress was gradually reframed as a strategic asset to be managed.

Seen against the wider political economy, this saturation coincides with what Fraser (2013) terms a redistributional crisis, in which responsibilities once borne by public institutions are displaced onto individuals and families—the "crisis of care" that shadows neoliberal restructuring. The platformization of learning sits squarely within this shift. Assessment and academic integrity are increasingly outsourced to commercial systems that monetize participation while narrowing the space for collective deliberation or democratic accountability. In parallel, the competitive state reorganizes schooling around knowledge as a strategic asset, aligning curriculum and evaluation with post-Fordist imperatives of productivity (Jessop, 2002, p. 22). Digitalization, from this perspective, is not a neutral delivery channel but a dispositif. This is an infrastructure that secures alignment with neoliberal logics by governing access, in the same time legitimating certain forms of knowledge, and circumscribing the possibilities of critical agency.

For students, these shifts mean that learning itself is increasingly recast as participation in data-driven marketplaces, where identities are shaped less through exploration, dialogue, or collective inquiry, and more through their capacity to align with metrics of performance. Participation becomes synonymous with visibility in metrics. A student is recognized insofar as their performance can be captured and compared. Recognition, once grounded in dialogic exchange or communal knowledge-building, is thus displaced by the performativity of numbers. Learning is reconfigured not as a shared project of meaning-making but as a continuous calibration of the self to data-driven norms—an economy of visibility in which educational subjectivities are governed as much by performance as by teachers and curricula.

The consequences for authority and knowledge are immediate. Classrooms are no longer insulated pedagogical spaces but nodes within transnational informational networks whose rules and protocols are determined elsewhere. Teachers, once positioned as interlocutors and intellectual authorities, are increasingly recast as data managers. They become administrators of preconfigured pathways, tasked with ensuring compliance with curricular assessment rubrics. Students, in turn, are interpellated as self-optimizing, perpetually upskilling subjects, evaluated by opaque algorithmic models that privilege what is easy to measure over what is educationally or ethically worthwhile (Knox, 2019; Williamson, 2017). Knowledge itself undergoes a profound transformation. From an oriented toward public reasoning and critique, it becomes a commodified asset circulating under platform logics, where legitimacy and visibility are products of code. To describe digitality as a "tool" is thus misleading. Digital infrastructures exercise a governing force. They delineate which knowledges appear, how learning is structured, and whose voices are amplified. With the entrance of educational technologies comes a redistribution of epistemic authority. Control moves away from pedagogical judgment and democratic participation and toward commercial platforms and algorithmic rule (Eubanks, 2018; Fawns, 2022; Noble, 2018).

The postdigital knowledge society embodies a striking paradox. On the one hand, digital platforms promise decentralization and open opportunities for counter-hegemonic voices, enabling new forms of participation that bypass institutional gatekeepers. On the other hand, these same platforms introduce new regimes of algorithmic control. Online environments are far from neutral. They operate through logics of datafication that regulates access and normalizes the self-monitoring subject. In this sense, platformized education functions through dynamics closely aligned with Foucault's (1977) analysis of governmentality. Individuals are induced to govern themselves. They calibrate their behavior in anticipation of algorithmic scrutiny, and internalize external norms of efficiency and employability. Education here is not simply adapting to technological innovation. It is being reconstituted by it. The boundaries between online and offline dissolve, while pedagogy is recast within neoliberal logics of self-optimization (Fawns, 2022).

This reconfiguration compels a fundamental reconsideration of what education is, what it should aim to accomplish, and whom it ultimately serves. Schools no longer operate solely as institutions of national cultural transmission or civic formation. They function within global knowledge ecologies shaped by technological infrastructures, economic imperatives, and political agendas. To sustain education as a space of intellectual emancipation, pedagogy must resist the language of technological neutrality. It must interrogate how digital systems govern knowledge, privilege particular epistemologies, and delimit what counts as legitimate learning. This requires moving beyond simplistic binaries of "good" or "bad" technology toward cultivating practices attuned to uncertainty and plurality—educational practices that refuse the reduction of learning to metrics of performance and instead reassert its democratic potential as a site of collective reasoning and epistemic justice.

The rise of artificial intelligence intensifies and complicates the ongoing reconfiguration of authority and knowledge in schools. Unlike static textbooks that transmit pre-sanctioned narratives, AI-driven platforms generate hypertextual and ostensibly personalized knowledge. Students engaging with such tools encounter not only new forms of content delivery but also new architectures of learning, where algorithms curate visibility, privilege certain perspectives, and assign value to particular knowledge. What appears as flexibility and openness is structured by opaque classificatory systems that govern what counts as relevant or legitimate information. In this sense, AI does not simply add a new layer to existing educational practices but reorganizes the epistemic terrain itself. My fieldwork shows that students quickly learn to adapt to these algorithmic logics. They adjust their queries and responses in anticipation of what "works" for the system, often reproducing patterns of compliance. Teachers, meanwhile, are left negotiating the tension between official suspicion of AI and its covert everyday use by students, which creates spaces of friction where authority and legitimacy are continuously contested.

At the same time, the promise of personalization that underpins educational AI is inseparable from the reproduction of inequality and the consolidation of commercial interests. Algorithmic pathways do not merely reflect individual learning needs. They encode and amplify existing asymmetries by privileging dominant epistemic frameworks. Students from more privileged backgrounds, with stronger digital literacy and greater access to supplementary resources, are able to appropriate these tools more effectively. Others risk being further marginalized by systems that misrecognize or undervalue their capacities. In practice, personalization becomes another modality of responsibilization. Learners are positioned as entrepreneurs of the self, accountable for their capacity to navigate opaque algorithmic environments. The use of AI in classrooms, then, exemplifies the ambivalence of the postdigital condition. It opens new possibilities for exploration and adaptability, but deepens asymmetries of epistemic authority, redistributing power from teachers and public institutions toward commercial platforms and infrastructures.

In Central and Eastern Europe, the postdigital transformation of education intersects with a long history of ideological and epistemic control, making digital shifts particularly charged with political and cultural significance. The discourse of the knowledge society in this region carries the imprint of two successive regimes of governance. These are the socialist model of central planning, which subordinated education to state authority, and the neoliberal restructuring of the 1990s, which reoriented schools toward market competition and international benchmarking. Both regimes positioned education as subordinate to external imperatives, whether of the state or the market, and in doing so cultivated a durable sense of dependency on external frames of legitimacy. Post-socialist reforms were repeatedly framed through the rhetoric of "catching up" with the West. It has produced enduring hierarchies of epistemic dependency in which innovation has been validated through external reference points, such as OECD reports, EU standards, or Anglo-American educational models. These hierarchies continue to shape how digital technologies are received and legitimated. AI-driven tools, frequently presented as democratizing and modernizing, reproduce these older asymmetries under the guise of algorithmic neutrality and personalization. The political economy of their adoption positions local schools as testing grounds for global solutions rather than as co-authors of innovation, entrenching patterns of external authority over local educational imaginaries.

Educational governance has shifted in recent years from decentralization toward assertive re-centralization, a trajectory underwritten by political imperatives that reassert state control over school system (Semjén, 2023). Within this framework, digital technologies and learning analytics have become entangled with nationalist and authoritarian agendas. Rather than serving as tools of emancipation, they function as instruments of surveillance and political control, narrowing pedagogical space under the rhetoric of modernization. Similar dynamics reverberate across the region. Although algorithmic systems and data-driven governance are promoted as markers of modernization and global competitiveness, they often reproduce long-standing tensions between authoritarian state and aspirations for development. At the same time, educational systems in CEE bear a complex civic and cultural legacy. As Janmaat and Piattoeva (2007) show, citizenship education in post-Soviet contexts such as Ukraine has been shaped by conflicting imperatives of democratization and nation-building, producing civic identities that are not stable. Against this backdrop, the integration of AI cannot be regarded as a neutral reform. It becomes another apparatus through which knowledge is legitimated by external actors—whether state authorities that instrumentalize AI for ideological ends or global corporations that consolidate epistemic authority through proprietary platforms. Resistance to AI in Polish schools, therefore, reflects not only pragmatic pedagogical caution but also broader anxieties over the erosion of epistemic sovereignty in a context where algorithmic infrastructures threaten to reproduce, under digital conditions, the very asymmetries of dependency and control that have long defined the region's educational landscape.

In this context, postdigital pedagogy in Central and Eastern Europe cannot be reduced to the technical matter of tool adoption or the instrumental integration of AI into existing curricula. It must contend with the historical weight of imposed knowledge regimes—socialist, neoliberal, and now algorithmic—that have repeatedly subordinated education to external logics of control. To reclaim education as a site of epistemic autonomy requires asking not only what AI enables in terms of efficiency or adaptive learning, but also what it forecloses. Which forms of knowledge are legitimized? Which perspectives are rendered peripheral and how local educational values are subordinated to global metrics? The encounter with AI thus crystallizes a broader regional dilemma. How to resist the reproduction of dependency and preserve the capacity of schools to define knowledge on their own cultural and ethical terms.

This tension between tradition and innovation is sharpened in Central and Eastern European classrooms by the persistent reproduction of entrenched epistemic hierarchies. Teachers, already navigating audit-driven systems saturated with assessment regimes, face contradictory expectations. They are expected to uphold their role as transmitters of state-sanctioned knowledge, while at the same time acknowledging that students' primary epistemic engagements increasingly unfold outside the classroom, within digital environments governed by logics of immediacy and algorithmic amplification. My fieldwork in Polish schools illustrates how this contradiction materializes in everyday practice. Teachers often spoke of students "outsourcing" their learning to generative AI or video-based platforms—sometimes jokingly, but more often with apprehension. Common strategies to contain this shift included requiring handwritten submissions, privileging oral examinations, or designing assignments aimed at "outsmarting" AI. These defensive tactics rarely touched the underlying problem. Students already inhabit epistemic worlds saturated by platforms where credibility is determined less by canonical authority than by affective resonance and algorithmic visibility. What is at stake, therefore, is not only classroom management but the authority of schools themselves in shaping what counts as knowledge and how it ought to be learned.

In this setting, the school emerges not as a site of seamless adaptation to the postdigital, but as a locus of epistemic friction. The culture of correct answers and state-sanctioned curricula collides with the fragmented, and affectively charged ways in which young people acquire and circulate knowledge online. Students themselves are acutely aware of this gap. In conversations, they often admitted to preferring YouTube or TikTok explainers over classroom instruction, describing these digital sources as more engaging, "alive," and directly connected to their everyday concerns. This preference cannot be reduced to laziness or a search for shortcuts. It reflects how digital epistemologies resonate with the forms of cultural belonging that shape young people's lifeworlds. As my observations confirm, these same platforms frequently reproduce algorithmic biases and hyper-simplifications of complex content. The paradox is thus stark. Students move toward digital platforms not only because they appear "easier," but because they offer recognition and affective alignment with their lived experience—precisely the dimensions that institutional schooling struggles to provide.

Such dynamics cannot be understood in isolation from the region's broader educational legacies. Evidence from Central and Eastern Europe indicates that school systems remain deeply marked by centralizing impulses and politicized priorities, privileging standardized performance and administrative conformity over deliberative or dialogic forms of learning (Semjén, 2023). In Poland, this legacy is visible in the persistence of transmission-oriented pedagogies and in the enduring figure of the "ignorant student," imagined as deficient, distracted, or irresponsible, and thus requiring discipline. The student is not recognized as an epistemic agent in their own right. Against this backdrop, resistance to AI and suspicion toward student-led digital learning appear less as simple technophobia than as professional strategies to preserve epistemic sovereignty. These strategies respond to perceived pressures from state-imposed curricula that prescribe what is legitimate to know and corporate platforms that structure how knowledge becomes visible and valued.

This contradictory positioning reveals a crucial dynamic. Institutional education does not merely lag behind technological innovation but actively re-inscribes epistemic hierarchies by delegitimizing student practices as "inauthentic" or "uncritical." Teachers' defensive strategies are not neutral pedagogical decisions but serve as mechanisms that police the boundaries of legitimate knowledge. At the same time, the reliance on platforms that students embrace demonstrates how epistemic authority has already shifted beyond the school's jurisdiction. A pedagogical stalemate emerges. Teachers and students are caught between the demands of tradition and the disruptions of postdigital culture, bound by mutual mistrust and disconnection. The result is an atmosphere of epistemic fragmentation, in which learning oscillates between compliance with inherited regimes of control and the algorithmically mediated practices that increasingly define students' sense of belonging and recognition.

The educational agendas of both the European Union and Poland frame digital transformation as an imperative, urging schools to cultivate young people's capacity to function within technology-driven economies. These policies emphasize digital literacy and lifelong learning, presenting digital skills as endlessly adaptable and central to employability. My fieldwork in Polish schools suggests that the reality of learning in postdigital classrooms extends far beyond this policy rhetoric. Students and teachers encounter technology as infrastructures that organize practices and relations of power. The mere provision of devices or platforms rarely translates into meaningful pedagogical innovation. Instead, technology tends to intensify systemic tensions—between policy demands for digital competence, institutional pressures of standardized testing, and students' own preference for the participatory, and affectively resonant logics of platforms such as TikTok and YouTube. Seen through the lens of Fraser's (2013) critique of neoliberalism, these tensions are symptomatic of a broader displacement of responsibility. The risks of economic volatility and technological disruption are transferred from collective institutions onto individuals who are compelled to continually self-optimize and remain competitive in precarious labor markets. Within this framing, digital schooling is not simply an adaptation to technological change. It is a mechanism through which neoliberal capitalism reshapes education itself, recasting learning as a form of survival conditions of constraint.

These contradictions are rooted in the organizational inertia of educational systems across Central and Eastern Europe. Despite policy commitments to digital innovation, schools remain embedded in industrial-era structures of standardization, surveillance, and linear progression. In this setting, digital technologies are deployed less as catalysts of transformation than as instruments of compliance and governance. What students encounter in the classroom—filtering software, digital gradebooks, or learning management systems—rarely reflects the exploratory, networked, and affectively charged epistemic environments they navigate outside of school. Instead, classroom uses of technology often reinforce monitoring, assessment, and control, perpetuating a view of digital tools as extensions of bureaucratic authority rather than as resources for critical inquiry or creative engagement. This contradiction echoes what Silova (2010) identifies as the post-socialist condition of education. Institutions may be are rhetorically aligned with global modernization and European integration agendas, however they remain structurally bound by inherited traditions of centralization and epistemic hierarchy. Digital schooling in this context thus reveals a double bind. It embodies the language of innovation while reproducing historical legacies of governance, producing a hybrid formation in which the postdigital condition both promises transformation and entrenches continuity.

Faced with these contradictions, students develop their own coping strategies that expose the gap between institutional structures, and lived experience. In my fieldwork, many described "outsourcing" their schoolwork to generative AI, online explainers, or video-based tutorials, which they perceived as clearer than classroom instruction. TikTok summaries of historical events or YouTube walkthroughs of mathematical procedures were valued not only for their immediacy but for the sense of recognition and cultural proximity they provided—qualities often absent in textbook-driven lessons. Teachers, however, frequently viewed such practices with suspicion, interpreting them as evasions of authentic learning or threats to professional authority. This dynamic produced defensive pedagogical strategies that sought to restore institutional control but rarely addressed the deeper issue. Students already inhabit epistemic environments governed by algorithms, where credibility derives less from canonical authority than from visibility and resonance.

This tension between students' everyday digital practices and the defensive strategies of schools extends directly into the didactic domain. The didactic dimension of this contradiction is particularly visible in teachers' practices. Training programs in Poland and across the region emphasize operational competence with digital tools—how to use a learning management system, how to incorporate multimedia into lessons—but rarely engage with the deeper epistemological shifts that digital infrastructures introduce. Teachers in my study often responded to students' reliance on AI and platform-based learning with strategies of restriction, mostly imposing outright bans on generative tools. It reveals a defensive stance aimed at preserving pedagogical authority in systems already dominated by performative metrics and test-oriented logics. At the same time, it emphasizes a missed opportunity. Postdigital pedagogy cannot be reduced to tool proficiency or access to devices. It demands cultivating reflexive awareness of algorithmic bias and the commodification of knowledge, while also recognizing and legitimizing the epistemic terrains in which students already learn.

Recognizing informal digital practices as legitimate educational terrains is crucial if schools are to remain epistemically relevant. Polish students themselves describe YouTube explainers or TikTok animations as more engaging and accessible than textbooks, even when they acknowledge that these resources oversimplify content. To dismiss such practices outright is to ignore where and how knowledge is actively encountered by young people. Instead, formal education must prepare learners to interrogate and contextualize these sources, fostering forms of critical literacy that extend beyond functional digital skills to encompass epistemic awareness.

In this sense, the challenge for postdigital schooling in Poland and the wider CEE region is not simply how to integrate technology into existing structures, but how to reconceive education itself—how to create pedagogical spaces that confront both the emancipatory possibilities and the structural inequalities of the digital condition.

While EU and Polish educational policies present schools as primary vehicles for preparing students for participation in a digital society, the realities of the postdigital condition demand more than infrastructural investment or skills-oriented training. These policies tend to frame digitalization in instrumental terms, as a matter of equipping students with competencies for employability and lifelong learning. Such framing underestimates how profoundly digital technologies transform the very conditions under which knowledge is produced. Postdigitality, as theorized in recent scholarship, does not describe the simple integration of digital tools into existing systems but signals a condition in which digital media have become inseparable from the fabric of everyday life and learning (Jandrić et al., 2018). To treat technology merely as an add-on to curricula is to miss this epistemic shift. What is required instead is a reconfiguration of educational practice that engages critically and reflexively with the epistemological and political dimensions of digital knowledge, rather than reducing digitalization to the technical integration of devices or platforms.

The complexity of this transition becomes particularly visible in empirical studies of technology-mediated learning. Research consistently shows that digital reforms succeed not simply through the provision of infrastructure but through the cultivation of institutional capacity and responsive pedagogy at every stage (Heinrich et al., 2020). In the Central and Eastern European context, however, educational systems remain strongly marked by historical legacies of centralization. Analyses of reform trajectories demonstrate how digital education agendas often reproduce rather than reduce existing inequalities, disproportionately favoring urban and well-resourced schools while leaving rural and disadvantaged areas marginalized (Semjén, 2023; Silova, 2010). Within such ecosystems, digital learning tools do not inherently foster innovation. Their meaning and impact are conditioned by the structures within which they are embedded. This emphasizes that educational technologies cannot be judged in isolation from the systemic contexts that govern their use, but must be analyzed in relation to broader regimes of governance and institutional culture.

Jessop's (2002) concept of strategic selectivity helps clarify these dynamics. Educational reforms, while framed in universalist rhetoric, are always mediated by institutional logics that privilege some trajectories over others. EU and Polish digital agendas emphasize lifelong learning, digital competence, and modernization, but their operationalization tends to align closely with neoliberal priorities of labor market readiness and performativity. This alignment shapes governance frameworks that valorize measurable outcomes, while sidelining practices that cannot be easily reduced to data or performance indicators. The "success" of digital education thus lies not in the presence or absence of infrastructure alone, but in the structural pathways that are enabled and those that are foreclosed. The postdigital challenge, then, is not whether schools adopt technology but how they navigate the selective pressures of governance regimes that determine whose knowledge counts and which futures are rendered possible.

These dynamics become visible in the lived realities of teachers and students across Central and Eastern Europe. While EU and national policies consistently promote digital innovation, actual implementation remains uneven and fragmented. In Slovakia, for example, gaps in teacher preparedness are evident in the uneven integration of digital technologies into mathematics teacher training (Slavíčková, 2021). Critical scholarship on digital education emphasizes that disadvantaged students often receive the least effective forms of digital learning, which risks deepening rather than alleviating inequalities (Selwyn, 2022). My fieldwork in Polish schools confirms this pattern. Teachers frequently sought to restrict students' use of AI and digital platforms, either through outright bans or by designing tasks that were deliberately inaccessible to generative tools. While such strategies were motivated by a desire to preserve pedagogical authority in an uncertain environment, they often had the unintended effect of exacerbating divides between students with access to informal, self-directed digital learning resources and those reliant exclusively on school-based instruction.

These tensions are compounded by the structural logics of governance that shape the role of technology in schools. Across many CEE systems, educational reform has been redefined through mechanisms of standardization, aligning the purpose of schooling with measurable outcomes and international benchmarks. Within this framework, digital tools, such as the school management systems in Poland, are instrumentalized for surveillance and datafication, translating learning into performance indicators (Williamson, 2017). What is framed as digital modernization thus functions as an extension of older regimes of control. Platforms designed to expand the horizons of learning are subsumed into routines of monitoring and accountability. In this way, digital transformation is not neutral but structurally selective, amplifying existing hierarchies of governance while narrowing the scope for pedagogical experimentation. The promise of digital schooling is undermined by its capture within state strategies of competitiveness and efficiency, leaving little space for the cultivation of intellectual agency and critical reflexivity—capacities central to any meaningful postdigital pedagogy.

At the classroom level, the effectiveness of digital education hinges less on the mere provision of technology than on the pedagogical logics within which it is enacted. Critical scholarship on digital pedagogy emphasizes the importance of moving beyond traditional teacher–student hierarchies toward participatory, learner-centered approaches (Fawns, 2022; Knox, 2019). My research suggests that such transformations remain constrained by institutional frameworks saturated with standardization and surveillance. Teachers in Polish schools most often integrated digital technologies in ways that reproduced directive, assessment-oriented practices—using platforms to monitor attendance, deliver pre-structured content, or administer tests. Students, by contrast, engaged with digital media in informal spaces that privilege exploration, from TikTok explainers to YouTube lectures. This disjuncture emphasizes the central contradiction of postdigital education in the region. While policy narratives celebrate "innovation," the everyday reality of classrooms reveals how technology frequently amplifies existing asymmetries of authority rather than destabilizing them.

Seen from this perspective, the call to reimagine the classroom as a space of co-construction cannot be reduced to a question of pedagogy, method, or teacher training. What is at stake is the recognition that digital technologies do not simply mediate learning but reshape its epistemological conditions. They determine what becomes visible and what counts as knowledge. Moreover, whose voices are amplified or silenced. In Polish schools, reluctance to acknowledge or legitimate students' digital epistemic practices reinforces the perception of school knowledge as disconnected from everyday life. This gap pushes learners toward parallel, platform-based economies of knowledge that often remain unexamined or even dismissed by educators. In this setting, digital literacy cannot be narrowly framed as functional competence or evaluative skill. It must be reconceived as an epistemological and ethical orientation, an ability to interrogate the credibility, provenance, and ideological framings of online knowledge while situating these practices within broader institutional, civic, and cultural contexts of learning.

These dynamics are not experienced solely as abstract inequalities of redistribution or recognition. They are lived and felt by students in various ways. Postdigital learning is mediated through experiences of anxiety, shame, and exposure. Students describe the stress of being "always on," the fear of failing to perform visibly, but also the relief of finding algorithmic shortcuts that ease cognitive and emotional burdens. At the same time, the affective appeal of personalization—the sense that platforms "understand" one's preferences, or that AI tutors simulate care and responsiveness—creates powerful attachments that shape learning identities as profoundly as institutional authority does. In this sense, AI operates not only as an infrastructure of knowledge but as a medium of affective governance, structuring how students feel themselves to be learners. Recognizing this affective dimension makes clear that digital education cannot be analyzed through cognition alone. It works through the body, through intensities of desire, shame, and belonging, which sediment into dispositions toward or against learning.

The postdigital classroom, then, is not simply a space where technologies are bolted onto existing routines but a contested arena in which epistemic authority is constantly renegotiated. It is precisely this friction—between state-sanctioned curricula and students' lived engagement with algorithmically mediated knowledge—that defines contemporary learning. Within these spaces, the dynamics I earlier described as reversive knowledge resurface with particular force. Students appropriate digital resources to bypass formal assignments, invert the intended hierarchy of expertise, and reconfigure the boundary between legitimate and illegitimate knowing. From the perspective of schools, such practices appear as plagiarism or erosion of discipline. From the perspective of students, however, they often operate as strategies of epistemic survival, enabling them to navigate between institutional demands and the affordances of digital platforms. These reversals are deeply ambivalent. They open possibilities for agency and resistance but also generate what might be termed dangerous epistemologies: modes of learning that derive their power precisely from eluding institutional oversight, but which simultaneously risk reproducing misinformation, algorithmic bias, or ideological closure.

Schools that ignore these dynamics risk rendering themselves increasingly peripheral to the knowledge lives of their students, ceding epistemic authority to platforms whose logics of visibility, affect, and algorithmic sorting remain uninterrogated. In such a scenario, the classroom becomes less a site of knowledge formation than a bureaucratic checkpoint, overshadowed by digital environments that already structure how students internalize information. Conversely, classrooms that succeed in cultivating digital agency—by legitimating students' informal epistemic practices, fostering critical reflection on algorithmic mediation, and confronting the ambivalence of reversive knowledge—can move beyond defensive strategies of prohibition. This does not mean uncritical embrace of digital tools but rather the development of pedagogical practices that situate them within epistemological inquiry.

In doing so, education is repositioned not as a reactive institution struggling to adapt belatedly to technological change, but as a transformative force capable of shaping the terms of engagement with the postdigital condition. Such an orientation equips learners not only with functional skills but with the capacity to interrogate and reimagine the dangerous epistemologies that proliferate in algorithmically mediated spaces. It reclaims the classroom as a site where students can learn to navigate the contradictions of a knowledge society governed by platforms and markets, while also cultivating forms of agency, reflexivity, and solidarity that resist their reduction to metrics of performance or commodities of data extraction. In this sense, the task of postdigital pedagogy is not simply to "integrate technology," but to reclaim education as a domain of epistemic autonomy and democratic possibility.

Interpreted through the lens of political economy, the class-based differences observed in my fieldwork reveal how social capital determines not only what students know but how they learn and how they inhabit their identities as learners. Among students from more privileged backgrounds, I observed what could be described as a developed epistemic habitus. These students did not rely on a single platform or authority. Instead, they triangulated between TikTok explainers, long-form podcasts, parental expertise, and transnational sources such as English-language media or online courses. Their learning practices reflected a middle-class orientation toward knowledge as something provisional, requiring contextualization, and verification (Bourdieu, 1984, p. 12; Bourdieu & Passeron, 1990). In interviews, such students described deliberately cross-checking school materials against digital sources or consulting parents to "*see if it makes sense*," (S_IC_School_1; S_IC_School_2) cultivating dispositions that aligned with broader middle-class strategies of reflexivity and epistemic vigilance.

By contrast, students with low social capital—often from rural or working-class families—approached digital learning in ways that were more reactive. They expressed a strong desire to form independent opinions and resisted what they perceived as "*imposed truths*" (S_IC_School_1) from teachers, but their reliance on a narrower repertoire of sources limited their capacity to contextualize or verify. In practice, this often meant leaning heavily on a single platform, such as TikTok or YouTube. These students articulated pride in "*finding things out themselves*" (S_IC_School_1; S_IC_School_2), but lacked access to alternative epistemic repertoires—whether linguistic resources, parental expertise, or extracurricular opportunities—that could support critique or anchor their perspectives within broader debates.

What united both groups, despite their differences, was the marginalization of the school as a meaningful site of epistemic authority. For both groups the school appeared redundant when compared with the richness of family networks and digital resources already available. They described classes as "repetitive" or "behind" what they could learn online (S_IC_School_1; S_IC_School_2). However, for the less privileged, the school failed to provide the support needed to transform affective responses into structured critique, leaving them vulnerable to digital platforms. In this way, the institution did not mitigate but rather deepened inequalities. It left the epistemic agency of middle-class students largely dependent on their external resources, while leaving their less advantaged peers to navigate digital environments with fewer tools for critical interrogation. The result was a stratified capacity to appropriate digital tools, one in which class position shaped not only the quantity of resources but the very Alongside these class-based differences, my fieldwork also revealed moments of convergence, where students—regardless of social background—gravitated toward extra-institutional figures of authority. The case of Andrew Tate was particularly striking. Among boys especially, his persona became a nodal point around which affective attachments, perceptions of injustice, and discourses of resistance coalesced. What stood out was not simply the circulation of his videos, but the insistence, voiced repeatedly, that this controversy was the issue from which they had "*learned the most*." Such statements illustrate how postdigital learning frequently operates less through rational verification or deliberative comparison than through discursive identification. In Laclau's (2005) terms, Tate functioned as a nodal point, an apparently unified figure that condensed diffuse frustrations—about school discipline, gender relations, social inequality, or mistrust of mainstream media—into a populist discourse that positioned "the people" against hostile elites. In this way, Tate exemplified how platform logics allow affectively charged figures to aggregate diverse discontents into the semblance of coherence.

In this setting, learning unfolded not as critical engagement with competing perspectives but as affective alignment with a discourse of antagonism and solidarity. The epistemic authority of Tate's persona derived less from evidence or argument than from style, virality, and the sense of recognition it offered to students who felt unseen by institutional education. For many, engagement with his content offered both affirmation and community—a way of articulating grievance in a system where their voices felt marginalized. This dynamic exposes both the fragility of schools' claims to epistemic authority and the potency of postdigital publics in shaping learner identities. It reveals that within algorithmically mediated environments, learning cannot be reduced to the acquisition of information. It is bound up with belonging, affective resonance, and the performance of grievance. Far from being peripheral distractions, these encounters with populist discourses constitute central episodes in students' epistemic lives. It takes place where the logics of platform capitalism, affective politics, and classroom disengagement intersect in ways that unsettle conventional understandings of what it means to "learn."

This convergence across class lines emphasizes the ambivalence of what I describe as reversive knowledge. Within the postdigital classroom, where the mechanized subject is shaped by assessment regimes, surveillance logics, and algorithmic infrastructures (Knox, 2019; Williamson, 2017), reversive practices emerge as students appropriate, parody, or invert official knowledge. These practices expose the instability of pedagogical authority, showing that control is never absolute and that meaning-making is always contested. The direction of these practices is undecidable. Reversive knowledge can undermine exclusionary hierarchies and create openings for critique, but it can just as easily reproduce reactionary worldviews and authoritarian identifications. The defense of Andrew Tate exemplifies this ambiguity. For many boys in my study, affectively charged identification with his persona produced a sense of epistemic agency denied in school. At the same time, this identification sustained epistemologies hostile to pluralism—what might be described as dangerous epistemologies. In these forms of learning power derives from escaping institutional oversight, risking amplifying antagonism and algorithmic bias.

This tension becomes sharper when these practices are situated within broader formations of power and meaning that exceed the classroom. Reversive knowledge does not circulate freely but is shaped by infrastructures that filter visibility and reward particular forms of engagement. What gains traction is often that which resonates affectively and confirms prior orientations, while other forms remain marginal or invisible. In this sense, students' appropriations of knowledge are not only acts of resistance but also moments of alignment with wider discursive currents. The same gesture that disrupts pedagogical authority can therefore reinforce alternative hierarchies structured through platform logics. This ambivalence points to a condition in which critique and compliance are intertwined, making it difficult to separate acts of autonomy from forms of dependence.

Crucially, in the CEE context, such reversive practices are often accompanied by a pronounced distrust of liberal discourses—those associated with the promises of post-1989 modernization and the perceived failures of neoliberal transition. For many students, aligning with populist figures or algorithmically amplified narratives offered a way of articulating insecurities about marginalization and lack of recognition. Reversive knowledge thus functioned not only as parody or resistance to school authority but also as a means of giving shape to diffuse anxieties, translating them into simplified antagonisms that pit "ordinary people" against elites, liberal institutions, or mainstream media. These identifications provide affective solidarity and a sense of agency. However they also may foreclose pluralism and critical deliberation. What emerges is a paradox. The very practices that allow students to express and negotiate their insecurities simultaneously leave them vulnerable to capture by algorithmic amplification and populist discourse, deepening their dependency on external epistemic authorities rather than cultivating autonomy.

In this sense, the postdigital classroom is not only a site of institutional reproduction (Bourdieu; Fraser, 1997) but also a site of epistemic contestation, where legitimacy is negotiated across state curricula, peer cultures, and algorithmic publics. Here, solidarity and antagonism operate as powerful forces of learning, shaping how students form identities and navigate knowledge. Class structures continue to condition access to epistemic repertoires, but digital publics add another layer, where affective attachments to figures like Tate cut across class lines and generate new, unstable subjectivities.

The discourse of digital emancipation in education rests on a profound misrecognition: the assumption that technology alone can level structural inequalities in learning. In practice, the invitation to self-regulated, digitally mediated learning is distributed unevenly, filtered through mechanisms that convert economic into cultural capital under the guise of meritocracy (Bourdieu, 1984; Bourdieu & Passeron, 1990). Students with high social capital, for example, were not simply more "digitally competent". They were better positioned. Their habitus, shaped by middle-class resources, equipped them with the dispositions of comparison, reflexivity, and epistemic triangulation that aligned with the unspoken norms of digital education. By contrast, other students, though equally immersed in TikTok and other platforms, lacked broader repertoires of reference and thus engaged learning more affectively and reactively. The supposed universality of digital tools concealed their function as instruments of symbolic violence, rewarding those already endowed with cultural and social capital while framing systemic exclusion as individual failure.

Here, digital competence itself becomes a new site of distinction, a marker of privilege that masquerades as neutrality. Just as Bourdieu (1984) showed how aesthetic taste functions as a form of symbolic power, the ability to navigate platforms reflexively—to triangulate sources, contextualize information, or critically interrogate algorithmic mediation—emerges as a form of epistemic capital. It is no less stratifying than classical forms of literacy. Those who possess it are celebrated as autonomous, innovative learners, while those without it are pathologized as disengaged or deficient. In this way, technical skills function as the new distinction, naturalizing educational inequalities by embedding them in the very discourse of digital empowerment. What appears as "self-regulated learning" or "digital agency" is in fact the capacity to mobilize inherited cultural capital within postdigital infrastructures.

The finding is therefore crucial. The promise of digital emancipation obscures how platform-mediated learning rearticulates older inequalities in new symbolic forms. Schools, by failing to address these dynamics, reproduce the very exclusions they claim to overcome, allowing privilege to be reframed as competence and deprivation as failure. The postdigital classroom, far from leveling the playing field, becomes a site where inequalities are recalibrated and legitimized through the language of meritocracy, producing hierarchies that are all the more resilient because they are cloaked in the rhetoric of neutrality and innovation.

My argument is that learning in the postdigital knowledge society is simultaneously stratified and discursively unstable. This complexity is not fully captured by frameworks that emphasize redistribution or recognition alone (Fraser, 2008). Fraser's categories remain vital in foregrounding material access and cultural legitimacy, however they require supplementation to grasp how inequalities are rearticulated in postdigital contexts. Bourdieu's notion of capital helps reveal how inequities do not merely exist externally but sediment into habitus—embodied dispositions that shape how learners encounter and internalize knowledge. At the same time, Laclau (2005) directs attention to the instability of the very categories that circulate within educational discourse: notions such as "*AI literacy*" or "*competences of the future*" gain their force as hegemonic signifiers not because of their intrinsic content, but because of their capacity to unify disparate demands under an apparently universal horizon. Taken together, these perspectives allow us to conceptualize postdigital learning as a process in which structural inequalities, embodied dispositions, and discursive struggles intertwine.

Fieldwork confirmed this point. Even as both groups of students consumed the same algorithmically curated content, their practices diverged sharply. Students with higher levels of social and cultural capital often triangulated between digital, familial, and institutional sources, cultivating reflexive comparisons and critical dispositions. Their habitus aligned with middle-class orientations toward knowledge as something to be interrogated, contextualized, and cross-verified. By contrast, students with limited capital engaged more affectively and reactively, expressing strong opinions but lacking access to epistemic repertoires that could scaffold critical engagement. This divergence emphasizes how algorithmic infrastructures do not erase inequalities. They recalibrate them by amplifying the dispositions already available to learners. The case of Andrew Tate revealed a striking counterpoint. Across class lines, students coalesced affectively around his figure, framing him as a source of "real learning." What mattered here was not factual verification or deliberative judgment but the emotional intensity of identification and the sense of recognition denied in institutional contexts. Students' insistence that they had "learned the most" from this controversy illustrates how learning in postdigital publics is propelled as much by affect and antagonism as by cognition, and how epistemic authority can be claimed through emotional alignment rather than rational deliberation.

A more integrated framework emerges when Fraser's emphasis on redistribution and recognition is read alongside Bourdieu's theorization of capital and Laclau's account of empty signifiers. Fraser helps us see the structural and cultural conditions for parity of participation: who has access to infrastructures, and whose practices are legitimated as "knowledge" (Fraser, 1997, 2003). Bourdieu (1984) adds a relational dimension, showing how these conditions sediment into embodied digital habitus—whether students approach digital platforms as spaces of inquiry and creativity or encounter them primarily as mechanisms of surveillance and compliance (Pangrazio & Sefton-Green, 2020; Selwyn, 2022). Laclau (2005) extends the analysis to the level of discourse, highlighting how terms such as "AI literacy," "*criticalthinking*," or "*competences of the future*" acquire hegemonic authority precisely because they appear universally desirable. Their power lies in concealing inequality by presenting mastery as a neutral benchmark of modern education, even as access to such competences remains profoundly stratified.

Taken together, these perspectives illuminate how structural, cultural, and discursive mechanisms intersect in reproducing inequality in postdigital learning. Redistribution determines infrastructural access, recognition shapes whose practices count as legitimate knowledge, capital informs the embodied dispositions through which learners navigate digital resources, and hegemonic signifiers frame these processes in ways that obscure their stratification. The result is a field where learning is experienced not only as differentiated access to knowledge but also as differentiated modes of being a learner: reflexive, comparative, and epistemically agentic for some; affectively charged, precarious, and reactive for others.

In this sense, the digital classroom, celebrated in global policy discourses as a democratizing space, often functions instead as a site where neoliberal logics of responsibilization and performativity intersect with dangerous epistemologies circulating in algorithmic publics. Agency here is not the freedom to learn critically but the obligation to optimize oneself, while pedagogical authority is hollowed out and re-inscribed elsewhere—in influencers, platforms, and peer discourses. Schools, tasked with codifying legitimate knowledge (Bourdieu & Passeron, 1990), increasingly find their symbolic authority destabilized by digital spaces that operate as parallel epistemic terrains. These terrains do not merely supplement formal education but contest it, opening up a struggle over what counts as knowledge and who has the power to define it. In Laclau's (2005) terms, this is not simply a pedagogical alternative but a hegemonic contest: between the fixed narratives of standardized schooling and the fluid, affectively charged discourses of digital counterpublics. The risk is clear—without critical interruption, reversive knowledge practices can just as easily sustain reactionary populisms as they can foster democratic critique, leaving education suspended between emancipation and stratification. This ambivalence is lived by students in the form of unstable learning identities: oscillating between critical exploration and reactionary closure, their educational subjectivities are shaped in terrains where the line between learning and unlearning is constantly redrawn.

What emerges is a field of discursive struggle distinctive to Central and Eastern Europe, where competing historical legacies and contemporary forces intersect in contradictory ways. The bureaucratic rationality of late socialism left behind systems of centralized curricula and a vision of schooling as an instrument of the state. These legacies—emphasizing particular ideology and suspicion of alternative epistemologies—continue to shape classroom culture decades after 1989. The transition to neoliberal democracy introduced the language of markets and efficiency, reframing schools as service providers and students as future human capital (Fuller, 2006, p. 29). This neoliberal turn unfolded unevenly across CEE, producing hybrid systems in which the old disciplinary infrastructures persisted alongside new performative logics of testing and competition. More recently, re-traditionalizing educational policies—framed around patriotism, religion, and cultural homogeneity—have sought to reclaim schools as instruments of national identity and ideological control (Zarycki, 2014). Layered upon these institutional trajectories is the disruptive presence of platform capitalism, whose logics of algorithmic visibility and affective engagement increasingly shape how young people encounter knowledge (Selwyn, 2022; Srnicek, 2017).

The intersection of these trajectories generates a paradoxical educational space. On the one hand, schools still perform the residues of socialist bureaucratic authority, presenting knowledge as a closed canon to be mastered and examined. On the other hand, they embrace neoliberal performativity, urging students to be self-managing and "future-ready," while simultaneously being re-traditionalized into guardians of collective identity. Digital publics cut across these layers, offering however another epistemic terrain in which legitimacy is redefined through visibility. In this crowded space, the learner is neither fully a disciplined subject of the state, nor solely a self-optimizing neoliberal individual, but also an affectively oriented participant in algorithmic publics. The "mechanized subject" produced by bureaucratic procedures, and grade surveillance (Au, 2011; Foucault, 1977) is thus destabilized by the competing claims of national, neoliberal, and digital orders. Students move fluidly between these subject positions, generating knowledge practices that parody or invert curricular content, embedding it within the vernacular logics of TikTok, YouTube, or online forums.

At the same time, the dangers of these reversive practices become especially visible in CEE, where democratic institutions remain contested and fragile. Post-socialist disillusionment with liberal democratic promises—combined with sharp social inequalities and the erosion of trust in mainstream institutions—renders students particularly receptive to antagonistic discourses circulating online. The attraction to figures like Andrew Tate, whose authority rests not on evidence but on affective resonance and populist antagonism, demonstrates how disaffection with both neoliberal and nationalist schooling can be redirected into new forms of epistemic dependency. These discourses help articulate insecurities that stem from structural precarity, but they do so by reinforcing hierarchies under the guise of emancipation. The result is not merely a privatization of authority but its rearticulation: from the bureaucratic state and neoliberal market to algorithmic platforms and populist influencers.

Fraser's later work (2008) offers an essential addition here. Redistribution and recognition of diverse knowledges remain insufficient if the very processes of defining digital competencies are exclusionary. Policy debates about "AI literacy" or "competences of the future" in CEE often unfold without meaningful participation from students, teachers, or communities most affected by these reforms. This representational deficit means that what counts as "future-ready" knowledge is articulated largely by corporate actors, policymakers, and international agencies, while the situated experiences of learners remain unvoiced. The result is a democratic shortfall distinctive to CEE. Education is not only stratified by material access and cultural recognition but also by the absence of institutional representation in shaping the discursive terrain of digital learning. In this sense, the instability of postdigital classrooms in the region is not accidental but symptomatic of deeper socio-historical tensions—between socialist bureaucratic legacies, neoliberal reforms, nationalist retrenchments, and the algorithmic governance of platform capitalism.

Learning in the postdigital knowledge society is increasingly mediated by artificial intelligence, where the everyday practices of students are reorganized by predictive and generative systems. AI powered platforms do not simply supplement pedagogy. They reshape what counts as learning by rearticulating knowledge as something to be optimized, personalized, and accelerated. For many students, "learning" is less about the slow accumulation of understanding than about finding the shortest path to a correct answer—a shift that illustrates how "*survival*" and "*to pass*" functions as empty signifiers (Laclau, 2005) within students learning discourses.

To "*survive*" becomes more than a minimalist strategy of passing exams through AI shortcuts. It increasingly denotes the literal endurance of schooling itself. In classrooms saturated with repetitive tasks and pedagogical routines perceived as monotonous or irrelevant, students frequently described the need simply to "*get through the day*" (S_IC_School_2). Falling asleep during lessons, drifting into distraction, or covertly resorting to AI tools to complete assignments were not only avoidance tactics but embodied strategies of survival in an environment experienced as overwhelming and physically draining. In this sense, the recourse to AI is symptomatic of a deeper malaise. It is less an expression of instrumental rationality than a coping mechanism for navigating the fatigue and alienation generated by the institutional logics of schooling. Survival thus captures both the symbolic dimension of "*doing enough to pass*" (S_IC_School_1) and the corporeal reality of sustaining attention and motivation in a system whose structures often suppress rather than cultivate curiosity and engagement.

The official educational discourse is organized around radically different empty signifiers. "*Development*" is reframed in policy discourse as acquiring "*competences of the future.*" It is less a trajectory of holistic growth than a managerial rearticulation of learning in terms of employability. Within this frame, the promise of digital development masks the reproduction of inequalities, presenting skill acquisition as an individualized project rather than a socially stratified process. "*Critical thinking*" is reduced not to the interrogation of social, political, and historical conditions under which knowledge is produced, but to algorithmic skepticism—learning how to detect bias in AI outputs or to cross-check search results, while leaving untouched the larger logics of surveillance capitalism and data extraction that organize the very conditions of digital learning.

At the same time, students' practices show that AI is both a prosthesis of knowledge and a disciplining apparatus. It extends memory and reasoning capacities while simultaneously normalizing surveillance and responsibilization (Foucault, 1977; Noble, 2018; Zuboff, 2019). The tension between accelerated shortcuts and deeper epistemic engagement becomes central to how learning is experienced. If textbooks once anchored knowledge within a linear, authoritative form, AI-driven media fragment learning into modular, on-demand outputs, blurring the line between inquiry and consumption. In this sense, AI is not merely infrastructure but a medium that actively inscribes new logics of learning within the broader regime of digital capitalism.

Algorithmic governance further destabilizes the promise of autonomy. Platforms claim to personalize learning, but as Noble (2018) and Zuboff (2019) show, such personalization operates through logics of selection, surveillance, and commercial exploitation. Laclau's (2005) insights into hegemony illuminate how discourses of choice and flexibility form equivalential chains that obscure the vertical relations of power inscribed in these infrastructures. What appears as freedom is structured by algorithms that amplify dominant narratives and suppress alternative epistemologies. In this way, digital systems do not simply mediate learning but actively configure its possibilities, delimiting what can be known and who can be recognized as a legitimate knower.

At the level of everyday practice, these dynamics reshape how learning is enacted. Algorithmic systems organize access to information in ways that privilege speed and pre-structured answers, shifting attention away from interpretation and sustained inquiry. Students navigate interfaces instead of engaging with problems, selecting from available outputs instead of constructing knowledge through extended engagement. In this sense, epistemic authority is displaced from pedagogical relations toward infrastructural arrangements that remain largely opaque. What appears as neutral support for learning operates as a silent regulator, shaping not only what is accessed but also how engagement itself takes form. These shifts accumulate over time, normalizing dependency on algorithmic guidance and narrowing the space for independent judgement.

For students, this means that AI and platformized learning are simultaneously experienced as tools of empowerment and as instruments of dependency. On the one hand, they appear to offer escape routes from rigid curricula and uninspiring pedagogy, enabling shortcuts, community-building, or access to alternative discourses. On the other, they risk channeling disaffection into new forms of epistemic dependency on algorithmic platforms and populist discourses, reproducing hierarchies under the guise of autonomy. In CEE especially, where distrust in liberal democratic narratives often intersects with nationalist or populist mobilizations, such algorithmic publics become powerful arenas for articulating insecurities and alternative epistemologies. What circulates here is not only entertainment or distraction but reversive knowledge—appropriations and re-significations of curricular content that both destabilize school authority and expose students to reactionary closures.

Against this backdrop, equity requires a shift from technocratic solutions to pedagogies that foreground critique, reflexivity, and collective participation. Fraser's (1997) insistence on the interdependence of redistribution and recognition is essential. Devices alone do not create parity of participation if students are not also granted recognition as epistemic agents. Nor can equity be secured without confronting the political economy of educational technology, which deepens stratification by aligning learning with the imperatives of surveillance and datafication (Williamson, 2017). As Biesta (2013, pp. 1–3, 19–23) suggests, pedagogy must resist allowing technology to define educational ends and instead orient tools toward responsiveness and meaningful educational purposes. Knox (2019) further emphasizes how the postdigital entangles learning in infrastructural and ideological systems that must themselves be critically scrutinized. Together, these insights support the argument that digital education needs pedagogies that interrogate its epistemological and ideological foundations—not merely deploy new platforms.

In Central and Eastern Europe, the uneven rollout of digital infrastructures renders visible the fractures within what is often imagined as a homogeneous "postdigital turn." Metropolitan centers increasingly adopt digital pedagogies, data-driven assessment systems, and AI-enhanced platforms (Grek, 2020). At the same time, peripheral or underfunded regions and schools continue to operate under conditions of structural lack. They face shortages of qualified teachers, and minimal institutional support for technological innovation (Erkkilä & Piironen, 2018). This unevenness undermines the assumption of a unified postdigital knowledge society contained within national borders. Instead, it exposes how digitalization functions as a mechanism of stratification, producing differentiated educational ecologies that mirror wider patterns of uneven development across the region.

The divide is not simply between schools but also within them. Access to and use of digital tools is filtered through students' social and cultural capital, which profoundly shapes their capacity to engage meaningfully with technology. As Bourdieu (1984) insists, cultural resources and embodied dispositions—the habitus—determine not only whether students can access digital infrastructures but how they are able to translate them into recognized forms of value. In the same classroom, some students mobilize technology critically and reflexively, connecting online practices to broader epistemic frameworks, while others are confined to repetitive or entertainment-driven uses that carry little symbolic capital in educational or occupational fields. What appears as a uniform provision of digital access is therefore fractured by deeper inequalities of recognition and redistribution.

This fragmentation means that postdigitality in CEE contexts is less a singular condition than a field of unequal trajectories. For students with higher volumes of social and cultural capital, digital tools become vehicles for exploration, authorship, and transnational networking, positioning them advantageously within global knowledge economies (Grek, 2020; Macgilchrist et al., 2020). Their peers with fewer resources often remain locked into more constrained uses—passive consumption, compliance with school surveillance, or algorithmically driven engagement that narrows rather than expands epistemic horizons. These divergences are not the outcome of individual choice but of structured opportunities: differences in parental mediation, community support, linguistic repertoires, and the legitimacy afforded to certain forms of knowledge.

From the perspective of Fraser's (1997) theory of justice, these dynamics reveal a compounded inequality. On the distributive level, disparities in infrastructure and institutional support limit equal participation. On the cultural level, students' practices are differentially recognized. Those aligned with middle-class norms of reflexivity and critical inquiry are valorized, while others are devalued as deficient or unserious. The result is not a digital commons but a stratified epistemic field, where recognition and misrecognition intersect with redistribution to determine who can participate in meaningful knowledge-making. In this sense, CEE classrooms demonstrate that postdigitality is not a universal horizon but a contested terrain, where digital tools both reflect and reproduce the hierarchies of social and cultural capital.

What becomes clear, then, is that postdigital education in CEE cannot be conceived as a linear transition into a digital future but as a fractured landscape where infrastructures and subjectivities collide. Digital tools, far from neutral, are embedded in the wider political economy of knowledge, where they can act as mechanisms of distinction, symbolic violence, or cultural exclusion as easily as they can enable creativity and participation. The mechanized subject of schooling—disciplined by tests, metrics, and procedural routines—now encounters the volatile energies of digital publics, producing reversive and sometimes dangerous epistemologies that unsettle the authority of institutional discourse. These struggles demonstrate that the meaning of digital learning cannot be read off the presence of devices or platforms alone. Rather, it must be understood as an ongoing negotiation over knowledge, identity, and power, situated within the uneven histories and contested futures of the region.

The critical question that follows is not only how digital media are currently reshaping education in CEE, but what their potential might be if mobilized otherwise. What forms of pedagogy, agency, and epistemic justice could emerge when technologies are redirected away from surveillance and stratification toward the democratization of knowledge production?

5.1 What Is the Potential of Postdigital Educational Media?

The final part interrogates the role of digital technologies within neoliberal transitional societies by reframing them not as neutral instruments of educational delivery but as cultural infrastructures that both enable and constrain the possibilities of learning. In postdigital contexts, where the boundaries between the digital and the social have collapsed, students often experience themselves as autonomous learners while being subtly governed by algorithmic systems. This experience of autonomy is itself a discursive construction. The sense of freedom to act is produced within infrastructures that delimit what is possible. What is presented as individual agency is therefore inseparable from the architectures of data capture and algorithmic curation that channel attention and normalize particular modes of engagement (Williamson, 2017; Zuboff, 2019).

In this light, the role of technology in education cannot be reduced to a set of tools or affordances. It must be understood as constitutive of the epistemological and social landscapes in which education unfolds (Jandrić et al., 2018; Knox, 2019). To treat technologies as co-constitutive forces—shaping identity and knowledge production—is to recognize that they structure hierarchies of credibility and recognition, valorizing some forms of learning while rendering others invisible. From this standpoint, pedagogy cannot remain at the level of functional skills or "digital literacy." It requires a critically reflexive, embodied practice that situates learners within these contested infrastructures, foregrounding how digital systems mediate what counts as knowledge, who is authorized to speak, and under what conditions. Schools must therefore reimagine themselves not as gatekeepers of canonical content but as sites of epistemic disobedience and digital critique—equipping students not only to navigate but to reshape the architectures of postdigital learning.

This transformation demands an epistemic reorientation. Students must be understood not merely as passive consumers but as active producers within technologically mediated worlds. Their interactions with Google, TikTok, YouTube, and AI systems are not peripheral distractions but central sites of meaning-making, forming their identity, political engagement, and economic prospects (Macgilchrist et al., 2020). These platforms constitute what Bourdieu (1984) would call new fields of cultural production, where dispositions and capacities are cultivated through the accrual of digital forms of symbolic capital. Like all fields, they are structured by deep inequalities. Algorithmic logics render some knowledges hyper-visible while obscuring others (Noble, 2018).

Such hierarchies of recognition illustrate Fraser's (2003) insight that redistribution of resources is insufficient without recognition of the epistemic conditions under which students' practices are valued or devalued. Simply providing devices or access risks leaving students vulnerable to misrecognition if the infrastructures themselves remain unexamined. The effect is that students come to inhabit learning as stratified terrain. Some cultivate reflexive dispositions and agency, while others internalize compliance or exclusion as the very horizon of what learning can mean. Here, CEE contexts provide a particularly sharp view of this stratification. Middle class students acquire forms of digital habitus that allow them to link their online practices to global epistemic frameworks, while students with lower social capital remain confined to reactive and entertainment-driven uses that hold little value in academic or economic fields.

Schools that respond to digital technologies primarily through bans, surveillance, or rigidly standardized policies reproduce a Foucauldian model of disciplinary control, treating students as objects to be monitored rather than subjects capable of inquiry and resistance (Williamson & Eynon, 2020). These strategies obscure the constitutive role of digital systems and deny learners the opportunity to engage with the infrastructures that increasingly organize their everyday lives. A different pedagogical orientation is needed. Postditital pedagogies acknowledges how digital technologies shape the very conditions of subjectivity and knowledge, and positions learners as capable of interrogating and contesting these formations. In this sense, education becomes a space where digital subjectivities can be rearticulated, not simply regulated. This requires participatory approach that not only encourages students to deconstruct digital practices but also to reassemble them creatively, exposing the contingencies and exclusions built into technological systems. Such pedagogies move the debate from digital literacy—understood as functional skill acquisition—to digital reflexivity. They highlight a practice of critical self-positioning within the infrastructures of platform capitalism and datafication (Couldry & Mejias, 2019). In this sense, the postdigital classroom is not simply a site of technological adaptation but a political field in which the conditions of epistemic justice, recognition, and collective agency are negotiated.

Reconsidered in light of contemporary developments, De Corte's (1994) paradigm of "learning with media" acquires renewed relevance. The task of postdigital education is not to prepare students for a predefined digital future, but to co-construct that future within contested conditions.

Artificial intelligence has become a paradigmatic form of educational media, not a neutral tool for instruction but an infrastructure that organizes knowledge and subjectivity. AI generative models do not merely supplement learning. They transform it into a continuous process of data extraction and circulation, where student activity is captured and repurposed for commercial and governance ends. In this configuration, pedagogy is increasingly subordinated to logics of optimization and prediction, embedding education within the broader dynamics of surveillance capitalism (Zuboff, 2019). Learning is reframed less as a dialogic encounter than as a controlled process.

This shift redefines the position of learners. They are addressed as both consumers and producers of data, caught in recursive loops where their actions refine algorithmic systems, while those same systems delimit the epistemic horizons available to them. Personalization—celebrated in policy discourse as a democratizing force—functions primarily as a mechanism of differentiation. It stratifies learners according to their compatibility with algorithmically valorized behaviors and outcomes. What appears as responsiveness is in practice a form of anticipatory governance, where students' pathways are pre-structured by probabilities and correlations rather than negotiated through pedagogical dialogue.

In this sense, AI does not simply mediate learning but establishes the conditions under which learning is recognized as legitimate. It acts as a new modality of cultural capital (Bourdieu, 1984), rewarding those able to navigate and appropriate algorithmic infrastructures while rendering others deficient or unprepared. Symbolic hierarchies are thereby reinforced, as fluency in AI-mediated practices becomes a marker of educational legitimacy. At the same time, the very categories of "competence," "critical thinking," and "autonomy" may become reduced to measurable behaviors that can be optimized by machines. The paradox is that while AI promises emancipation through personalization, it often intensifies dependence on opaque systems that make so many tasks easier and more personalized that functioning without them becomes difficult.

The task of postdigital education is not to prepare students for a predefined digital future, but to co-construct that future within contested terrains of power and culture. This requires reframing education as a site where technological infrastructures are not merely adopted but critically examined and reworked. As Fraser (2008) and Bourdieu (1984) remind us in different ways, genuine transformation must be both structural and symbolic. It demands a redistribution of material resources that shape access to technology, while simultaneously disrupting the hierarchies of recognition that determine whose knowledge practices are legitimized within digital ecologies. Such a dual reorientation shifts the school from being a gatekeeper of technological capital to a locus of knowledge activism. The school where students and teachers engage with the politics of data and AI not as abstract themes but as lived experience that define their position in the global knowledge economy. In this sense, postdigital pedagogy is neither a technophilic embrace nor a technophobic retreat but an emancipatory praxis that equips learners to intervene in, rather than submit to, the architectures of algorithmic governance.

Technology in education thus functions as a distinctive form of cultural capital, one that both reflects and reproduces social divisions. Digital capital—the capacity to navigate, critically engage with, and strategically deploy technology—is not distributed evenly but is mediated by family resources, cultural and social capital, previous experiences, institutional infrastructures, and cultural expectations. In policy rhetoric, technology is celebrated as a democratizing force, capable of bridging educational divides. In practice, its deployment often re-inscribes inequality. Students embedded in socioeconomically privileged environments encounter technology as a resource for creativity and self-realization. Their families invest in coding programs, AI-driven platforms, and extracurricular opportunities that cultivate dispositions aligned with the symbolic capital valued in global labor markets (Selwyn, 2022, p. 22). For these students, technology extends their agency and consolidates their position within transnational circuits of knowledge and cultural production.

As my research showed, students situated in resource-poor environments may encounter technology under conditions of restriction, surveillance, or lower educational ambition. Schools may impose device bans, restrict Internet use, or rely on digital tools that reduce learning to repetitive exercises (Williamson, 2017). In such contexts, technology is less a vehicle of empowerment than a medium of control or distraction. This divergence produces not only material inequalities but also divergent digital habitus. Privileged students develop practices of intentional, strategic engagement with technology, while disadvantaged students internalize constrained dispositions, experiencing digital tools as means if survival or instruments of escapism. The digital divide, therefore, is not only about access to devices or connectivity but about the structuring of subjectivities—about who is positioned to become a producer of digital knowledge and who remains confined to its consumption.

These dynamics reflect a broader social stratification whereby digital literacy itself becomes a marker of distinction. In elite schools, digital education is reframed as cultural capital with future-oriented exchange value. Coding fluency, computational thinking, and media production are cultivated as signs of innovation and entrepreneurial potential (Bourdieu, 1984). In under-resourced schools, by contrast, digital instruction is reduced to rudimentary competencies—basic document preparation, learning management system navigation—that lack symbolic and economic recognition. The result is a polarized digital economy of education. Privilege produces digital innovators, while marginalization produces compliant digital users (Pangrazio & Sefton-Green, 2020). What emerges is not a universal postdigital condition but multiple, stratified postdigitalities, differentiated by social capital and habitus.

The most urgent issue lies not only in redistribution of devices and infrastructures but in recognition of epistemic agency. Fraser's (2008) framework insists that parity of participation requires more than access. It requires that marginalized students be acknowledged as subjects whose ways of knowing and using technology count within educational fields. Without this recognition, digital tools risk functioning as instruments of neoliberal socialization, channeling students into consumerist subjectivities where knowledge is fragmented into measurable outputs and identities are reduced to data profiles. The hidden curriculum of digital education thus extends beyond technical skills, embedding a vision of the learner as a compliant node within platform capitalism. To resist this trajectory, schools must cultivate reflexive pedagogies that reveal the power dynamics of digital infrastructures and create space for counter-hegemonic practices of knowledge production. Only by foregrounding recognition alongside redistribution can digital education move from reproducing social inequality to enabling the collective re-making of postdigital futures.

In Central and Eastern Europe (CEE), the import of Western-designed curricula and standardized AI platforms frequently overwrites local modes of meaning-making, positioning students less as participants in culturally situated learning than as consumers of ostensibly "universal" competencies. Empty signifiers such as "AI literacy," "*critical thinking*," or "*competences of the future*" circulate across policy documents as if they were neutral benchmarks of modernity, however they conceal the epistemic coloniality through which regional histories and knowledges are systematically devalued. Such discourses perform what Laclau (2005) described as hegemonic operations of equivalence. They bind heterogeneous aspirations—economic competitiveness, or social mobility—into a single vocabulary of progress, obscuring the power asymmetries inscribed in these categories. In practice, the invocation of "AI literacy" rarely acknowledges students' situated repertoires of digital practice. Rather, it enforces conformity to Anglo-Western models of knowledge, presenting them as universal and unquestionable.

Against this backdrop, students' everyday practices become more than mundane acts of digital participation. They constitute subtle, if fragile, forms of epistemic disobedience (Mignolo, 2011). By switching between multilingual repertoires, remixing memes grounded in local political histories, or circulating peer-driven interpretations of contested pasts, students resist the homogenizing thrust of imported curricula. These practices reframe learning not as assimilation into Western-modern epistemologies but as ongoing negotiation within postdigital publics—spaces where local knowledge intersects with algorithmically curated global flows. What appears from the outside as peripheral or even deficient engagement is, in fact, an effort to inscribe meaning into contexts that official discourses render invisible. This subaltern creativity is precarious. It takes place under conditions where institutional structures continue to cast students as dependent consumers, whose identities are scripted through external frameworks rather than sustained by locally meaningful pedagogical practices.

In the fractured terrain of the postdigital knowledge society, school learning in CEE must therefore be understood less as the acquisition of technical skills than as a contested discursive process through which students construct identities and social positions. AI systems, recommendation algorithms, and platforms are not neutral supplements to classroom instruction. They operate as infrastructures that actively delimit the epistemic horizons within which young people are authorized to imagine themselves as learners or future workers. For students endowed with strong cultural and digital capital, these infrastructures can function as extensions of inquiry and creativity, enabling experimentation and transnational connectivity that align with the symbolic economy of global knowledge work. For others, particularly in underfunded schools or marginalized communities, the same infrastructures materialize as instruments of surveillance or rote repetition—practices that generate docility rather than reflexivity.

Learning thus emerges as a stratified discursive terrain, structured by what Bourdieu (1984) described as the unequal distribution of capital and the differential formation of habitus. Within the same classroom, some students inhabit AI as a field of exploration and authorship, accruing digital forms of symbolic capital that reinforce their educational advantage, while others encounter it as a regime of constraint, where their contributions are rendered invisible or trivial. The consequence is a polarized system of subjectivation. On one side, producers of knowledge recognized as future innovators. On the other, consumers of content interpellated into compliance with the logics of platform capitalism. In this configuration, recognition is not simply uneven but conditional, tethered to students' ability to embody the dispositions valorized by neoliberal educational discourse.

A decolonial perspective reveals that the stratification of learning in Central and Eastern Europe is inseparable from longer histories of epistemic dependency. Since the early 1990s, the region has been persistently framed as a periphery obliged to "catch up" with Western modernity. Educational reforms as well as fast adoption of standardized AI platforms have repeatedly installed Anglo-Western epistemologies as normative, while regional histories and pedagogical traditions are relegated to the margins. Within schools, this translates into learning practices where AI functions as an agent of epistemic extractivism. Students' local learning is translated into standardized outputs—essays formatted for plagiarism detectors, projects uploaded into global learning management systems—while the forms of knowledge that do not fit these templates are erased. Students are thus not only learning through AI but also learning to inhabit identities defined by global North discourses of identity, society, entrepreneurship, and modernization.

In this landscape, AI is not merely a delivery mechanism of content but a mechanism that stabilizes the meaning of key educational signifiers. Within classrooms, terms like "competence," "innovation," or "digital literacy" operate not as descriptive categories but as what Laclau (2005) would call empty signifiers. They condense diverse aspirations—passing exams, surviving economic uncertainty, aspiring to mobility—however are repeatedly filled with the logics of neoliberal governance and postdigital infrastructures. Algorithmic profiling, standardized assessment, and platform pedagogies rearticulate these signifiers in ways that valorize particular subjectivities—resilient, competitive, entrepreneurial—while constructing others as deficient. Learning thus ceases to be reducible to knowledge acquisition and instead becomes the contested terrain on which students are discursively positioned, compelled to negotiate whether they embody the valorized subject of the postdigital order or remain excluded from its promise.

Bourdieu's concepts of capital and habitus illuminate how these antagonisms are lived and embodied. In elite schools, students acquire a digital habitus that treats AI as a field for experimentation and authorship, producing symbolic capital that aligns them with the figure of the future innovator. In marginalized contexts, however, the same systems are experienced as external authority or as low-stakes entertainment, cultivating a constrained habitus in which AI functions as surveillance rather than as creativity. These divergent dispositions are not natural outcomes but the result of discursive structuring. They reflect how schools, media, and policies articulate what it means to be "educated" or "digitally competent." For many students, the inability to embody the valorized identity of the digital subject produces a profound experience of misrecognition, reinforcing inequalities not only in achievement but in self-understanding, in the very terms through which they see themselves as learners.

Fraser's framework helps to clarify why this situation cannot be resolved through redistribution alone. Providing devices, connectivity, or standardized AI systems does not dismantle the hierarchies of recognition that govern how knowledge and subjectivity are valued. If AI-mediated education continues to privilege Western epistemologies while rendering local repertoires invisible, students in CEE remain doubly excluded: materially, through unequal infrastructures, and symbolically, through epistemic misrecognition. School learning, in this sense, becomes a site where neoliberal governance and coloniality converge, producing stratified subjectivities under the banner of digital modernization. The promise of inclusion through technology thus masks the deeper reproduction of dependency, where the very infrastructures meant to "modernize" education simultaneously delimit whose knowledge counts and whose identities are legible within the postdigital order.

Learning in the postdigital knowledge society cannot be reduced to the mastery of tools or the accumulation of competencies. It is the very process through which subjectivities and hierarchies stabilized, and possibilities for resistance opened or foreclosed. In Central and Eastern Europe, the encounter with AI and imported digital curricula dramatizes this condition. Students are not simply acquiring "future skills" but negotiating whether their practices, languages, and histories can be recognized as legitimate within global circuits of knowledge. What appears as personalization or innovation is often the re-inscription of dependency, where algorithmic infrastructures channel learning into predictable pathways of competitiveness and compliance. Within this terrain, students also generate counter-practices. These are acts of epistemic disobedience, hybrid uses of media, vernacular reinterpretations, that contest the universality of Western-modern epistemologies. To frame learning in CEE today is therefore to acknowledge its dual character. It is both a site of stratification and misrecognition, and a space where new forms of agency and knowledge can be imagined. The challenge for pedagogy is not to insulate students from postdigital infrastructures but to cultivate practices that make visible their power, contest their exclusions, and open learning to genuinely plural futures.

5.2 Education, Equality, and the Political Economy of Knowledge

The potential of postdigital educational media, as discussed earlier, is often framed in terms of democratization. New tools are expected to widen participation and personalize learning (Jandrić et al., 2018). This celebratory narrative, however, rests on a selective imagination of technology as an equalizing force, detached from the social relations in which it operates. What it obscures is that the very infrastructures heralded as empowering are themselves embedded in the political economy of knowledge, where inequality is not an unfortunate side effect but a constitutive feature. In practice, the promise of equity is recoded. Rather than addressing the structural conditions that distribute resources and opportunities unevenly, equity is reframed as the individual capacity to adapt and remain employable in competitive markets. This redefinition aligns with neoliberal rationalities of governance (Ball, 2012; Jessop, 2002), in which systemic dispossession is rearticulated as personal deficit, and responsibility for overcoming exclusion is devolved onto learners themselves. Fraser's (2008) account of justice helps make visible how redistribution is displaced by a narrow version of recognition, where students are "included" only insofar as they can demonstrate responsibilized participation. In Bourdieu's (1986) terms, the supposed democratization of access masks the privileging of those already equipped with the cultural and social capital to convert postdigital tools into valued forms of achievement. Postdigitality, then, does not dissolve inequality. It reorganizes it, embedding hierarchies into the infrastructures of participation while legitimizing them through the rhetoric of personalization and empowerment.

This tension reflects the broader transition from the "knowledge society" to "knowledge economies" (Bell, 1973; Castells, 1996; Drucker, 1993). What was initially imagined as emancipatory, an epoch in which knowledge would displace material labor as the central resource, was quickly rearticulated in managerial terms: "knowledge management" and "human capital" (Ball, 2012; Fuller, 2006). In this reconfiguration, inequality was not addressed but redefined. Systemic dispossession, rooted in structural distributions of capital and opportunity, was translated into the language of personal failure or lack. The solution offered was not redistribution but continuous upskilling, lifelong learning, as well as entrepreneurial self-inventing, placing the burden of adjustment squarely on individuals (Giroux, 2014; Jessop, 2002). As Fraser (2008) emphasizes, this relies on narrowing justice to recognition, where the capacity to adapt is valorized, while redistributive claims are sidelined. Equity thus becomes conditional and procedural. It is measured by one's demonstrable ability to remain employable and flexible, rather than being structural or transformative. In effect, the promise of equity is tethered not to the dismantling of inequalities but to survival within competitive markets, rendering precarity itself a normalized horizon of educational justice.

Postdigital infrastructures extend this logic in novel ways. As Knox (2019) has shown, "data imaginaries" recast learning as quantifiable flows of information calibrated for optimization. In privileging what is measurable and visible, such imaginaries marginalize narrative or experiential forms of knowledge, narrowing equity to the ability to perform within metrics designed for comparison. Bourdieu's (1986) account of cultural capital makes visible how this operates in schools: students whose dispositions and resources already align with the expectations of audit cultures can convert postdigital tools into legitimate achievement, while those lacking comparable resources are positioned as deficient. What appears as neutrality in data thus conceals a politics of distinction, rewarding those who embody the "right" forms of capital. Simons and Masschelein (2008) describe this shift as the governmentalization of learning. Students are responsibilized as self-tracking actors, while teachers are tasked with translating educational encounters into outputs legible to audit culture. The result is a redistribution of risk, where failure is individualized and equity is redefined as personal adaptability. In 's (2008) terms, redistribution is displaced by recognition, but recognition itself is narrowed to responsiveness to postdigital norms. Epistemic injustice (Fricker, 2007) intensifies under these conditions, as forms of knowledge outside dominant frameworks—embodied, affective, cultural, and, now, also digital—become illegible within the datafied infrastructure.

Findings from schools illustrate these dynamics with particular clarity. AI, for instance, was frequently prohibited in classrooms under the pretext of fairness, with teachers penalizing computer-generated work. These prohibitions did not eliminate the use of AI. They stratified it. Students with greater cultural capital were able to mobilize AI discreetly, framing it as an aid to legitimate intellectual work and embedding it within practices already valued by teachers and institutions. Others, lacking such resources and strategies, either refrained from using AI altogether or were penalized when their use was exposed. In this way, a technology widely advertised as democratizing knowledge became another mechanism through which advantage and disadvantage were unevenly distributed.

These dynamics confirm Jessop's (2002, 2020) observation that neoliberal governance does not resolve inequality but systematically recodes it into matters of individual responsibility and adaptability. For students positioned differently within the social field, AI became a test of alignment with the dominant rules of the game—a practical manifestation of Bourdieu's (1986) insight that capital confers advantage precisely by making certain practices legible and legitimate. Equity, in this setting, was less about structural redistribution and more about the capacity to perform compliance with institutional expectations. In Fraser's (2008) terms, redistribution was displaced by recognition, but recognition itself was conditional and stratified, extended more readily to those whose practices aligned with dominant epistemic frameworks. What was framed as fairness and personalization thus functioned, in practice, as the normalization of inequality through the idiom of datafication.

Learning analytics and dashboards emphasize this paradox. Promoted as instruments of personalization and inclusion, they translate student activity into metrics of engagement and progress. As Williamson (2017) demonstrates, such systems encode prior inequalities, rewarding students already positioned to succeed while narrowing the educational horizon to conformity and efficiency. The promise of personalization thus operates within a tightly circumscribed field, where the ability to meet the expectations of the dashboard becomes the measure of educational worth. Jessop's (2020) notion of strategic selectivity captures this dynamic. Infrastructures themselves act as filters, privileging forms of participation that are easily quantifiable, while rendering other, less measurable practices invisible.

In this context, equity is redefined as comparability. Students are recognized insofar as they can be aligned within pre-given metrics. But comparability rests on terms defined by dominant epistemologies, privileging behaviors and dispositions congruent with middle-class cultural capital while marginalizing those outside these norms. Fraser's (2008) dual framework clarifies what is at stake: redistribution is displaced by the focus on recognition, recognition itself is conditional on alignment with audit cultures, and misrecognition becomes normalized as students whose practices exceed or diverge from these parameters are coded as deficient.

Rather than acting as neutral mediators, learning analytics and dashboards legitimate exclusions by cloaking them in the rhetoric of modernization and objectivity. In classrooms, this often translated into students anxiously monitoring their own "performance data," while teachers were compelled to frame educational progress in terms of outputs in the e-journal. Far from democratizing knowledge, these systems intensified the responsibilization of both students and teachers, naturalizing inequality under the guise of fairness and innovation.

The political economy of knowledge under postdigital conditions renders equity both central and hollow. The rhetoric of democratization legitimizes education, but its infrastructures operate by responsibilizing and stratifying learners. Those already endowed with privileged dispositions and resources can align themselves with the codes of audit cultures, transforming personalization and datafication into opportunities for distinction, while others are cast as deficient when their practices fail to register within the dominant metrics (Bourdieu, 1986; Simons & Masschelein, 2008). What is presented as fairness—such as the banning of AI—often conceals a form of symbolic violence, where dominant norms are reproduced as neutral and natural (Bourdieu, 1991).

The infrastructures of learning, far from neutral mediators, function selectively. They reward students who are already positioned to succeed, while marginalizing those whose knowledge practices fall outside the narrow range of what is measurable or optimizable. In classrooms, this was evident when AI prohibitions stratified students. As I have shown, some discreetly incorporated it into their intellectual work, framing its use as legitimate, while others lacked the strategies or confidence to do the same and were penalized. In these ways, inequality is not eliminated but reorganized, reframed as a question of individual competence or responsibility rather than structural distribution (Jessop, 2002, 2020).

The promise of equity narrows to recognition within the system's own terms. Adaptability, self-management, regulation and compliance are translated into digital traces of performance. Structural inequalities are displaced from view, while students and teachers alike are compelled to translate lived educational practices into forms legible to data systems (Knox, 2019; Williamson, 2017). Recognition becomes conditional and misrecognition normalized, as contributions outside dominant epistemologies are erased (Fraser, 2008; Fricker, 2007). In practice, the very infrastructures celebrated for expanding participation also harden the gap between inclusion and exclusion, namely between those who can convert digital affordances into advantage and those who cannot.

What appeared in the previous subchapter as a horizon of possibility thus emerges here as a terrain of contestation. Postdigital media do not simply open or close pathways to equity. They institutionalize inequality while presenting it as modernization. The same tools that claim to democratize learning function as mechanisms through which stratification is rendered objective, and durable. Equity, far from resolved, remains the legitimizing promise of education—and its most persistent absence.

The political economy of knowledge under postdigital conditions legitimizes the promise of democratization, that coexists with infrastructures framing responsible learners and stratifying opportunities. What counts as equity is reduced to adaptability within pre-given metrics. While those whose practices or dispositions fail to register are cast as deficient. The result is a hollowing out of justice: redistribution is displaced. Moreover recognition becomes conditional, and misrecognition naturalized (Fraser, 2008). Schools illustrate this paradox with particular clarity. Prohibitions on AI framed as fairness stratified students by cultural capital. Technology encoded prior inequalities into metrics of progress. What is more personalization became indistinguishable from fitting into dominant epistemologies (Knox, 2019; Williamson, 2017).

The postdigital condition also discloses spaces of contestation. Against the narrowing of equity to responsibilization, Jandrić and Hayes (2020) propose the idea of *we-learn, we-act, we-think*, a collective praxis that reimagines learning as situated between humans and machines without simply reproducing existing hierarchies. This shift does not deny the role of technology but rejects the determinist illusion that it defines our future. Instead, it imagines inclusivity as collective engagement, where technology becomes part of a shared space of unlearning neoliberal imperatives and opening possibilities for new human-machine solidarities. Such a project resonates with what Lewis and Alirezabeigi (2018) describe as *study*—a suspension of outcomes and measurements that define the learning economy. To study in this sense is not to reject the digital but to dwell in its potentiality. It means to see the saturated field of communication not as noise but as the ground for new meanings to emerge. It is a practice of withholding closure, but also a refusal of the metricized temporality of the postdigital school.

This alternative orientation echoes postcolonial and critical pedagogical traditions, where the act of profanation—releasing knowledge from its sacralization within dominant epistemologies—becomes a political gesture (McLaren, 1992; Spivak, 1999). It is a move from equity as comparability to equity as possibility, grounded not in compliance with infrastructures of measurement but in collective practices that imagine learning otherwise. In this sense, the inequities embedded in postdigital educational media are not the final word. These are the conditions that make urgent the search for alternative pedagogies that refuse to naturalize inequality and instead cultivate a democratic, postdigital *we-learn* (Jandrić & Hayes, 2020).

References

Au, W. (2011). *Unequal by design: High-stakes testing and the standardization of inequality*. Routledge. https://doi.org/10.1080/00220272.2010.521261

Ball, S. J. (2012). *Global Education Inc.: New Policy Networks and the Neo-Liberal Imaginary*. Routledge.

Bell, D. (1973). *The coming of post-industrial society: A venture in social forecasting*. Basic Books.

Biesta, G. J. (2013). *Beautiful risk of education*. Routledge.

Bourdieu, P. (1984). *Distinction: A social critique of the judgement of taste*. Harvard University Press.

Bourdieu, P. (1986). The forms of capital. In J. G. Richardson (Ed.), *Handbook of theory and research for the sociology of education* (pp. 241–258). Greenwood Press.

Bourdieu, P., & Passeron, J.-C. (1990). *Reproduction in education, society and culture* (R. Nice, Trans.; 2nd ed., Vol. 4). Sage.

Bourdieu, P. (1991). *Language and symbolic power*. Polity Press

Castells, M. (1996). *The rise of the network society*. Blackwell. https://doi.org/10.1002/9781444319514

Couldry, N., & Mejias, U. A. (2019). *The costs of connection: How data is colonizing human life and appropriating it for capitalism*. Stanford University Press.

Davies, C., & Eynon, R. (2013). *Teenagers and technology*. Routledge.

Drucker, P. (1993). *Post-capitalist Society*. HarperBusiness.

Erkkilä, T., & Piironen, O. (2018). Rankings and global knowledge governance. In *Rankings and global knowledge governance*. Palgrave Studies in Global Higher Education. Palgrave Macmillan. https://doi.org/10.1007/978-3-319-68941-8_7

De Corte, E. (1994). Toward the integration of computers in powerful learning environments. In *Technology-based learning environments: Psychological and educational foundations* (pp. 19–25). Springer Berlin Heidelberg. https://doi.org/10.1007/978-3-642-79149-9_3

Eubanks, V. (2018). *Automating inequality: How high-tech tools profile, police, and punish the poor*. Martin's Press.

Fawns, T. (2022). An entangled pedagogy: Looking beyond the pedagogy–technology dichotomy. *Postdigital Science and Education, 4*, 711–728. https://doi.org/10.1007/s42438-022-00302-7

Fraser, N. (1997). *Justice interruptus: Critical reflections on the "postsocialist" condition*. Routledge.

Fraser, N. (2003). Social justice in the age of identity politics: Redistribution, recognition, and participation. In N. Fraser & A. Honneth (Eds.), *Redistribution or recognition? A political-philosophical exchange* (pp. 7–109). Verso.

Fraser, N. (2008). *Scales of justice: Reimagining political space in a globalizing world*. Polity.

Fraser, N. (2013). *Fortunes of feminism: From state-managed capitalism to neoliberal crisis*. Verso.

Fricker, M. (2007). *Epistemic injustice: Power and the ethics of knowing*. Oxford University Press.

Foucault, M. (1977). *Discipline and punish: The birth of the prison*. Pantheon.

Fuller, S. (2006). *The Philosophy of Science and Technology Studies*. Routledge.

Giroux, H. A. (2014). *Neoliberalism's war on higher education*. Haymarket Books

Grek, S. (2020). Prophets, saviours and saints: Symbolic governance and the rise of a transnational metrological field. *International Review of Education, 66*, 139–166. https://doi.org/10.1007/s11159-020-09844-z

Heinrich, C. J., Darling-Aduana, J., & Good, A. G. (2020). *Equity and quality in digital learning: Realizing the promise in K-12 education*. Harvard Education Press.

Jandrić, P., Knox, J., Besley, T., Ryberg, T., Suoranta, J., & Hayes, S. (2018). Postdigital science and education. *Educational Philosophy and Theory, 50*(10), 893–899. https://doi.org/10.1080/00131857.2018.1454000

Jandrić, P., & Hayes, S. (2020). *Postdigital we-learn. Studies in Philosophy and Education, 39*(3), 285–297. https://doi.org/10.1007/s11217-020-09711-2

Janmaat, J. G., & Piattoeva, N. (2007). Citizenship education in Ukraine and Russia: Reconciling nation-building and active citizenship. *Comparative Education, 43*(4), 527–552. https://doi.org/10.1080/03050060701611920

Jessop, B. (2002). *The future of the capitalist state*. Polity.

Jessop, B. (2020). *Putting civil society in its place: Governance, metagovernance and subjectivity*. Polity Press

Knox, J. (2019). What does the 'postdigital' mean for education? Three critical perspectives on the digital, with implications for educational research and practice. *Postdigital Science and Education, 1*(2), 357–370. https://doi.org/10.1007/s42438-019-00045-y

Laclau, E. (2005). *On populist reason*. Verso.

Lewis, T. E., & Alirezabeigi, S. (2018). Studying with the Internet: Giorgio Agamben, education, and new digital technologies. *Studies in Philosophy and Education, 37*(6), 553–566.

Macgilchrist, F., Allert, H., & Bruch, A. (2020). Students and society in the 2020s: Three future "histories" of education and technology. *Learning, Media and Technology, 45*(1), 76–89. https://doi.org/10.1080/17439884.2019.1656235

McLaren, P. (1992). Critical literacy and postcolonial praxis: A Freirian perspective. *College Literature, 19*(3/1), 7–27.

Mignolo, W. D. (2011). *The darker side of Western modernity: Global futures, decolonial options*. Duke University Press.

Noble, S. U. (2018). *Algorithms of oppression: How search engines reinforce racism*. NYU Press.

Pangrazio, L., & Sefton-Green, J. (2020). The social utility of 'data literacy.' *Learning, Media and Technology, 45*(2), 208–220. https://doi.org/10.1080/17439884.2020.1707223

Selwyn, N. (2022). *Education and technology: Key issues and debates* (3rd ed.). Bloomsbury.

Semjén, A. (2023). (Re)centralisation of education governance in Hungary: Its causes, declared goals, motives and some potential hidden goals. *Podstawy Edukacji, 16* https://doi.org/10.16926/pe.2023.16.13

Silova, I. (2010). Rediscovering post-socialism in comparative education. In I. Silova (Ed.), *Post-socialism is not dead: (Re)reading the global in comparative education* (pp. 1–24). Emerald. https://doi.org/10.1108/S1479-3679(2010)0000014004

Slavíčková, M. (2021). Implementation of digital technologies into pre-service mathematics teacher preparation. *Mathematics, 9*(12), Article 1319. https://doi.org/10.3390/math9121319

Spivak, G. C. (1999). *A critique of postcolonial reason: Toward a history of the vanishing present*. Harvard University Press.

Srnicek, N. (2017). *Platform capitalism*. Polity Press.

Williamson, B. (2017). *Big data in education: The digital future of learning, policy and practice*. Sage.

Williamson, B., & Eynon, R. (2020). Historical threads, missing links, and future directions in AI in education. *Learning, Media and Technology, 45*(3), 223–235. https://doi.org/10.1080/17439884.2020.1798995

Zarycki, T. (2014). *Ideologies of eastness in Central and Eastern Europe*. Routledge.

Zuboff, S. (2019). Surveillance capitalism and the challenge of collective action. In *The New labor forum* (Vol. 28, No. 1, pp. 10–29). Sage.

CHAPTER 6

Conclusion

This book has traced how learning unfolds in the postdigital condition—both at school and within the wider postdigital knowledge society. In schools, education is saturated by technological infrastructures, but also constrained by pedagogical traditions that reproduce narrow hierarchies of knowledge (Klus-Stańska, 2012). What policy documents and research literature often describe as "digital transformation" (Fawns, 2022; Knox, 2019; Williamson, 2017) emerges less as rupture than as intensification. Neoliberal logics of human capital acquire new force through digital mediation. In the broader postdigital knowledge society, these dynamics are extended and strengthened. Algorithms and data economies not only shape what counts as knowledge but also determine whose voices are heard and which subjectivities are legitimized. In both contexts, recognition and authority are increasingly governed by technological infrastructures rather than dialogic or democratic processes.

Teachers and students, positioned at the intersection of these regimes, respond not with uniform compliance but with ambivalence, pragmatism, but also, with moments of resistance. The school becomes a site of friction where algorithmic publics, teachers' demands, standardized assessments, and state-sanctioned curricula collide with students' emotionally saturated digital practices. Learning, in this sense, is not a neutral process of transmission but a contested practice. It is shaped by institutional demands and

M. Popow, *Learning in the Postdigital Knowledge Society*, Palgrave Studies in Educational Media,
https://doi.org/10.1007/978-3-032-21956-5_6

digital architectures, but also reconfigured through the everyday tactics by which students and teachers negotiate or redirect them.

A central theme across the chapters has been the redefinition of learning itself, both in the postdigital school and in the wider post-digital knowledge society. The ideal of the knowledge society once promised openness, democratization, and pluralism (Bell, 1973; Castells, 1996; Drucker, 1993). In practice, this promise has been displaced by the operational logic of the knowledge economy, where learning is rendered a form of capital accumulation—whether measured in standardized competencies, quantified performance, or digital literacies aligned with employability (Jessop, 2002; Szkudlarek, 2016). In the postdigital condition, this economization of learning is intensified by algorithmic infrastructures that make adaptation and productivity the very conditions of epistemic recognition. The governing rationality of neoliberalism responsibilizes individuals for their own adaptability while shifting risks away from institutions (Fraser, 2013). Within this regime, students are cast as self-managing subjects compelled to reskill and align with metrics of performance, while teachers are repositioned as data managers and supervisors of compliance. As Biesta (2019) warns, such "learnification" narrows the purpose of education to measurable outcomes, displacing questions of subjectivity, self-awareness, but also of democracy, and ethical responsibility. In Central and Eastern Europe, where schools are already navigating the weight of social transformation legacies and the imperatives of neoliberal reform, this narrowing takes on a double edge. Learning is not only subordinated to the market but also instrumentalized within nationalist projects, leaving little space for pluralism or epistemic sovereignty.

The ethnographic findings highlight the consequences of this transformation. Teachers often frame students as deficient, lacking intrinsic motivation or curiosity, while students respond by treating school as a set of hurdles to be navigated with minimal effort. The culture of testing reinforces this dynamic, reducing knowledge to standardized fragments and penalizing deviation (Klus-Stańska, 2012; Zalewska, 2015). Within this environment, the learner becomes a mechanized subject. The subject calibrated to survive, to pass, to conform to formats that reward replication over exploration. Students' use of digital tools reflects this orientation. Generative AI, websites with pre-prepared answers, or shared test archives are not embraced as vehicles of deeper learning but as pragmatic shortcuts—means of meeting institutional expectations efficiently.

These practices, however, are not merely cynical. They reveal an acute awareness of the performative logics of schooling. By appropriating digital tools, students participate in what I have called reversive knowledge. These are strategies that bypass institutional demands. These reversals, while destabilizing authority, rarely escape the gravitational pull of the system. Instead, they often circulate within its logics—at times reproducing exclusionary ideologies, reinforcing hierarchical power relations, or aligning with nationalist narratives. What appears as resistance thus remains ambivalent. It simultaneously unsettles pedagogical authority while risking complicity in broader projects of closure and domination.

Algorithms, predictive analytics of learning, as well as personalization systems determine which knowledges are visible, which voices are amplified, and which forms of participation are recognized (Knox, 2019; Williamson, 2017). The authority of pedagogical judgment is displaced. The visibility of learners is tied to data metrics rather than dialogic or communal recognition (Noble, 2018, p. 53; Eubanks, 2018). The paradox of the postdigital condition is that the same platforms that open spaces for alternative epistemologies also entrench new regimes of algorithmic control. Students may find in YouTube or TikTok more engaging and affectively resonant knowledge than in textbooks, but they are also exposed to biases, simplifications, and stereotypes patterned into platform logics. Teachers, for their part, often respond defensively—restricting AI, requiring handwritten work, or designing tasks meant to "outsmart" digital tools. These practices reflect not technophobia but an attempt to preserve professional authority and epistemic sovereignty in the face of external incursions.

The Central and Eastern European context magnifies these tensions. Educational reforms after 1989 were driven by neoliberal restructuring, cultural nationalism, and the imperative to "catch up" with the West (Silova, 2010). As Novotný, Dvořák, and Dvořáková (2023) demonstrate, these dynamics produced a hybrid governance of schooling in which Western-oriented standards of efficiency and accountability intersect with national traditions and state-led agendas. Patriotic curricula and state centralization thus coexist with projects of digital modernization. As Dudzikowa (2001, p. 109) observed, schools continue to cultivate the illusion of formative development while in practice reproducing narrow epistemic hierarchies. My fieldwork illustrates how these legacies persist. Teachers rely on transmissive methods and standardized assessments, while students pursue knowledge outside school through engaging, digitally mediated practices. The collision between these logics produces disconnection and fragmentation. Schools are caught between the rhetoric of innovation and the weight of tradition. Promises of democratization intertwine with realities of control.

Taken together, the analyses in this book suggest several conclusions. First, postdigital education should not be understood as a matter of tool adoption or technical modernization. It represents a transformation in the very coordinates of learning. Digital infrastructures do not simply enhance pedagogy. They restructure authority, shape identities, redefine legitimacy, and delimit epistemic possibilities. To call education "postdigital" is to recognize that online and offline, but also human and technological, are now inseparably entangled (Fawns, 2022).

Second, the promise of digital democratization has often obscured the reproduction of inequality. Postdigital schooling exemplifies the duality between maldistribution and misrecognition (Fraser, 2009, 2013). Material access remains uneven, and students' informal practices are frequently delegitimized as "inauthentic" or "uncritical." Instead of reducing inequalities, digital infrastructures frequently encode pre-existing hierarchies and shift responsibility for overcoming them onto individuals. Third, the figures of the mechanized subject and reversive knowledge highlight the ambivalence of student practices. Learners are neither passive victims nor emancipated actors. Their engagements with digital tools are pragmatic and often ironic. These practices reveal both the fragility of pedagogical authority and the persistence of systemic pressures. They demonstrate that meaning-making remains contested, even within environments saturated by control. They also caution against romanticizing resistance. Reversive practices may equally reinforce reactionary worldviews or reproduce superficial engagement. Finally, the Central and Eastern European experience proves the importance of context. Postdigital education here is not merely a reflection of global trends but an assemblage shaped by historical legacies and neoliberal reforms. This hybridity complicates narratives of linear modernization. It also foregrounds the stakes of epistemic sovereignty. Knowledge may be governed by state authority, global corporations, algorithms, or the lived practices of students themselves.

The task for postdigital critical pedagogy in this setting is not to reject technology nor to celebrate it uncritically, but to interrogate the infrastructures through which knowledge is organized. As Biesta (2019) argues, education cannot be reduced to measurable learning outcomes.

It also concerns subjectivity, democracy, and ethical responsibility. This suggests moving beyond functional digital skills toward capacities for critique and contextualization.

The analyses in this book suggest that the future of education under postdigital conditions will not be determined by technology itself but by how institutions, educators, and students negotiate its logics. The collapse of the online/offline divide has not dissolved the need for schools. It has transformed schools into contested arenas where epistemic authority and political legitimacy are continuously at stake. These struggles are not class-neutral. As Bourdieu (1984) demonstrates, education functions as a central mechanism for the reproduction of social hierarchies through the unequal distribution of cultural capital and the privileging of dominant forms of knowledge. In the postdigital classroom, these dynamics are reconfigured but not erased. Digital repertoires may offer students alternative routes to recognition, they also intensify symbolic struggles over legitimacy and distinction. The challenge, therefore, is to reclaim education not as a mechanism of compliance but as a space of deliberation and epistemic justice.

This conclusion is not a closure but an opening. The postdigital condition demands a rethinking of what it means to learn, to teach, to participate and to know. It calls for vigilance against the ways in which digital infrastructures reproduce inequalities, but also for imagination in seizing the possibilities they create for new forms of knowledge and solidarity. Education will remain a contested field. It will remain in between market logics and democratic aspirations, in between algorithmic governance and critical agency, as well as mechanization and reversive practice. The question is not whether schools will adapt to the postdigital, but how they might be reimagined so that learning, in all its ambivalence, can still serve as a site of intellectual emancipation and collective possibility.

References

Bell, D. (1973). *The coming of post-industrial society: A venture in social forecasting*. Basic Books.

Biesta, G. (2019). Should teaching be re (dis) covered? Introduction to a symposium. *Studies in Philosophy and Education, 38*(5), 549–553.

Bourdieu, P. (1984). *Distinction: A social critique of the judgement of taste*. Harvard University Press.

Castells, M. (1996). *The rise of the network society*. Blackwell. https://doi.org/10.1002/9781444319514

Drucker, P. (1993). *Post-capitalist Society*. HarperBusiness.

Dudzikowa, M. (2001). *Mit o szkole jako miejscu wszechstronnego rozwoju. Eseje etnopedagogiczne*. Oficyna Wydawnicza "Impuls".

Eubanks, V. (2018). *Automating inequality: How high-tech tools profile, police, and punish the poor*. Martin's Press.

Fawns, T. (2022). An entangled pedagogy: Looking beyond the pedagogy—technology dichotomy. *Postdigital Science and Education, 4*(3), 711–728.

Fraser, N. (2009). *Scales of justice: Reimagining political space in a globalizing world* (Vol. 31). Columbia University Press.

Fraser, N. (2013). *Fortunes of feminism: From state-managed capitalism to neoliberal crisis*. Verso.

Jessop, B. (2002). *The Future of the Capitalist State*. Cambridge: Polity Press.

Klus-Stańska, D. (2012). Wiedza, która zniewala–transmisyjne tradycje w szkolnej edukacji. *In Forum oświatowe* (Vol. 24, No. 1 (46), pp. 21–40).

Knox, J. (2019). What does the 'postdigital' mean for education? Three critical perspectives on the digital, with implications for educational research and practice. *Postdigital Science and Education, 1*(2), 357–370. https://doi.org/10.1007/s42438-019-00045-y

Noble, S. U. (2018). *Algorithms of oppression: How search engines reinforce racism*. NYU Press.

Novotný, P., Dvořák, D., & Dvořáková, M. (2023). Czech School Reforms: Between East and West. In: Krejsler, J.B., Moos, L. (eds) School Policy Reform in Europe. *Educational Governance Research*, vol 22. Springer, Cham. https://doi.org/10.1007/978-3-031-35434-2_10

Silova, I. (2010). Rediscovering post-socialism in comparative education. In I. Silova (Ed.), *Post-socialism is not dead: (Re)reading the global in comparative education* (pp. 1–24). Emerald Group Publishing.

Szkudlarek, T. (2016). *On the Politics of Educational Theory: Rhetoric, theoretical ambiguity, and the construction of society*. London: Routledge. https://doi.org/10.4324/9781315712505

Williamson, B. (2017). *Big Data in Education: The Digital Future of Learning, Policy, and Practice*. SAGE.

Zalewska, E. (2015). Porównywanie wyników testów egzaminacyjnych. Wiadomości Statystyczne. *The Polish Statistician, 60*(12), 70–81.

Materials Under Analysis

Policy Documents

European Commission. (2018). *Key competences for lifelong learning*. European Union.

Ministry of Education and Science of Poland. (2024, October 11). *Draft resolution on the Digital Transformation Policy for Education 2024–2035. Eurydice.*

Ministerstwo Edukacji i Nauki. (2019). *Ramy kwalifikacji, ECTS i ECVET dla uczenia się przez całe życie.* Warszawa: Ministerstwo Edukacji i Nauki.

Ministerstwo Edukacji i Nauki. (2024). *Nowelizacja podstawy programowej kształcenia ogólnego (MEN, 2024).*

Ministerstwo Edukacji i Nauki. (2024). *Projekt podstawy programowej edukacji obywatelskiej (MEN, 2024).*

Ministerstwo Edukacji i Nauki. (2024). *Polityka transformacji cyfrowej w edukacji 2024–2035 (MEiN, 2024).*

Selected materials from *Zintegrowana Platforma Edukacyjna (PZE).*

The European Commission's Digital Competence Framework for Educators (DigCompEdu).

Vuorikari, R., Kluzer, S., & Punie, Y. (2022). *DigComp 2.2: The Digital Competence Framework for Citizens—With new examples of knowledge, skills and attitudes* (JRC128415). Publications Office of the European Union.

M. Popow, *Learning in the Postdigital Knowledge Society*, Palgrave Studies in Educational Media,
https://doi.org/10.1007/978-3-032-21956-5

Textbooks

Cisek, A., Rysak, L., Wilczyński, K., & Modzelewska-Rysak, I. (2022). *Historia i teraźniejszość. Podręcznik. Część 1. Liceum i technikum. Zakres podstawowy.* Warszawa: Wydawnictwa Szkolne i Pedagogiczne. Nr dopuszczenia: 1155/1/2022.

Faszcza, M. N., Lolo, R., & Wiśniewski, K. (n.d.). *Historia 1. Zakres podstawowy. Nowa edycja.* Warszawa: Wydawnictwa Szkolne i Pedagogiczne.

Kulesza, R., & Kowalewski, K. (2024). *Zrozumieć przeszłość 1. Podręcznik. Liceum i technikum. Zakres rozszerzony.* Warszawa: Nowa Era.

Malarz, R., & Więckowski, M. (2024). *Oblicza geografii. Podręcznik. Klasa 1. Zakres podstawowy. Liceum i technikum.* Warszawa: Nowa Era. Nr dopuszczenia: 1216/1/2024.

Praca zbiorowa. (n.d.). *Język polski. Sztuka wyrazu. Podręcznik do liceum i technikum. Część 1 (Starożytność i średniowiecze) i Część 2 (Renesans, barok, oświecenie). Zakres podstawowy i rozszerzony.* Gdańskie Wydawnictwo Oświatowe.

Reports and Methodological Guides for Teachers

Białek, K., & Swat-Pawlicka, M. (2025). *Kompetencje (w) przyszłości: Praktyczny przewodnik.* Warszawa: Instytut Badań Edukacyjnych – Państwowy Instytut Badawczy.

Chmielecka, E., Saryusz-Wolski, T., Sławiński, S., & Stęchły, W. (Red.). (2019). *Ramy kwalifikacji, ECTS i ECVET dla uczenia się przez całe życie.* Warszawa: Ministerstwo Edukacji i Nauki.

Instytut Badań Edukacyjnych. (2020). *Krytyczne myślenie, ocena wiarygodności informacji: Wnioski z międzynarodowych badań edukacyjnych i przeglądu literatury.* Warszawa: Instytut Badań Edukacyjnych.

Płonka, P. (2022). *Misja: być świadkiem historii. Poradnik metodyczny do programu nauczania historii dla III etapu edukacyjnego (liceum ogólnokształcącego i technikum).* Warszawa: Ośrodek Rozwoju Edukacji.

Index

M. Popow, *Learning in the Postdigital Knowledge Society*, Palgrave Studies in Educational Media,
https://doi.org/10.1007/978-3-032-21956-5

FSC
www.fsc.org
MIX
Papier | Fördert gute Waldnutzung
FSC® C083411

Kolibri 360 GmbH
Ferdinand-Jühlke-Straße 7
99095 Erfurt, Deutschland
produktsicherheit@kolibri360.de